EXPLORING IN AND AROUND

BOSTON

ON BIKE AND FOOT

SECOND EDITION

LEE SINAI

ILLUSTRATED BY
JOYCE S. SHERR

APPALACHIAN MOUNTAIN CLUB BOOKS
BOSTON, MASSACHUSETTS

Cover Photographs: Kindra Clineff
Illustrations by Joyce S. Sherr
Maps by Lee Sinai
All photographs by the author unless otherwise noted.
Book design by Stephanie Doyle
Cover design by Elisabeth Leydon Brady

Ⓣ Reproduced by Permission of the MBTA. © MBTA 1996.
Patrick J. Moynihan, General Manager

Library of Congress Cataloging-in-Publication Data
Sinai, Lee
    Exploring in and around Boston on bike and foot / Lee Sinai: illustrated by Joyce S.
Sherr. —2nd ed.
        p.   cm.
    Includes index.
    ISBN 1-878239-81-3
    1. Boston Region (Mass.)—Guidebooks. 2.Boston (Mass.)—Guidebooks. 3.
Walking—Massachusetts—Boston Region—Guidebooks. 4. Walking—Massachusetts—
Boston—Guidebooks. 5. Bicycle touring—Massachusetts—Boston Region—
Guidebooks. 6. Bicycling touring—Massachusetts—Boston—Guidebooks. I. Title.
F73.18.S56   1999
917.44'610443—dc21   99-14062
                                                                    CIP

The paper used in this publication meets the minimum requirements of the American
National Standard for Information Sciences—Permanence of Paper for Printed Library
Materials, ANSI Z39.48–1984.∞

Due to changes in conditions,
use of the information in this book
is at the sole risk of the user.

Printed on recycled paper using soy-based inks.

Printed in the United States of America.

10 9 8 7 6 5 4 3 2 1   99 00 01 02 03 04

CONTENTS

ON BIKE

On-Road

BOSTON

NORTHERN SUBURBS

WESTERN SUBURBS

SOUTHERN SUBURBS

Off-Road

NORTHERN SUBURBS

WESTERN SUBURBS

SOUTHERN SUBURBS

ON FOOT

BOSTON

ACKNOWLEDGMENTS

I am most grateful to Allen, Lauren, and Todd for their constant encouragement and support. Many thanks to my friends who graciously and patiently accompanied me as I designed and tested routes, and to others who checked the directions. Ellen Citron, Melissa Norton, Carol Reiling, and Fern Schaffer deserve special mention as *accompaniers par excellence*.

I am much obliged to all the superintendents, rangers, directors, and public information officers who guided me around their facilities and fact-checked the chapters. Rene Morin, superintendent of the Middlesex Fells Reservation, merits a special commendation for all his help, as do Maggie Brown and Tim Carew, rangers at Blue Hills Reservation. Thanks to Barbara Pryor, public information director at Garden in the Woods; Richard Schulhof, assistant director of education and public affairs at the Arnold Arboretum; Bob Caruso, superintendent of Breakheart Reservation; Ray Faucher, superintendent of Great Brook Farm; Nancy Childs, naturalist, and Laurie Bennett, director, at Habitat; Elisse Landry, director of Broadmoor; and Carol Decker, director of Ipswich River. I am grateful to the superintendents and supervisors at the Trustees of Reservations: Tom Foster, Al Yalenezian, and Marc Bailey. Ron Wolanin, naturalist, and Patrick Dorcus, director of Moose Hill, were most informative, as were Don Frazer, harbor regional supervisor, and Matt Tobin, ranger, from Boston Harbor Islands State Park. Pete Carlson, regional trails coordinator, showed me around Bradley Palmer, and Wil Tapin, superintendent of Harold Parker, guided me through his park. Members of the Friends of Lynn Woods: Steve Babbitt, Marc McInerney, and Ken Agacinski were most accommodating. Sara Germain, assistant to the director of the Peabody Museum at Phillips Academy, and Laurel Stavis, director of public information at Wellesley College, deserve mention, as do Nick Capasso, associate curator of DeCordova Museum; Jean Rogers, ranger at Fresh Pond; and Eric Soucey.

*To Myra
and Morry*

TOURING LOCATIONS

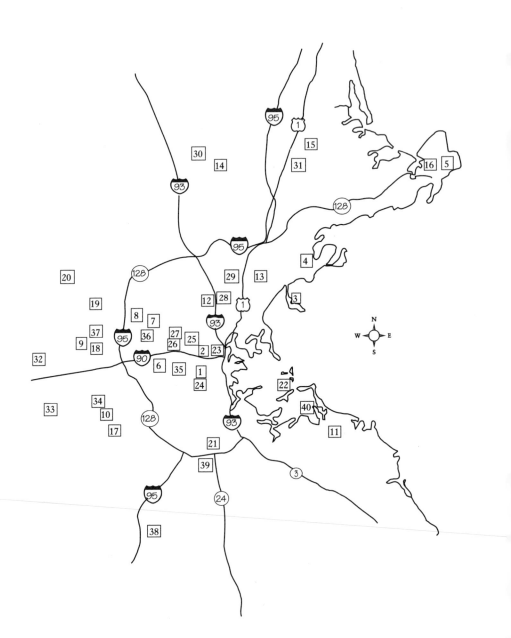

MAP LEGEND

MAP SYMBOLS

.... Biking or Hiking Route

🚲 Beginning of bike route

🚶🚶 Beginning of foot trail

🚶🚶 Beginning of walking route

2 Direction Numbers

③ Intersection Numbers

........➤ Secondary arrow--used when routes overlap

Lighthouse

Scenic Lookout

Ⓟ Automobile Parking

Ⓗ Hospital

Ⓡ Railroad

Ⓣ Rapid Transit Station

Bathhouse/Boathouse

Drinking Water

Swimming

Canoeing and Kayaking

Marsh

Field

- - - Reservation Boundary

ooooooo Stone Wall

Highlights Chart

Bikes/Hikes	Miles	Difficulty*	Suitable for Children
1. Emerald Necklace	16	E	
2. Charles River Loop	18	E	✔
3. Nahant	10	M	✔
4. Swampscott—Marblehead	19	E	
5. Gloucester—Rockport	26	M	
6. Newton—Brookline	17	M	
7. Minuteman Bikeway	24	E	✔
8. Lexington—Concord	20	M	✔
9. Lincoln—Sudbury	25	M	
10. Wellesley—Dover	23	M	
11. Hingham—Cohasset	21	E	
12. Middlesex Fells—West	7	M	
13. Lynn Woods	5	M	
14. Harold Parker	7.5	M	
15. Bradley Palmer	4	M	
16. Dogtown	5.5	M	
17. Noanet Woodlands	5	E/M	
18. Weston Woodlands	5–7	E	
19. Great Meadows—Concord	10.5	E	✔
20. Great Brook Farm	5–6.5	M	✔

*Difficulty: E=Easy, M=Moderate, S=Strenuous

Handicapped Accessible	Entry Fees	In-line Skating	Cross-country Skiing	Swimming	Dogs Allowed
✔		✔	✔		✔
✔		✔	✔		✔
		✔	✔	✔	✔
	✔	✔		✔	
	✔			✔	
		✔			✔
✔		✔	✔		✔
✔	✔				
	✔	✔	✔	✔	
			✔		✔
			✔		✔
			✔		✔
			✔		✔
			✔		✔
	✔		✔		✔
			✔		✔
✔			✔		✔
			✔		✔

Highlights Chart

Bikes/Hikes	Miles	Difficulty*	Suitable for Children
21. Blue Hills	10	M	
22. Boston Harbor Islands	2	E	✔
23. Back Bay—Beacon Hill	2	E	✔
24. Arnold Arboretum	3	M	✔
25. Harvard Univ.—Harvard Square	2	E	✔
26. Mount Auburn Cemetery	2	E	✔
27. Fresh Pond	2.5	E	✔
28. Middlesex Fells—East	5	S	
29. Breakheart	3	M	✔
30. Phillips Academy	2.5	E	✔
31. Ipswich River	4	E	✔
32. Garden in the Woods	3	E	✔
33. Broadmoor	2.7	E	✔
34. Wellesley College	3.5	E	✔
35. Hammond Pond	2	E	✔
36. Habitat	2	E	✔
37. DeCordova—Sandy Pond	3.5	E	✔
38. Moose Hill	3	E	✔
39. Ponkapoag Pond	4.6	E	✔
40. World's End	3.7	E/M	✔

* Difficulty: E=Easy, M=Moderate, S=Strenuous

Handicapped Accessible	Entry Fees	In-line Skating	Cross-country Skiing	Swimming	Dogs Allowed
			✔	✔	✔
	✔		✔	✔	✔
✔	✔	✔	✔		✔
✔			✔		✔
✔	✔				
✔					
✔		✔	✔		✔
			✔		✔
		✔	✔	✔	✔
✔			✔		
	✔		✔		
✔					
	✔				
✔					
			✔		✔
	✔				
	✔		✔		✔
	✔		✔		
			✔		✔
✔	✔		✔		✔

INTRODUCTION

Welcome to the Boston area, renowned for its history, culture, and charm! This compact region is also blessed with miles and miles of rocky shores, sandy beaches, plentiful ponds, and craggy bluffs. Thanks to more than a century of preservation-minded policies, Massachusetts boasts hundreds of thousands of acres of undeveloped woodlands. How best to take advantage of this area's plentiful physical, historical, and cultural attributes? Use your feet, bicycle, in-line skates, or cross-country skis and allow *Exploring in and around Boston on Bike and Foot* to introduce you to the top spots within a 30-mile radius of Boston.

After selecting my favorite places in and around Boston, I asked the supervisor or public information officer of each property to guide me through the most interesting and scenic sections. I then designed routes that highlight the best attributes of each area, including historic and noteworthy sights as well as botanical and geological features. Drawings help identify flora and fauna described in the text.

I've included plenty of gems stashed away in the suburbs: tiny but terrific museums, quaint historic homes, serene sanctuaries, and colorful arboretums. Among your 40 choices are cycling Boston's famous Emerald Necklace; hiking around World's End, a magnificent promontory off the South Shore; exploring the islands in Boston Harbor; taking a bike ride through historic Lexington and Concord; and off-road biking on tree-lined trails in tranquil reservations. Detailed directions serve as an introduction to and a field guide for each exploration, with the hope that you will enjoy it, respect it, and wish to return.

Exploring in and around Boston on Bike and Foot is divided into two parts: On Bike and On Foot. The biking half of the book is also divided into two sections, one devoted to road biking and the other to off-road. Within the On-Road biking section are scenic tours of Boston and the region, from the northern suburbs, edged by rocky cliffs or sandy shores, to the historic, bucolic western towns and picturesque South Shore communities. When possible, the rides run along scenic back roads and avoid congested streets. The length of the rides ranges from nine to 27 miles. Because of the opportunity for frequent stops and the relatively untaxing terrain, most cyclists will not be daunted by the distances.

The section on off-road biking offers rides of varied lengths and degrees of difficulty. The main route is usually rather tame, but rigorous optional loops are included for those seeking more challenging biking.

Many of the walks in the On Foot section wind through reservations and parks, selected because of their exceptional scenery, well-groomed trails, and varied vegetation and wildlife. Most are of moderate length, from two to five miles. For those who wish to lengthen their excursions, extensions are suggested. Two historic walks also are included: one through the Back Bay and Beacon Hill sections of Boston and the other around Harvard University and its environs in Cambridge.

I've chosen explorations that are accessible via public transportation in order to prevent the frustration that results from trying to navigate a car in and around Boston. Buses, trains, and the subway (Ⓣ) provide regular service throughout the city and its outlying areas. Bicycles are allowed on commuter rail trains daily during nonpeak hours. On Sundays bikers can haul their bikes on the Ⓣ. Check the appendices for information on how to obtain a bike pass and the stations and hours where bikes are permitted. The appendices also list addresses and telephone numbers of in-line skate, cross-country ski, and bicycle rental and repair shops, as well as museums and historic houses. (An emergency number and public transportation information are included as well.)

THE CHART

The chart at the front of this guide (pp. x–xiii) allows the reader to find quickly the explorations of most interest. It lists the routes suitable for school-age children and also summarizes activities available at each location. A quick peek will reveal the length and level of difficulty of each exploration; the availability of handicapped access; and the areas suitable for in-line skating, swimming, cross-country skiing, and dog-walking.

HOW TO USE THIS BOOK

All chapters include directions to each exploration via both public transportation and automobile, a map of the area to be explored, information on where to park, approximate walking times and biking distances, admission fees, food and drink spots, public restroom locations, and a background of the region.

Numbered directions guide you through each outing. Each successive number indicates a change in direction. If faced with choices and no directions are provided, continue straight on the main path or road. Because street signs are often missing, bike odometers are helpful in determining the distance between turns. For example, when you know the next turn is a half-mile away, you can approximate when to turn. Additional information, historical, botanical, and/or geological, follows the directions and is indented. This format gives you the choice of reading the information or skipping over it to focus only on the directions.

Since hiking allows for a more leisurely examination of the natural world than biking, the On Foot chapters contain more nature information. In these chapters you will find more words in **boldface type** that point out a noteworthy site, tree, flower, animal, or bird with accompanying drawings to help with identification.

The maps have been designed for use in conjunction with the written directions. Numbers enclosed in squares refer to the numbered directions in the text, whereas numbers inside ovals indicate trail intersections and help determine your specific location within the reservation.

In order to maximize your enjoyment of each exploration, I strongly recommend reading the chapter before you set out and then allowing enough time. (Tip: add one hour to your original estimate.) For the rides, photocopy the pages of the chapter(s) you intend to use. It is much easier to follow directions on separate pages in a transparent pocket attached to a handlebar bag than to open the book continually to check directions.

Although each chapter has been pretested, words and directions can be misinterpreted, and intersection markers may be missing. If you lose your way, don't worry; rediscovering the route is part of the adventure.

In order to preserve what nature has kindly bestowed, please stay on marked trails, leave nothing behind, and take out only what you bring in.

WORDING

T intersection: The road on which you are traveling ends, requiring a right or left turn onto the intersected road. This junction forms a **T**.

Bear or bend left or right: Turn at a wide angle (about 120°).

Merge: The road or trail joins another road.

Ⓣ: Massachusetts Bay Transit Authority. Under and above ground trains or subways.

NECESSARY GEAR

Biking	Hiking
Insect repellent	Insect repellent
Water	Water
Sunscreen	Sunscreen
Sunglasses	Sunglasses
Tissues	Tissues
High-energy snacks	High-energy snacks
Bandanna or small hand towel	Bandanna or towel
Small first-aid kit	Small first-aid kit
Windbreaker	Long pants tucked into
Helmet	socks if hiking in the
Bike lock	woods
Tool kit	Binoculars (optional)
Odometer	
Handlebar bag with	
transparent map holder	

MOUNTAIN BIKING

The East Coast has finally become aware of what the West Coast knew decades ago: Mountain biking is a great way to exercise and enjoy the scenery. Unfortunately, irresponsible riding has contributed to significant erosion, forcing a number of areas to close trails to mountain bikers. Each year more towns and reservations are posting signs forbidding biking on the trails.

Many state-owned properties have remained open but are not well maintained. As a result, these picturesque areas that offer great riding have insufficient trail markers. It's very confusing to follow directions with few signs, so be prepared to lose your way a few times. The first time you explore an area you may have to dismount frequently to check directions and the trip will probably take twice as long as subsequent visits. In general, the trails on interior sections of the forests and reservations tend to be narrower, rockier, and hillier. If you are biking in the state forests during hunting season in November or December, wear fluorescent orange or green.

In order to preserve the areas that have remained open to mountain bikers, please follow these rules:

1. Keep off trails posted with No Biking signs.

2. Stay on the trails. Never create new ones.

3. Do not ride between January 1 and April 30.

4. Practice low-impact cycling: Dismount in areas where your tires will leave an imprint, such as wetlands, moist stream beds, or on certain soils after a heavy rain; avoid skidding when ascending or descending steep slopes.

5. Always relinquish the right of way to other trail users.

6. When meeting horseback riders, dismount until the horse has passed.

7. Ride in control.

8. Alert other trail users if you intend to pass.

9. Don't ride alone.

1

EMERALD

NECKLACE

 Distance and Difficulty: 16 miles of easy biking. Some short sections with heavy traffic.

A unique and charming feature of Boston's landscape is the string of gardens, parks, and malls, named the Emerald Necklace, that winds through the city. The credit for this design goes to Frederick Law Olmsted, who shaped the nine contiguous parks that stretch for eight miles.

This bike tour follows Olmsted's green belt from the Boston Public Garden to Arnold Arboretum and returns via the bike trail through the Southeast/west Corridor Linear Park. The linear park trail begins a block from the arboretum and runs through newly landscaped parks and quaint South End neighborhoods to Copley Place in the Back Bay. Although most of the ride is on bike paths and through parks, you will have to navigate short sections of busy roads.

Transportation: By automobile: Take the Arlington Street/Downtown Boston exit off Storrow Drive. From the exit ramp, turn left at the traffic lights. Follow Arlington Street; you'll see the Public Garden on the left. To reach the Boston Common Underground Parking Garage, make a sharp left at the second set of traffic lights onto Boylston Street, keeping to the far left. Turn left at the next traffic light onto Charles Street. The entrance to the parking garage is on the right.

By commuter rail: From South Station, follow Summer Street and take a left onto Bedford Street to West Street, which leads to Boston Common. Cut through the common in a westerly direction to the Boston Public Garden. Walk through the garden, over one of the world's smallest suspension bridges, straight ahead to the Arlington Street entrance to the garden.

From North Station, follow Causeway Street (its name changes to Staniford Street) until you reach Cambridge Street. Cross Cambridge Street, turn right and ride up Temple Street for two blocks until you reach the State House. Ride around the State House to Joy Street, turn left, and go downhill one block to Beacon Street. Cross Beacon and cycle in a westerly direction through Boston Common toward Charles Street. Cross Charles Street and walk your bike through the garden.

Food and Drink: Jamaica Pond Boathouse; a variety of shops on Centre Street in Jamaica Plain.

Restrooms: Boston Welcome Center on Tremont Street, across from the tourist information booth on Boston Common; Jamaica Pond Boathouse; Hunnewell Visitor Center in Arnold Arboretum.

Recreational Options: Walking all or part of the route; in-line skating along Commonwealth Avenue Mall, Back Bay Fens, the Riverway, Olmsted Park, and Jamaica Pond; boating on and fishing in Jamaica Pond.

Background: Frederick Law Olmsted had a vision: He sought to create rustic environments where Bostonians could leave noisy, polluted, and over-crowded cities to partake of recreational pursuits and enjoy nature. One of America's first professional landscape designers, Olmsted started his firm in New York, where he designed Central Park. When Olmsted was hired to create a string of parks for Boston, he decided to move his firm to Brookline, Massachusetts, where it remained for nearly a hundred years.

Olmsted did not design Boston Common, the Public Garden, or the Commonwealth Avenue Mall, but he did incorporate them into the Emerald Necklace, one of his finest works.

THE RIDE

1. The ride begins at the Arlington Street entrance to the **Boston Public Garden**.

Although bike riding is not allowed in the garden, you can wheel your cycle in and around the well-manicured landscape. America's first public botanical garden displays intricate floral plantings and exotic trees, along with man-made ponds where you can watch the famous swan boats paddle by. Don't miss the bronze replica of Mrs. Mallard and her eight ducklings, featured in Robert McCloskey's popular book *Make Way for Ducklings*, waddling along the northern-most walkway.

2. Cross Arlington Street to **Commonwealth Avenue Mall** and bike down the middle of its wide center strip.

Begun in 1858 as the Boston version of a Parisian boulevard, Comm. Ave., as it is now known, was developed during a span of 30 years. Trainloads of gravel were deposited daily, first along Arlington Street and then throughout the entire length of Commonwealth Avenue, until the former tidal flats of the Back Bay were filled. The homes on each side of the road were built sequentially, and, as you progress down the boulevard, you'll see the evolution of prosperous Bostonians' architectural taste from the mid- to late-1800s.

Silver maple

The entire boulevard was planted originally with four rows of elm trees, Olmsted's favorite. He hoped each row would create its own canopy to protect walkers, bench-sitters, and carriage-riders. Unfortunately, the elms fell victim to Dutch elm disease and were replaced with smaller but hardier trees, such as **silver maple** and Japanese elms.

Each block boasts its own statue. One of Alexander Hamilton, the first granite sculpture in the United States, stands between Arlington and Berkeley Streets. Unfortunately, the sculptor, William Rimmer, was not familiar with chiseling this type of stone and Hamilton's limbs occasionally have fallen off.

3. Continue down the length of the boulevard, crossing under the Massachusetts Avenue overpass. Turn left onto Charlesgate East and

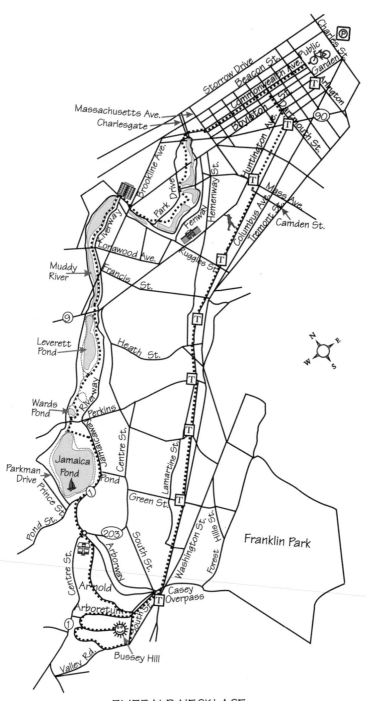

Massachusetts Ave.
Charlesgate

Muddy River

Leverett Pond

Wards Pond

Parkman Drive

Jamaica Pond

Arnold Arboretum

Bussey Hill

Franklin Park

Casey Overpass

EMERALD NECKLACE

walk your bike up the sidewalk on the Storrow Drive exit ramp that leads to the Fenway section of the ride.

4. This next section is tricky: lots of traffic and three separate streets to cross. Basically, head straight toward the bridge that spans the Muddy River. This maneuver requires crossing at one set of lights next to the sign Boylston Street Outbound and then crossing again at Boylston Street Inbound sign.

5. The bridge at this busy intersection in the **Back Bay Fens** begins the Olmsted-designed section of the Emerald Necklace.

    Before mounting your bike, stand at the bridge and look out over the Muddy River. This aptly named waterway was a foul-smelling fen, or bog, before Olmsted transformed it by rerouting and speeding up the flow of water. Seeking green spaces that would bring relief from the stresses of city life, Olmsted created a series of English-style, unpretentious pastoral landscapes. By tearing down and building up hills, creating ponds, and moving trees, he transformed a neglected area to a landscape that appears to have been there forever.

6. Facing the water, turn right and follow the paved walkway down toward an endless array of community gardens, each more elaborate than the last.

    These "victory gardens" were first planted during World War II because of the shortage of fresh vegetables. Now residents wait years for the tiny plots, leased annually from the city for $15.

7. After biking around the gardens, head into the next section of the Fens toward the flags that surround the war memorials.

    Well-spaced benches provide a convenient rest and snack stop where you can look out across the Muddy River for a great view of the Museum of Fine Arts.

    The vista back toward the victory gardens includes a stone bridge designed by H. H. Richardson, the architect of Trinity Church in Copley Square. The bridge was constructed with a local variety of conglomerate rock called Roxbury puddingstone. Formed from outwash of ancient rivers, the stone has an uneven speckled appearance.

8. From the memorials, angle off to your right and keep your eyes open for the well-hidden Rose Garden. You're in for a treat if you have arrived

when the garden is unlocked. (Starting in mid-April, 8:00 A.M. to 3:00 P.M., Monday through Friday. In June, when the roses are at their peak, the garden is open daily from 8:00 A.M. to 7:00 P.M., as it is weekdays during the summer. Autumn hours are the same as in spring.)

9. Continue on the walkway that parallels Park Drive until you reach the intersection with Brookline Avenue.

> The huge Sears, Roebuck and Co. building at the junction of Boylston Street, Brookline Avenue, and Park Drive, a Boston landmark, is being revived as a shopping center with a parking garage. A park is planned for the parking lot across the street.

10. The building sits next to another challenging intersection where you must cross three busy streets: Brookline Avenue, Park Drive, and Boylston Street. With the former Sears building on the right, go straight, turning left when you see the sign for the **Riverway**. Once you reach the Olmsted-designed green belt that borders the river, you'll find the bike path. Paths line both sides of the Riverway, so you can ride on either the gravelly east side that belongs to Boston or the paved west side in Brookline.

> Designed in the 19th century, the Riverway originally was conceived as a carriage path. Today this narrow road with tree-lined curves limits cars' visibility, so cycling on the path through this section is much safer than driving on this busy road.

> Unfortunately, roads carrying heavy traffic intersect with the bike path. Stop and dismount at each intersection before proceeding to the next section.

11. After you cross the intersection with Huntington Avenue, you'll notice that the paths diverge. An unpaved path runs along Leverett Pond, while the paved section passes under the Riverway and remains on the right side as it parallels the river. If you follow the unpaved route, continue to bear left and you'll pass three separate bodies of water in this section, named **Olmsted Park**.

12. At the third body of water, named Ward's Pond, look on your left for six steps and then head up the path toward the road. If you cycle past the path, you will have to carry your bike up a flight of stairs.

13. **Jamaica Pond**, a geologic kettle hole more than 50 feet deep, appears after the intersection with Perkins Road. If on the paved route, bear left and follow the signs to the Jamaicaway. The bike path continues to follow what is now called the Jamaicaway, while a narrow, pedestrian-only path circles the pond. The path surrounding the pond is frequently dotted with fishermen trying to catch trout, which the state stocks each year.

    The Jamaica Pond Boathouse, open daily in spring, summer, and fall, rents rowboats and sailboats from noon to dusk. Refreshments and restrooms are available at the boathouse and along Centre Street (reached by biking down Pond Street, which is opposite the boathouse).

14. To continue on to Arnold Arboretum, remain on the paved walkway until you reach a break in the necklace requiring a few minutes of traffic navigation. Enter the first rotary at the intersection of the Jamaicaway, Parkman Drive, and Prince Street and proceed straight ahead onto the Arborway, following the signs for Route 1 south.

15. At the next rotary do *not* follow Route 1 south. Instead, stay to the left and follow the signs to **Arnold Arboretum** and Route 203 east toward Dorchester. The entrance to Arnold Arboretum is just ahead.

16. Turn right and pass through the entrance gate into the Arboretum, open daily throughout the year.

    Although designed by Olmsted and developed as an integral part of the Emerald Necklace, the 265-acre Arboretum is maintained by Harvard University, which pays the city $1 per year to use the land. More than 5,000 varieties of woody plants grow in this scenic living museum. For more information on the Arnold Arboretum, turn to chapter 24.

17. Follow the entrance road as it winds through the Arboretum, continuing straight past the left fork that leads to the Forest Hills gate. The first side road on your right leads to the bonsai house and greenhouses, where much of the propagation and research take place. Some of the bonsai plants in this famous collection are more than 100 years old.

18. Take your next left and ascend to the crest of Bussey Hill. If you arrive either before or after foliage season, you may catch a view of the city.

19. Descend the hill. Take your first left and then another left onto Valley Road.

20. Proceed straight on Valley Road until you reach the South Street gate. Turn left onto South Street.

21. Remain on South Street until you reach Washington Street. Cross Washington heading toward the Forest Hills subway station.

22. Ride to the front of the station (the northeast side). At the traffic lights, pass beneath the overpass and cross New Washington Street to reach the Southeast/west Corridor Park (11.3 total miles).

> The return is via the Pierre Lallement Bike Path, a 3.5-mile ride through the Southeast/west Corridor Park. Heavily landscaped with trees and bushes, the park runs above the Orange Line MBTA (Ⓣ) tracks, passing by six MBTA stations before it ends at the Back Bay Station. (The park's name changes from Southeast to Southwest depending on which side of the tracks it is located.) Basketball courts, playgrounds, and tennis courts border the path.

> It may seem odd that a bike path running through Boston should have such a decidedly French name. Lallement invented the bicycle in France in 1862; he succeeded in getting a patent for the machine but lacked the business acumen to profit from it. He spent the latter part of his life in Boston, where he died a pauper at age 47. By naming the bike path in Lallement's honor, his supporters are according him the credit he deserved but never received.

23. Remain on the path as it runs for 1.5 miles on the west side of the tracks before it switches to the east.

> On the west side you'll have a straight-shot view of the John Hancock and Prudential skyscrapers. On the east side, you'll first pass the sprawling brick campus of Roxbury Community College.

24. After passing the Northeastern University parking garage, playing fields, and tennis courts, turn left on Camden Street. The bike path continues halfway down the block on the right side.

25. At the intersection with Massachusetts Avenue, head toward the Massachusetts Avenue Ⓣ station. Next to the station a bike ramp leads to the continuation of the Southwest Corridor Park.

> This section highlights the charm of the South End. The quaint brick row houses were constructed during the late 19th century.

26. From the end of the bike path at Copley Place, turn left onto Dartmouth Street.

27. Remain on Dartmouth, passing Trinity Church and Boston Public Library, for four blocks until you reach Commonwealth Avenue. Turn right on Commonwealth to return to the starting point at the Public Garden.

Although **Franklin Park** is the last link in Olmsted's necklace, and what he regarded as his major achievement in Boston, it is not included in this tour. Regrettably, hazardous traffic en route and a few unsafe areas in and around the park necessitate its omission.

A hundred years ago, the park was extremely popular; its roads were lined with carriages that carried passengers through the grounds to their favorite picnic spots. While some sections of the park retain Olmsted's original ideas of developing natural features into ideal scenes reminiscent of the English countryside, much of the 527-acre park has been changed. In 1911, the zoo replaced the Greeting, designed by Olmsted to be the park's formal entrance. Of particular interest in the zoo is the African wildlife section, where animals are allowed to move freely in settings similar to their actual African habitats. Four major African ecologies are represented: desert, tropical forest, veldt, and bush forest.

Franklin Park also contains a golf course, woodland preserve, and the Playstead, an area for active recreation and sports. If you wish to visit, travel in a group by automobile or public transportation.

2

CHARLES

RIVER

LOOP

Boston—Cambridge—Watertown

 Distance and Difficulty: 17.8 total miles consisting of two loops, the 10.8-mile Cambridge-Boston loop and the seven-mile Watertown loop.

On warm sunny days, students, residents, and tourists head for the broad grassy expanses bordering the banks of the Charles River. The river and its surrounding parks teem with people soaking up the sun, the scenery, and the scene. Cyclists, in-line skaters, joggers, walkers, sunbathers, vendors, and musicians all compete for space. The Boston side is wider, offers a greater number of walkways, and is adorned with bridges, fountains, lagoons, and the Hatch Shell, home of popular summer concerts. However, on Sundays in the spring, summer, and fall, cars are not allowed on a 1.2-mile section of Memorial Drive, the Cambridge roadway adjacent to the Charles River, thereby increasing that side's playground potential.

If you prefer to exercise without swarms of people, tour any weekday between about 9:00 A.M. and 4:00 P.M., when the 18-mile Dr. Paul Dudley White Bicycle Path is not as crowded. Expect the river to provide plenty of visual entertainment, with sailboats and windsurfers tacking to and fro and rowers propelling their skiffs and sculls rhythmically over the water. Whether the path is crowded or not, the dramatic eastern view down the river to the Boston skyline, gold-domed State House, and shimmering facade on the John Hancock building makes this ride a winner.

The path follows the Charles River from Watertown to the locks and dam next to Boston's Museum of Science, in two loops, so you can choose the length of your ride: the seven-mile Cambridge-Watertown loop, the 11-mile Boston-Cambridge loop, or a combination of the two.

Transportation: By the Ⓣ : On Sundays, when bikes are permitted on the Ⓣ (with a $5 Ⓣ pass; see appendix), cyclists can hop on the Red Line, exit at the Harvard Square station, and head south toward the river.

By automobile: Free parking is available at the MDC (Metropolitan District Commission) parking lots on Soldiers Field Road, at the west end of Storrow Drive. From Boston head west on Storrow Drive. After you pass the Harvard Square exit, take your first left onto Soldiers Field Road, following the signs to Newton. There are at least three parking lots on the right side of this road.

To reach the parking area from the west take Route 2, follow the signs toward Boston and Storrow Drive. Where Route 2 bears left for Cambridge and Memorial Drive, continue straight toward Boston. Shortly the road forks again. Bear left through a set of lights, over a tiny bridge, and take your first right onto Soldiers Field Road.

There is also a small MDC parking lot on the river side of Memorial Drive two miles east of where Storrow and Memorial Drives split.

Food and Drink: The only food and drink directly on the route is at the booths, open seasonally, adjacent to the Esplanade on the Boston side. On Sundays when Memorial Drive is closed to traffic, vendors are stationed near the road. A variety of restaurants and snack shops are located in Harvard Square (via JFK Street) and in the Cambridgeside Galleria in Kendall Square.

Restrooms: MDC Daly Recreation Center on Nonantum Street at the third mile of the Watertown loop; near the Hatch Shell on the Esplanade (seasonal); the MDC boathouse between the Esplanade and the dam (seasonal); on the first floor of Cambridgeside Galleria mall.

Recreational Options: In-line skating, cross-country skiing, walking, sailing, windsurfing, canoeing, and kayaking.

Background: The Charles River not only beautifies and energizes the cities of Boston and Cambridge, it also has played an important historic role. Named for King Charles I of England, the river ironically slowed the progress of the British troops on their march to Concord in April 1775. Before the large dam was built at the east end in 1910, the river turned to marshland at low tide. Paul Revere frequently navigated the Charles River, so he knew when and where to cross. The British, having no such knowledge, rowed into the marsh grass and became mired.

After Revere heard of the British intentions to demolish the colonists' supply of arms in Concord, he alerted fellow patriots in Charlestown by a prearranged signal: two blinking lights from the steeple of North Church. Revere then left his home in Boston's North End and joined watermen who rapidly rowed him across the eastern end of the river to Charlestown. There friends were waiting with their fleetest horse. Cleverly evading British patrols, Revere arrived in Lexington five hours ahead of the Redcoats and warned residents that British troops were on their way.

The dam and locks built at Lechmere Canal eliminated the effects of the tide. Instead of swamps at low tide and flooding when high tide coincided with a storm, the Charles became a predictable river that boasted a nine-mile lake at its eastern end.

The crowds along the banks of the Charles River peak the third Sunday in October when tens of thousands of spectators navigate for the best spot to view the Head of the Charles, the largest one-day rowing regatta in the world. Here a procession of boats from all over the world, manned by oarsmen and -women of all ages, compete against the clock to see which craft covers the 3-mile course in the shortest time.

THE RIDE

1. Begin at one of the MDC parking lots on Soldiers Field Road for the seven-mile Watertown-Cambridge loop. From the parking lot, facing the river, turn left on Soldiers Field Road, heading west toward Watertown. (Boston bikers can pick up the ride at the Esplanade entrance at Arlington Street at direction #19. Cambridge bikers can pick up the ride at the intersection of Memorial Drive and JFK Street at direction #8.)

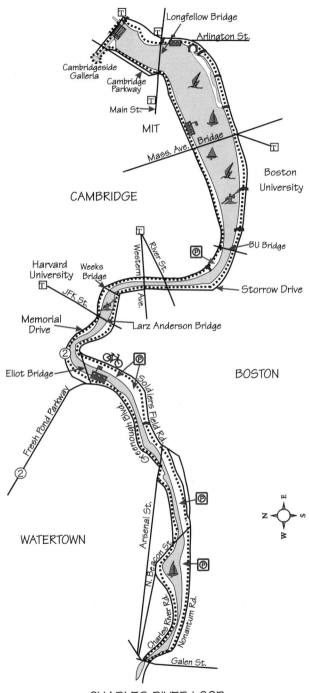

Longfellow Bridge
Arlington St.
Cambridgeside Galleria
Cambridge Parkway
Main St.
MIT
Mass. Ave. Bridge
CAMBRIDGE
Boston University
Western Ave.
River St.
Harvard University
Weeks Bridge
JFK St.
Memorial Drive
Larz Anderson Bridge
BU Bridge
Storrow Drive
Eliot Bridge
Fresh Pond Parkway
Soldiers Field Rd.
Greenough Blvd.
BOSTON
Arsenal St.
N. Beacon St.
WATERTOWN
Charles River Rd.
Nonantum Rd.
Galen St.

CHARLES RIVER LOOP

The wide grassy expanse adjacent to Soldiers Field Road appeals to large groups who gather on summer weekends to eat, drink, and partake of land and water sports. On this side, you'll pass a number of boathouses; concessions that rent canoes and kayaks; and the Harter Community Gardens, where residents lease parcels of land for gardens.

After pedaling one mile and passing Northeastern University's Henderson Boathouse, the wide grassy expanse changes to woods. By the third mile there are neither woods nor grass and the bike path becomes a sidewalk that runs alongside the river.

2. You will have to dismount at three light-regulated intersections: Arsenal Street, North Beacon Street, and Galen Street, where a sign indicates the end of the bikeway. Turn right on Galen Street and cross the bridge over the Charles River into Watertown to return on the opposite side of the river.

On the corner, a delightful park next to the river offers a relaxing respite in busy Watertown Square. A number of Armenian families have settled in Watertown and many shops and restaurants in and around the square reflect that heritage.

3. The first mile on the return borders the river, parallels Charles River Parkway, and passes the Watertown Yacht Club. During the second mile, the path runs through a grassy section with bike racks and picnic benches.

Just before the traffic light at North Beacon Street, 1.4 miles from Watertown Square, a sign marks the Prehistoric Site 1500 B.C., where stone-cutting tools, now on display at the Peabody Museum at Harvard, were excavated during construction.

4. At the traffic lights at the North Beacon Street intersection, bear left and follow the signs for the bike path. (Do not go over the bridge or you'll return to the Soldiers Field Road side.)

5. At the next light, at Arsenal Street, again bear left and remain on Greenough Boulevard. Here you can either ride on the bike path or on the side of Greenough Boulevard, a wide, relatively untraveled road.

6. Before you reach the next busy intersection, get on the bike path so you can cut through the parking lot at the Buckingham, Brown and Nichols Boathouse, owned by the private school across the street. Follow the parking lot until it ends.

7. At the end of the parking lot, veer right as the path descends under Eliot Bridge and emerges on the Memorial Drive side of the Charles River, where the eleven-mile Cambridge-Boston loop begins.

If you prefer to bike only one loop and wish to return to the parking lot on Soldiers Field Road, do not go under the bridge. Instead, cross the Charles via the sidewalk on the diminutive Eliot Bridge. Turn right onto the paved walkway that returns to the bike path beside Soldiers Field Road.

8. From Memorial Drive, your first stop, literally, is at the traffic light at the congested intersection with the Larz Anderson Bridge and JFK Street.

The bridge leads to Harvard Stadium and Harvard Business School, and JFK Street heads into Harvard Square. If you wish to turn left and explore Harvard University and Harvard Square, see chapter 25.

Dogwood

John F. Kennedy Park, a memorial to the former president, sits on the corner of JFK Street. This five-acre site is landscaped with a fountain surrounded by **dogwood** and cherry trees, lilacs, and viburnum. All display fragrant, colorful blossoms in May, the month of Kennedy's birth. Beyond the park lies Harvard's Kennedy School of Government, where famous faculty share their knowledge with future world leaders.

Along this stretch of Memorial Drive, Harvard's red-brick dormitories line the road, providing a classy but cozy feeling.

On the right, you'll pass the John W. Weeks Pedestrian Bridge.

9. Four additional intersections require dismounting and walking your bike across busy streets.

To put a positive spin on these cycling interruptions, take advantage of the enforced stops and gaze down the river toward the Boston skyline. Each stop will improve the vista, which includes Beacon Hill and the gold-domed State House.

10.   After crossing the Western Avenue Bridge, River Street Bridge, and Boston University (BU) Bridge, you'll reach the Massachusetts Avenue (MIT) Bridge, which leads to the Massachusetts Institute of Technology, another world-renowned university. Educating 10,000 students, half of whom are enrolled in its many graduate schools, MIT is regarded as one of the top schools for the study of science and engineering.

> Set back from the drive sits the imposing Rogers Building with its four pairs of columns and domed roof. Named after the founder of MIT, the building is the main entrance to the teaching buildings. The MIT boathouse appears ahead on the right.

11.   At the next intersection, the Longfellow Bridge (also called the salt-and-pepper bridge because of its shakerlike center columns), you will have to navigate a rather narrow sidewalk that heads out into the river before it curves back toward land.

> It's a bit tricky to maneuver through this next section to the Cambridgeside Galleria. The operative command is "Follow the river!"

12.   After you have pedaled over the bridge, take your first right onto a wide bike path, with the river on your right and large condominium buildings on your left.

13.   Continue straight toward the Museum of Science, the building that appears to bridge the Charles River.

14.   Proceed on the path as it turns left, follows the Lechmere Canal, and descends below a bridge. After the bridge, the paved path becomes gravel and leads to a circular lagoon sporting a soaring fountain.

> For a great rest/snack stop, head to the left of the lagoon to the Cambridgeside Galleria, a shopping mall with an extensive food court. You can use the facilities, purchase a drink or snack, and revive at the waterside tables. If you are interested in a water excursion, lock your bike and take a river tour on one of the boats that embark from this basin.

15.   To continue, after having traveled four miles from the western end of Memorial Drive, circle around the lagoon, go under the bridge, and emerge on a driveway next to the Museum of Science.

16. Follow the driveway to the road and turn right onto the sidewalk in front of the Museum of Science, regarded by many as one of the best science museums in the world.

Once you've passed the museum, look below to your right at the Charles River Dam, which controls the water levels of the Charles River Basin. The original dam was replaced in 1978 by a system of locks with six huge propeller pumps that can move 8,400 cubic feet of water per second. The system allows both fish and boats to pass from Boston Harbor to the Charles River. The MDC, which operates the dam, offers tours by appointment (617-727-0488).

17. Having completed the Cambridge half of the second loop, go around the parking area of the MDC/State Police Station and head down the Boston side of the Charles River.

A number of pedestrian bridges cross Storrow Drive to the Charles River: the first at Charles and Cambridge Streets; the next, at the end of Arlington Street, leading to the Hatch Shell; a third at Fairfield Street in the Back Bay; and a fourth, off Massachusetts Avenue.

For the next 3.6 miles, no intersections interrupt your cycling. You can choose among several parallel paths: next to the river, farther away, or alongside the road. Because of the variety of paths and level terrain, this section is popular with in-line skaters.

A half-mile from the east point on the Boston side, you will pass the Community Boating Boathouse, operated by the MDC, which organizes one of the country's oldest and largest public sailing programs.

Shortly thereafter, you'll spot a partially covered stage, named the Hatch Shell after its benefactor, Edward Hatch, where free Esplanade concerts and the famous Fourth of July fireworks are held. The current Hatch Shell is actually the third outdoor band shell. Because of the awful acoustics emanating from the first wooden version, the designers of the second shell were determined to remedy the sound problem. The second, a steel roof, radiated superior sound, along with stifling heat that roasted the musicians and conductor. Few acoustical complaints result from the third roof, a combination of terrazzo, marble, teak, and concrete.

Tall fountains add a touch of class to the basins along the Charles River Esplanade.

The grassy seating area (covered with blankets and beach chairs during musical events) is surrounded by statues that oversee the hoopla. This section is always the busiest, filled with people in motion and others watching the activity. Here you can find refreshments, telephones, plenty of benches, and restrooms.

The Esplanade was beautifully crafted in 1936 by Arthur Shurcliff, who filled in the land and created a series of lagoons that can be crossed via charming minibridges.

An unusual sculpture sits in the center of one of the parks. Sculptor Ralph Helmick layered lengths of aluminum to form a likeness of Arthur Fiedler, founder of the Esplanade concerts and former conductor of the Boston Pops.

18. Two and a half miles from the science museum, the path divides; off-road bikers and joggers favor the dirt path, while in-line skaters and riders of touring bikes prefer the paved route.

   The students reclining on the grassy banks probably attend **Boston University**, the school that occupies many of the buildings on the left side of Storrow Drive. One of the largest private institutions in the country, BU enrolls 28,000 students in its undergraduate program and in its 17 other specialized schools.

19. At the BU Sailing Pavilion, the path leads to a wooden bridge that extends out on the water before narrowing into a sidewalk next to Storrow Drive.

20. You will have to dismount at three bridge intersections: two heading to and from Cambridge's Central Square, the third to Harvard Square and Harvard Stadium.

21. After cycling a little more than a mile past the Larz Anderson Bridge to Harvard, you will come to the Eliot Bridge. To return to the parking lots on Soldiers Field Road, *do not go over the bridge!* Instead, bear right onto the path just before the bridge; it passes under the bridge and follows the river along Soldiers Field Road.

3

NAHANT

 Distance and Difficulty: 10 miles of relatively easy riding with several short hills.

If the weather outside is sweltering and you're looking for a place to exercise where it's cool and inviting, cycle around Nahant. Favored by wealthy 19th-century Bostonians, this charming former resort community now is occupied year-round by residents who enjoy the ocean views and close proximity to Boston. While exploring the scenic rocky coast along the two peninsulas of Little Nahant and Nahant, the perspiring pedaler can jump into the ocean for a swim at any one of the 11 beaches en route.

The 10-mile loop around Nahant is a perfect family excursion. Although no bike paths exist on the peninsula, traffic is light because only residents are permitted to park in town and at beaches. Bikers do not have to worry about parking fines whenever they stop to swim, explore coves, or walk along the beach.

It's worth the effort to pedal up the bluffs that overlook the ocean. Walkways circle peaks, adorned with soft green grass and numerous park benches, where you can rest, picnic, watch the ocean crash against the rocks, or search the water for the fabled sea serpent that supposedly surfaces every 50 years.

Bordering the beach for a mile and a half, a bike path on the causeway links Lynn to Nahant. On this stretch bikers are accompanied by refreshing breezes, along with skaters and walkers who enjoy exercising alongside the surf.

Cyclists who wish to extend the ride can follow the tour into Swampscott and Marblehead (see chapter 4).

Transportation: By automobile: From Boston, follow Route 1A to Lynn. In Lynn, Route 1A is also called the Lynnway. Stay on the Lynnway when it forks to the right and heads east toward Nahant. Go around the rotary toward Nahant and turn into the parking lot for the Lynn–Nahant Beach Reservation.

From Routes 128/95, take Exit 44B onto Route 129 east toward Lynn. Remain on Route 129 for approximately four miles into Lynn. When Route 129 makes a sharp left at the traffic light, continue straight on Chestnut Street for 1.3 miles, following the signs to North Shore Community College. Turn right on Broad Street, which is also Route 1A (continuing to follow the North Shore Community College signs). The Mary Baker Eddy House, where Eddy lived when she wrote *Science and Health* in 1875 and founded the Christian Science Church in 1879, sits on the left, immediately after the turn (free guided tour). Turn left onto Market Street/Carroll Parkway (Lynnway) toward Nahant. The Lynn Heritage State Park sits on the right side of the Lynnway. Limited parking is available in the park. The MBTA may be offering free parking in its modern commuter rail parking garage (from Broad Street, turn right onto Washington). To park at the Nahant Beach parking lot, enter the Nahant rotary and turn left into the lot. In summer a fee is charged at the lot, which holds 1,300 cars but fills quickly on a hot day.

By commuter rail: From North Station, take the Rockport Line to Lynn. The train station is less than a half-mile from the causeway to Nahant. Exit the station and turn left onto Market Street, which crosses Route 1A and becomes Carroll Parkway (Lynnway). Turn left on Carroll Parkway to the Nahant rotary. Circle right around the rotary toward Nahant.

Food and Drink: Water fountains are located near the bathhouse and at the main entrance to Nahant Beach Reservation. A concession stand, open seasonally, sits near the bike path 0.3 mile from the main gate. The Ocean's Edge restaurant, located just before the left turn to Little Nahant, has takeout service during the summer. Along Nahant Road in Nahant Center is Richdale's, a small market, and Captain Seaside, a coffee/pizza shop.

Restrooms: Three locations along Nahant Beach: in the bathhouse immediately after the rotary, in the halfway house located 1 mile from the bathhouse, and at the main gate, 1.3 miles from the rotary. All restrooms are open from May 1 through September 30.

Fees: The parking lot along Nahant Beach charges several dollars.

Recreational Options: In-line skating along the bike path next to Nahant Beach, off-season in the huge parking lot, and around Nahant if you don't mind hills. Swimming.

Background: Since 1630, proximity to the ocean lured settlers to Nahant. In the 17th century, farmers used the surrounding water to protect their grazing sheep and cattle from hungry wolves. A century later, the farmland was divided into individual lots, but only three permanent homes were built on what was then a hard-to-reach peninsula.

The lucrative shipping trade created a wealthy upper class that could afford to summer in Nahant. In 1820, Colonel Thomas Perkins, a Boston merchant, purchased land along the rocky north coast. His daughter and son-in-law, Samuel Cabot, desperate for a climate that would cure their sickly son, encouraged the colonel to build a cottage. The curative effects of the sea and salt air convinced Perkins to buy Nahant's entire east end and build a hotel. The first resort in the United States had been created.

Although Thomas Perkins discovered Nahant, farsighted Frederick Tudor, who made vast sums of money shipping ice from Fresh Pond (see chapter 27) to places as distant as the West Indies, developed the peninsula. Having successfully developed a section of Beacon Hill, Tudor felt confident enough to purchase land, divide it into 62 lots, and build simple summer cottages. He then convinced his business buddies to join him.

Nahant was well on its way to becoming a full-fledged seaside resort if it could solve the accessibility problem. Vacationers disliked traveling over the barrier beach that often was submerged during high tide. In 1847 a cart road was built, but the strong sea breezes continually covered the road with sand. The problem was solved by planting beach grass on either side of the road to stabilize the sand.

The next generation to summer in Nahant included Harvard professors who had married the daughters of the well-to-do merchants. Free from teaching duties in the summer, these husbands enjoyed accompanying their wives and children and writing by the sea. Among the most prominent were poet Henry Wadsworth Longfellow, who began summering there in 1850, and Louis Agassiz, the zoologist/geologist. Even though Longfellow's wife, Fanny Appleton, was the daughter of one of Boston's wealthiest merchants, Henry insisted on paying for their lodging, so his wife and children often boarded with families of fishermen.

During the two decades prior to the Civil War, Nahant developed into the country's most popular summer resort. Attracted by frequent steamboat trips, publicity of sea serpent sightings, and the construction of posh hotels, celebrities and nobility summered in this picturesque spot. Nahant hotel owners decided that Lynn's restrictive temperance laws were hurting their business and convinced officials to allow the peninsula to separate from Lynn. In 1853, Nahant incorporated and became the smallest town in Massachusetts.

In the mid-1800s, Newport stole the "most fashionable resort" crown. Nahant's fancy hotels closed and were replaced by establishments on the south coast that catered to the working class. The addition of a wharf and steamboat landing at Bass Point stimulated the construction of two hotels and 24 tent colonies.

During the Spanish-American War, the government deemed the two eastern hills to be of strategic importance in the defense of Boston Harbor and built forts on their summits and tore down the cottages on surrounding land.

The introduction of the trolley in 1905 created a carnival-like atmosphere in this once staid resort. On a hot sticky Sunday, 30,000 perspiring people took the train to Lynn and then lined up to ride the electric car to Nahant. Families and couples headed for the Midway Amusement Park at Bass Point, where they rode on the longest roller coaster in the East, listened to band concerts, or rode round and round on the carousel.

THE RIDE

1. Begin on the bike path that runs through the Nahant Beach Reservation and cycle beside the ocean.

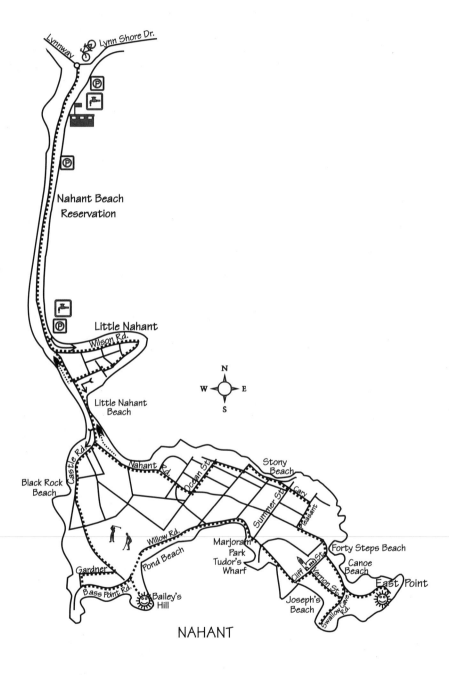

NAHANT

Managed by the Metropolitan District Commission (MDC), which oversees the park system in and around Boston, the reservation runs north and south of the rotary for 2.5 miles and includes a boat ramp, tennis courts, bathhouse, restrooms, and a lifeguard-supervised beach.

2. At 1.3 miles, pass the Ocean Edge restaurant and turn left on Wilson Road into Little Nahant. Follow the road as it circles around and returns to the causeway.

   Little Nahant was not developed until 1906, the year after the trolley line connecting Lynn with Nahant allowed the working class to visit in greater numbers than before. These workers liked what they saw and demanded inexpensive summer camps. The developers carved out tiny plots where they built modest homes both on Little Nahant and on the east side of the main peninsula. Both areas have retained the character of that era.

3. Turn left onto the sidewalk and pass Little Nahant Beach.

4. At 2.5 miles, carefully cross the terminus of the causeway and bear right onto Castle Road. Follow Castle Road past Black Rock Beach where there is a super, straight-shot view across Massachusetts Bay to Boston.

5. Remain on Castle Road until it ends, and then turn right. The road loops around and passes Bass Point, where apartments have replaced hotels and forts.

6. Continue on Bass Point Road as it takes a right-angle turn and runs along the south coast to **Bailey's Hill**. Eighty years ago this section looked quite different: Imagine a roller coaster and midway sitting next to Bass Point Road!

7. Stop at Bailey's Hill, where a bandstand serves as the sole reminder of the resort era. Pedal to the peak for a vista across the bay to the Boston Harbor Islands (chapter 22). Because of the clear view of Boston and its harbor, the government built a fort here to protect Boston Harbor during the Spanish-American War.

8. From the base of Bailey's Hill, head straight into the overgrown parking lot and onto the dirt path that leads to the golf course clubhouse and parking lot. Pond Beach is to your right.

9. Turn right into the golf course parking lot and pedal to the stop sign at Willow Road (four miles).

10. Follow Willow as it runs between the Ocean View Country Club and Nahant Harbor.

   Henry Wadsworth Longfellow and his family spent several summers in the boardinghouse at 162 Willow Street. Across from Longfellow's former residence lies **Marjoram Park**, which offers views of the Boston skyline.

   At the end of Wharf Street, the next right after Marjoram Park, rests **Tudor's Wharf**, built initially by Nahant's first developer, Frederick Tudor, as a steamboat dock, now serving both fishermen and sailors.

11. Return to Willow Road and turn right. Willow ends at Cliff, where you must turn left.

   The house at 211 Willow is one of the few remaining homes from the original summer development. The house has been restored and modified during the last 150 years.

12. Take your next right onto Vernon Street (there may not be a street sign). The lovely stone, wood, and slate structure on the left, opposite Vernon, is the Nahant Village Church, an ecumenical Protestant establishment.

13. Turn right onto Swallow Cave Road.

   The first house on the right, #20, was designed and built by Cornelius Coolidge, who worked with Frederick Tudor in the development of both Beacon Hill and Nahant.

   At the end of Swallow Cave Road, a white pillar next to #3 marks the path to Swallow's Cave. This narrow steep path descends the slope to a cave carved out of the jagged cliff.

14. Retrace your route down Swallow Cave Road to Nahant Road. Turn right to enter the famed **East Point** section of Nahant.

   This scenic spit of land figured prominently in Nahant's development. Thomas Perkins built his first home here and followed it with the Grand Nahant Hotel which hosted Boston bluebloods, merchants, and visiting nobility. The hotel was replaced by estates built by Brahmins from Boston. Henry Cabot Lodge summered here for decades in a huge mansion landscaped with luxurious gardens.

During the Spanish-American War, when the government had taken over Bailey's Hill, Lodge permitted a coastal defense signal station to be installed on his peak. The station was equipped with electric searchlights that scanned the sea for 20 miles. Telephones linked the station to forts on the Boston Harbor Islands.

After Cabot died, his mansions remained vacant until World War II, when the army tore down the houses and built a fort. Now Northeastern University Marine Science and Maritime Studies Center occupies the site. Although cars are not allowed through the gate, bikers are permitted to pedal up the hill where **Lodge Memorial Park** is perched. Your climb will be rewarded by a spectacular 360° panorama with benches strategically placed to rest and enjoy the view at the same time.

15. Return to the entrance and pass through the gate. To your right lies **Canoe Beach**, a secluded bay surrounded by cliffs.

Formerly owned by the Lodges, the beach is now open to the public. The sand often is littered with oxygen tanks belonging to scuba divers who dive among the unusual rock formations and search for remnants of the many ships wrecked on the rocks. A lighthouse once stood on tiny Egg Rock, perched out in the ocean, to warn ships away from the hazardous reefs. By 1922, the lighthouse was abandoned due to the reduced number of ships plying the waters.

Across from Canoe Beach sits a park, and across from the park a placard marks the site of the first American lawn tennis game, played in 1874. Jim Dwight, a nephew of the Appleton family, former owners of the home with the broad expanse of grass, returned from a trip to England with a set of lawn tennis equipment. He set up the net, convinced his friends to play, and became quite proficient. After entering a number of tournaments, with balls of assorted sizes and a variety of rules, Dwight organized the U.S. National Lawn Tennis Association and standardized the rules and equipment.

The Forty Steps Beach lies next to Canoe Beach. Townies were not allowed to swim in this section during the resort era because the posh summer people socialized and swam there.

16. Continue biking along Nahant Road.

The mansion just before Cliff Street that resembles a Greek temple was built in 1829 and belonged originally to the Mifflin family, who founded Houghton-Mifflin Publishing Company.

17. Remain on Nahant Road until you reach Pleasant Street, having cycled 6.8 miles. Turn right. On the corner of Nahant and Pleasant Streets sits the Nahant Public Library, where old photographs and memorabilia are displayed.

18. Follow Pleasant to the end and turn left onto Cary Street. Stony Beach will appear soon on your right.

19. Continue to hug the water until you reach Ocean Street. Turn left.

20. Ascend Ocean to Nahant Road. Turn right. Don't miss the spectacular south coastal view from the top of Ocean Street.

    The exclusive Nahant Country Club sits on the left side just before Nahant Road. Formerly the home of Frederick Tudor, Nahant's developer, it was purchased in 1889 by the summer swells, who transformed it into their private club.

    Tudor was responsible for planting thousands of trees on what was once barren farmland. In 1825, he methodically planted 150 fast-growing Balm of Gilead trees to protect slower-growing trees. By 1834 he had four thousand trees growing in his nursery. He offered his poplars, firs, elms, oaks, and hickories at no cost to the summer residents for planting around their homes.

21. At 7.5 miles, head down Nahant Road toward the causeway, passing the Coast Guard station, built originally to rescue survivors from boats wrecked on the treacherous north coast.

22. Return to the parking lot on the bike path along the causeway.

4

SWAMPSCOTT

MARBLEHEAD

 Distance and Difficulty: 18–20 miles (depending on your starting point) of level riding. Count on a correlation between good weather and increased traffic.

Sights and sites, both picturesque and historic, offer an unbeatable combination on this ride up the coast from Swampscott to Marblehead. The 20-mile tour begins in the former resort town of Swampscott, defined by grand homes, wide sandy beaches, and serene seascapes, and runs north paralleling the coast. The route leads to Marblehead Neck, a rocky headwall that suggests how the community acquired its name (its early settlers apparently were not aware that the town straddled a ledge made of granite, not marble). Little traffic, gorgeous homes, and spectacular scenery make this section ideal for cycling.

The town of Marblehead itself is also perched on a rocky outcropping. Pedaling through the historic district and then down to the waterfront reveals a mixture of tiny craft shops and carefully preserved buildings. Much of Marblehead Center has retained an Old World charm from the prosperous shipping era when many of its dwellings were built.

How best to explore these towns? By bicycle. Driving and parking, when visiting the out-of-the-way forts and historic mansions that line Marblehead's narrow winding streets, can cause major headaches. Cycling provides the

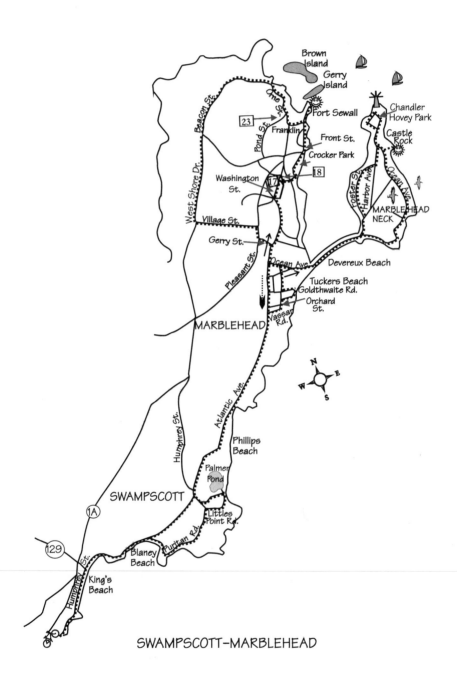

SWAMPSCOTT–MARBLEHEAD

mobility and flexibility for frequent stops to appreciate panoramic coastal views or cool off at one of Swampscott's beaches (the town limits automobile parking to town residents). Don't forget your bike lock!

Transportation: By automobile: From Boston, take Route 1A north. Drive through Lynn and turn right onto Route 129 (Eastern Avenue). Follow Route 129 east for one block to Lynn Shore Drive. Park anywhere along the drive.

From Route 128/95, take exit 44B onto Route 129 east toward Lynn. Follow Route 129 for approximately 4 miles and continue on Route 129 as it turns left onto Western Avenue. Remain on Western for 0.7 mile until Route 129 turns right onto Eastern Avenue. Continue on Eastern Avenue (Route 129) until it meets Lynn Shore Drive, which runs along the coast. Park anywhere on Lynn Shore Drive.

By commuter rail: From North Station take the Rockport Line to Lynn. Exit the station and turn left on Market Street. Cross Route 1A and turn left on Carroll Parkway (the Lynnway) toward Nahant. At the rotary, turn left onto Lynn Shore Drive toward Swampscott. Follow the directions for the ride.

Food and Drink: Abageal's, located in Swampscott on Humphrey Street (Lynn Shore Drive) just past the Lynn/Swampscott line, sells ice cream and snacks. Marblehead Center, at the junction of Atlantic Avenue and Washington Street, should appeal to "foodies" as it offers a variety of establishments within a narrow area, including Tony's Pizza, Five-Corner Deli, Sandbar and Grille, Jacob Marley's, J. Higby's for yogurt and ice cream, and Atlantic Avenue Seafood and Lobster for takeout seafood.

Restrooms: Bathhouses and restrooms are located opposite the rotary in the Lynn–Nahant Beach Reservation and at Devereux Beach on Ocean Avenue at the entrance to Marblehead Neck. Restrooms are also situated in Chandler Hovey Park in Marblehead Neck, along the Marblehead Town Wharf on Front Street, and at Fort Sewall, at the tip of Front Street. Most of the eating establishments listed above have restrooms.

Fees: Jeremiah Lee Mansion and King Hooper Mansion. Open from mid-May through mid-October. Both are open Monday to Friday from 10:00 A.M. to 4:00 P.M. and Saturday and Sunday from 1:00 P.M. to 4:00 P.M.

Recreational Options: In-line skating on the boardwalk by the beach on Lynn Shore Drive, walking around historic Marblehead Center and Harbor, swimming at one of the seven beaches.

Background: Close proximity to the sea has shaped the development of Swampscott and Marblehead. Both began as small fishing villages, prospered during the shipping era, and progressed to fashionable resort communities. Marblehead's incorporation in 1649 allowed the development of a sense of history, lacking in Swampscott, which did not separate from Lynn until 1852. Thoughtful restoration and preservation of its old buildings contribute to Marblehead's many charms.

THE RIDE

1. Swampscott's three square miles are wedged between Eastern Avenue to the south and Bellevue Avenue to the north. Begin at the town line at the intersection of Eastern Avenue and Lynn Shore Drive (Route 129 north), which is called Humphrey Street in Swampscott. Follow Humphrey Street north for 0.7 mile, riding either on the wide boardwalk or, if traffic is light, on the street until reaching Puritan Road.

   If you wish to start your ride with a swim, you can stop at any or all of Swampscott's four beaches that lie along a five-mile strip. Across from Monument Avenue, steps lead down to wide, sandy crescent-shaped King's Beach that runs south for a mile to Lynn Beach.

   Fisherman's (or Blaney's) Beach, the town pier, and Chaison Park lie behind the junction of Puritan and Humphrey Streets. Next to the pier sits the Fish House, built in 1896 by the town for its fishermen to use. It remains the only town-owned fish house in New England.

2. Turn right on Puritan Road. The Swampscott Yacht Club sits on the corner.

3. Follow Puritan for almost a mile until you reach Littles Point Road. Turn right and then right again to a drop-dead setting occupied by Marian Court Junior College.

   In 1925, when the estate served as President Calvin Coolidge's summer White House, it was called White Court. Classrooms with ocean views now occupy the ornate interior adorned with marble floors and hand-painted murals.

Phillips Beach lies just north of the college, behind Palmer Pond, a wetland bird sanctuary where you might see **mallard ducks**.

Mallard

4. From the college, continue on Littles Point Road to Phillips Beach Avenue, which returns to Puritan Road. Turn right on Puritan.

5. At 2.2 miles, turn right at Humphrey Street and continue to bear right onto Atlantic Avenue (Route 129) as Humphrey forks to the left. Remain on Atlantic as it heads into Marblehead.

6. Proceed 2 miles and turn right onto Vassar Road (4.2 miles total).

7. Take your first left onto Orchard Street.

8. Take the second right onto Goldthwaite Road, which leads to Tuckers Beach.

9. From Tuckers Beach at 4.5 miles, turn right and continue on Orchard for 0.3 mile until reaching Ocean Avenue.

10. Turn right onto Ocean for a 4-mile scenic loop around Marblehead Neck.

    This loop is made for bikers—little traffic, spectacular scenery, and bike route signs all over the Neck.

    Devereux Beach is located along the causeway linking Marblehead and Marblehead Neck. The sand here is not as fine as at the Swampscott beaches, but Devereux does offer a terrific southern view of Nahant and Boston's outer harbor.

11. Now on the neck, at 5 miles, bear right and follow Ocean Avenue as it parallels the coast.

12. A left turn on Risley Road leads to **Marblehead Neck Wildlife Sanctuary**, managed by Massachusetts Audubon Society. Fifteen acres of undeveloped swamp, thickets, and woodlands draw migrating birds in spring and fall.

13. Don't miss **Castle Rock**, the best picnic spot on the trip. An open headland, Castle Rock is perched on the right 1.3 miles after the causeway (6.3 miles total). A paved walkway to the rock lies next to a mansion surrounded by a wrought-iron fence. Painters climb this rugged bluff to capture the spectacular seascape.

14. For another fantastic view, continue straight on Ocean Avenue to **Chandler Hovey Park** and **Marble Light**, located at the tip of the peninsula. From here you can preview coming attractions as you peer across Marblehead Harbor to the quaint town center.

Chandler Hovey donated this picturesque park to the town in 1948. On a sunny summer weekend, you will see scads of sailboats from Marblehead's six yacht clubs skimming across the water.

Marble Light, formerly a white stone tower built in 1835 to guide seamen into Marblehead Harbor, was replaced by this practical steel lighthouse in 1895. Twenty-five years later, the oil lamp was electrified and now casts a green glow over the water.

Perched off to the northeast is Cat Island, the former site of a summer hotel and children's hospital. The Marblehead YMCA now operates a camp there.

15. Continue to circle around the neck, returning to Ocean Avenue.

16. Bear right at the fork to Harbor Avenue, which runs by Marblehead Harbor. If you wish to ride closer to the water, turn right on Ballast Lane, which leads to Foster Street. Foster bends, following the coastline, and joins Harbor Avenue.

17. Follow Harbor back to Ocean, cross the causeway, and turn right at the traffic light onto Atlantic Avenue.

18. At 9.7 miles, bear right on Washington Street at the intersection known as Five Corners, the location of many fast-food shops and restaurants.

Washington Street climbs to the historic district, filled with small gift shops and large historic homes. **Abbott Hall**, a huge brick Romanesque-style building, contains the town offices, museum, and gift shop, and is open daily year-round. Historic relics and pictures of prominent townspeople decorate its wood-paneled interior.

Across from Abbott Hall at numbers 187, 185, and 181 sit three mansions built in the 18th century by members of the Hooper family, leading Marblehead merchants. John Hooper lived at 187 Washington Street from 1803 to 1855. He designed the enclosed widow's walk above the roof so he could scan the sea for his ships laden with cargo from Europe, China, and the West Indies.

Farther down the hill, at 161 Washington, stands the impressive **Jeremiah Lee Mansion**, which is open to the public. Although its facade resembles stone, it actually is made of beveled wood covered with gray paint mixed with sand to give it a stony texture. The house was constructed in the Georgian style in 1803. No effort was spared to produce a detailed exterior, complete with cupola. The elaborate, elegant interior is filled with hand-carved woodwork, painted fireplace tiles, and handmade landscape wallpapers. Lee accumulated his wealth by curing fish and transporting it to the West Indies and Europe, where it was traded for salt, wine, iron, molasses, and sugar. Lee's ships also carried from England the Queen Anne, Chippendale, and Hepplewhite furniture that continues to decorate the mansion.

19. Turn right and head to 8 Hooper Street, home of the Marblehead Arts Association and the **King Hooper Mansion**.

The front of the house resembles the Jeremiah Lee Mansion, with its wood hewn to look like stone. Lee probably copied the effect, since Hooper's home preceded his by 50 years. The rear of the house was constructed even earlier, in 1728, by Robert's father. The three-story Georgian mansion was added to the dwelling 20 years later. Robert Hooper, like Lee, became fantastically rich because of the shipping trade. He was called "King" not only because of his great wealth and royal manner of life but also because of his generosity and integrity.

20. Continue down Hooper Street and turn left on Front Street. For a terrific view of the harbor, climb to the top of **Crocker Park**.

Once used to dry Jeremiah Lee's cod, the land was donated to the town in 1886 by Uriel Crocker, who was eager to share the panoramic views of the harbor and Marblehead Neck.

21. Wind your way down this quaint narrow street until it ends at Fort Sewall.

The town wharf rests on the right side of Front Street; on the left sits the home of the Boston Yacht Club, established in 1890 and the oldest in New England. The modest homes that line Front Street formerly belonged to fishermen, shoemakers, and carpenters. Many of the homes display plaques with the date the home was built along with the original owner's name and occupation.

On the way to the fort you'll spot a small rocky beach with the unsettling name Screeching Woman Cove, where a sea captain's daughter was said to have been murdered by pirates.

22. Continue straight past the Not a Through Way sign. A tiny metal sign bears the name **Fort Sewall**, the sole clue that a fort sits on the promontory.

Fort Sewall was constructed originally in 1644 and enlarged a hundred years later. The fort was scarcely used until the War of 1812 when it was further fortified and contained British prisoners. It was then named for Massachusetts Chief Justice Sewall. It was manned again during the Civil War. In 1892, Fort Sewall was dedicated as a public park and now offers yet another spectacular panorama, including Gerry Island, Brown Island, and the North Shore.

23. From Fort Sewall, retrace your route and take the first right on Franklin Street, which leads to Orne Street.

24. After having cycled 12 miles, bear right on Orne Street. Pedal for a quarter-mile until you reach the junction with Pond Street and **Old Burial Hill** on your left.

If you wish to wander among old gravestones while enjoying the view from one of Marblehead's highest points, but don't want to navigate the steep hill or steps up Old Burial Hill, turn left on Pond Street and pedal down the paved walkway to one of the oldest graveyards in New England. The cemetery contains stones that date to 1681, 600 graves from the 1700s, and an obelisk that memorializes 65 Marblehead fishermen lost in the gale of 1846. If you have time, wander around to view the delicate carvings and unique inscriptions on the stones.

Fountain Park, another hilly preserve that formerly held a fort, sits across Orne Street. Below the park, you'll find small, sandy Gas

House Beach where, during low tide, the water is shallow enough to walk to adjacent Gerry Island.

25. Continue on Orne as it skirts the coast.

Brown, or **Crowninshield, Island,** perched in the water to your right, is also accessible by foot during low tide. Managed by the Trustees of Reservations, it offers five acres of rocky shore, sandy beach, salt marsh, and meadow.

26. At 12.5 miles, Orne becomes Beacon Street as it travels through a wooded section. Remain on Beacon, now named West Shore Drive, for 1.4 miles (13.9 total) and turn left on Village Street.

27. Remain on Village for 0.6 mile until the **T** intersection at Pleasant Street (14.5 miles). Turn right.

28. Proceed 0.1 mile on Pleasant and turn left on Gerry Street (across from Marblehead High School).

29. Turn right at the **T** intersection onto Atlantic Avenue. Follow Atlantic Avenue through Swampscott back to your car or the railroad station.

5

GLOUCESTER

ROCKPORT

 Distance and Difficulty: 26 miles on level to rolling terrain. There is so much to see and do; allow a full day.

Even though Gloucester is endowed with the physical attributes that usually guarantee rampant commercialism—wide sandy beaches separated by scenic rocky shoreline—it has managed to retain an unpretentious, fishing-village quality. Rockport's polished, artistic image presents a striking contrast. These two dissimilar communities are connected by a magnificent craggy coast interspersed with coves, old quarries, sandy beaches, and art colonies. The combination of dramatically different towns, enhanced by spectacular scenery, creates such a splendid exploration that I extended my limit of 25 miles from Boston. I could not omit two of the brightest stars in the shining constellation around Boston.

Despite the traffic, cycling around Cape Ann, as this section of the North Shore is called, is a wonderful way to spend a day. The scenery truly compensates for the automobiles, which, because of their volume, do not speed by. Although exploring on a summer weekend is tempting, the traffic diminishes considerably on a weekday in spring or fall. But on a hot summer day, cooling ocean breezes and eight sandy beaches may compensate for the crowds.

The tour begins in historic Gloucester, as you ride past buildings erected during the 18th century, the town's most prosperous years. Pedaling toward the pervasive smell of fish leads you to the bustling waterfront where fishermen are busy unloading the day's catch, mending nets, or swabbing large draggers. The ride skirts the rocky coast along East Gloucester, where the art colony of Rocky Neck and Beauport Museum are located.

Farther up the coast sits Rockport, filled with artists painting and patrons viewing. Shoppers throng narrow lanes lined with galleries, craft shops, and restaurants. The road around Cape Ann's northern tip passes old quarries and Halibut Point State Park, which boasts a view encompassing three states. On the last leg, the quaint, unspoiled village of Annisquam creates the impression of traveling three hundred years back through history.

Transportation: By automobile: Follow Route 128/95 north to the rotary at exit 11. Turn right onto Washington Street. Follow Washington St. for a half mile and turn left onto Railroad Avenue. You can park in the large parking lot on the left, just past the train station. Do purchase some items from the Star Market to legitimize using their lot.

By commuter rail: From North Station, take the Rockport Line and exit at Gloucester Station on Railroad Avenue in Gloucester Center. If traveling on a weekend, call North Station at 222-3600 and make a reservation.

Food and Drink: You can pick up a picnic lunch at the above-mentioned Star Market on Railroad Avenue. Among the many spots to eat are Cameron's, 206 Main Street, in Gloucester (popular with locals, fabulous lobster rolls); Captain Carlo's Seafood, Harbor Loop, Gloucester (outdoor dining, fresh seafood); Amelia's Subs and Seafood and Long Beach Dairy, Thatcher Road (Route 127A), the road from Gloucester to Rockport. In Rockport, Helmut's Strudel, 49 Bearskin Neck; Peg Leg Restaurant, 18 Beach Street; and the Greenery in Dock Square. At the end of the route, Slav's Firehouse Restaurant, 1072 Washington Street, Gloucester.

Restrooms: Cape Ann Visitor Information Center, on Commercial Street at Fort Point, located at the intersection of Washington Street and Western Avenue; Good Harbor Beach; Dock Square on Bearskin Neck in Rockport; Halibut Point State Park.

Fees: Sargent House Museum, the schooner *Adventure,* Beauport (978-283-0800).

View from the bluff at Halibut Point State Park

Recreational Options: Swimming, fishing.

Background: The location and topography of Gloucester and Rockport, like many other Massachusetts towns, determined their character. Gloucester's protected harbor attracted some of America's first English settlers, fishermen who concluded that the port was ideally situated. Their initial impression was justified when Gloucester quickly became a major fishing and trading center, one that has endured longer than any other in the United States. But its wharves are no longer covered with salted fish drying in the sun; now the fish are refrigerated and rushed to stores or processing plants located near the harbor. Although Gloucester fishermen continue to haul in fish and lobster, its reputation now rests on processing plants that draw refrigerated freighters laden with fish.

For the first hundred years, Rockport was known as Sandy Bay and its residents made their living by fishing, lumbering, and farming. From the early to mid-1800s, many second- and third-generation Bostonians left these occupations to seek other work. Sandy Bay residents looked inland to the rocky landscape. By 1840, Sandy Bay became the town of Rockport and more than 1,000 men worked in the granite industry. They quarried granite to ship all over the country, where it was used to construct buildings, roads, and monuments. When, at the turn of the century, the granite industry began to decline, Rockport residents looked once more toward its scenic coast and encouraged visitors to do the same. Now this picturesque village is thronged with tourists, admiring its attributes and wandering through its numerous galleries, restaurants, and specialty shops.

THE RIDE

1. Train travelers, exit from the station and go east on Railroad Avenue; drivers, also go east.

2. Turn right on School Street.

3. Proceed on School Street four blocks to Middle Street. Turn right.

    Middle Street was named Cornhill Street in the mid-1700s during Gloucester's prosperous fishing and trading era. Before the town filled in sections of the harbor and replaced the old wharves with roads, Cornhill Street overlooked the harbor and was home to the wealthiest, most-prominent residents. On the right side are examples of their magnificent 18th-century homes.

    Farther down on the right, at #58, sits the **Rogers-Babson House**, where Roger Babson was born in 1875. An engineer by training, Babson was a savvy businessman and financier who made much of his money in the stock market, particularly from the Great Depression when he wisely sold high and bought low. Babson shared much of his wealth by founding three colleges, several museums, and the Open Church Foundation. He was responsible also for conserving Dogtown (see chapter 16), where, during the depression, he hired unemployed stonecutters to chisel edifying maxims on huge boulders.

    Across the street, at #49, is the **Sargent House Museum**. Built in 1768 by Winthrop Sargent, this stately, beautifully furnished Georgian-style home is open to the public on weekends from noon to 4:00 P.M. Sargent, an influential leader of early Gloucester, built this house for his daughter, who married John Murray. Sargent had discovered Murray when the latter was an itinerant preacher. Sharing his belief in universal salvation, Sargent invited Murray to Gloucester, introduced

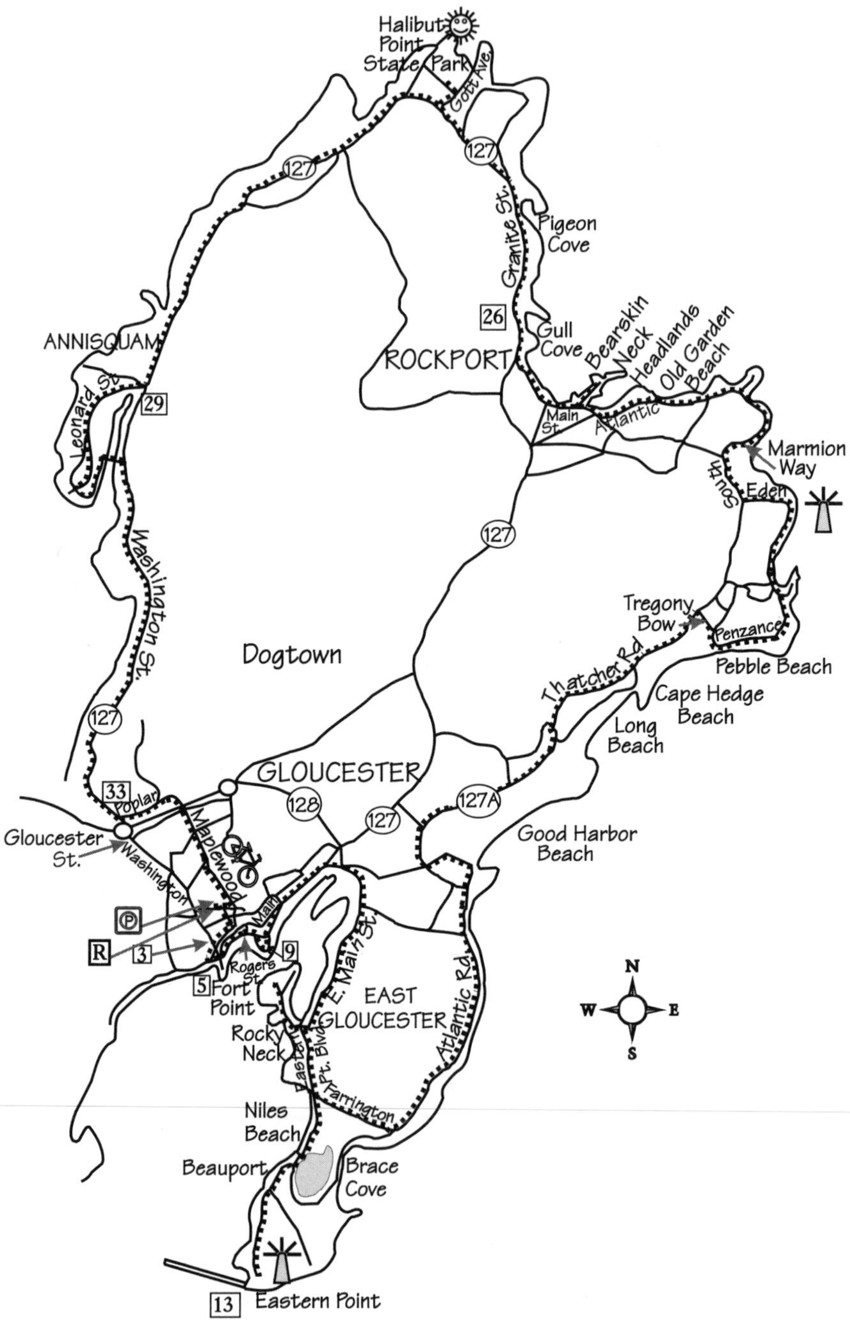

Halibut Point State Park
Gott Ave.
127
Pigeon Cove
Granite St.
26
ROCKPORT
Gull Cove
Bearskin Neck
Headlands
Old Garden Beach
Main St.
Atlantic
Marmion Way
South
Eden
ANNISQUAM
Leonard St.
29
Washington St.
Dogtown
Tregony Bow
Penzance
Pebble Beach
Thatcher Rd
Cape Hedge Beach
Long Beach
GLOUCESTER
128
127A
33
Poplar
Gloucester St.
Washington
Maplewood
Good Harbor Beach
P
R
3
Main
9
Rogers St.
5
Fort Point
E. Main St.
EAST GLOUCESTER
Atlantic Rd.
Rocky Neck
Eastern
Pt. Blvd.
Farrington
Niles Beach
Beauport
Brace Cove
13
Eastern Point
N
W
E
S

GLOUCESTER--ROCKPORT

him to his daughter, and supported him. Together the families became leaders in the Universal Salvation movement.

Overcoming strong opposition, eviction, and threats of imprisonment, Reverend Murray was instrumental in founding the first Universalist Church in America. On the right side of the next block stands his **Independent Christian Church**, the mother church of Universalism in the United States. If the church is open, note the original whale-oil chandelier that has been electrified.

4. Remain on Middle Street as it crosses Washington Street, passing the WW I memorial statue of a horse and rider.

5. Middle Street joins Western Avenue.

> The **Fishermen's Memorial** stands at the head of the harbor on the right. The inscription etched below the statue of the fisherman, "They that go down to the sea in ships, 1623–1923," refers to the Gloucester fishermen who lost their lives at sea. The statue was sculpted for Gloucester's 300th anniversary.
>
> Straight ahead lies Pavilion Beach and Western Harbor. To the right sits **Fort Point**, the visitor information center, and the inner harbor.
>
> The view from Fort Point encompasses the inner harbor, the art colony on Rocky Neck, and Ten Pound Island perched in the middle of the outer harbor. During the American Revolution, gun emplacements were constructed on Fort Point. Now a statue of Saint Peter, the patron saint of fishermen, stands prominently on the site. During the last weekend in June, a three-day festival dedicated to Saint Peter is held on Fort Point.

6. Facing Fort Point, turn left on Western Avenue and follow the signs for Route 127 north.

7. Bear right onto Rogers Street (Route 127), which runs by the harbor.

8. Take the next right onto Harbor Loop, an appropriate spot to stop for seafood.

> The multigabled granite dwelling that overlooks the harbor is the **Fitz Hugh Lane House**, where the famous 19th-century landscape painter lived and painted scenes of Gloucester's ships and sailors in and around the water. Some of his paintings are exhibited at the Cape Ann Historical Association, 27 Pleasant Street.

The **Captain Solomon Jacobs Park,** named after one of Gloucester's most respected ship captains, lies behind the Fitz Hugh Lane House. The Coast Guard station sits to the right of the park. Beyond the station stands a building with a square white tower where, in 1925, Clarence Birdseye paved the way for Gloucester's progression from drying fish to freezing and processing. Birdseye began freezing cabbages, moved on to meats, and then figured out how to quick-freeze fish. General Foods purchased his patents and labeled their frozen vegetables with his name.

The **Schooner Adventure,** docked in the harbor, offers a tour of an old 121-foot fishing schooner that includes exhibits, photographs, and a video on Gloucester fishing boats.

9. Follow the loop back to Rogers Street and turn right, with the ocean on your right (where it will remain for much of the ride).

10. Remain on Rogers Street and continue straight, passing where Route 127 bears to the left. Take your next right at the traffic light onto East Main Street toward East Gloucester.

11. Cycle for 1.1 miles until you reach **Rocky Neck** (2.8 miles total). Turn right to visit one of the oldest art colonies in New England, situated among a potpourri of shops and residences.

12. After exploring the area, return to East Main Street and turn right toward Eastern Point. Continue straight through the stone pillars onto Eastern Point Boulevard, ignoring the Private Road sign, toward Beauport and Eastern Point Lighthouse. Niles Beach is on the right.

This exclusive section of summer estates restricts automobile traffic. Biking allows passage to most places and is particularly convenient when cooling off at a beach such as Niles, with parking for residents only.

To reach **Beauport,** as the **Sleeper-McCann House** is commonly called, follow Eastern Point Boulevard for 0.5 mile.

Beauport, which offers hourly guided tours, is open 10:00 A.M. to 4:00 P.M. Monday through Friday from mid-May through mid-September. It is open on weekends 1:00 to 4:00 P.M. from mid-September to mid-October. The Society for the Preservation of New England Antiquities (SPNEA) owns and operates Beauport, which was built and furnished by designer Henry Davis Sleeper. In 1903, Sleeper transported a small house, built in 1728, to this site. For the next 30 years he added rooms, skillfully decorating them to show-case his antique furnishings and relics. After Sleeper died, Charles and Helena McCann purchased the 40-room mansion, to which they added their collection of Chinese porcelain. The McCann heirs donated Beauport to SPNEA.

13. To visit **Eastern Point Lighthouse**, continue straight on Eastern Point Boulevard to the tip of the point. This is a great spot for viewing water traffic in and out of Gloucester Harbor. On a clear day the panorama of the southern coast extends 30 miles to Boston.

You can park your bike and walk for a half-mile on Dog Bar Breakwater, composed of layers of granite from quarries in Rockport. The lighthouse and breakwater protect ships from colliding with this treacherous rocky headland and hidden sandbar.

14. Return on Eastern Point Boulevard to Farrington Avenue. Turn right.

15. Follow Farrington Avenue to Atlantic Avenue. Turn left and continue on Atlantic Avenue for 2.2 miles, with spectacular rocky coastal views on your right.

16. Just after the road bends to the left, turn right on Thatcher (Route 127A).

Good Harbor Beach, one of Gloucester's excellent long, sandy public beaches, lies off to the right. Bikers can take advantage of the facili-ties and avoid the parking fees.

17. Remain on Route 127A for 2.7 miles into Rockport, passing Long Beach and Capehedge Beach. Turn right onto Tregony Bow.

18. Follow Tregony as it merges with Penzance Road. If you wish to visit Pebble Beach, follow Penzance Road. If you want to continue biking, interrupt your downhill run and turn left on Eden Road.

Pebble Beach contrasts with the other fine, white sandy beaches, as it is composed of smooth round pebbles. Early fishermen scooped the stones from this beach to use as ballast when heading to their fishing grounds. If their trip was successful, they threw the stones overboard.

Look out to sea at Thatcher's Island for a glimpse of **Cape Ann Lighthouse**, originally constructed in 1771. Mariners are grateful for the bright beams cast by the powerful Fresnel lenses in the twin granite towers that were added in 1861.

19. Eden Road returns to 127A (South Street). Turn right.

20. Take your fifth right onto Marmion Way and continue to parallel the jagged coast.

21. As Marmion Way curves away from the water, take the first right onto Shetland Road to continue to parallel the coast while passing Old Garden Beach, a scenic, small sandy stretch protected by rocky outcroppings.

22. Hug the shore until you reach Atlantic Avenue. Turn right to visit the **Headlands**.

While admiring the magnificent seascape from this wide-open rocky promontory, don't miss the view inland of Rockport Harbor and Bearskin Neck.

23. Return on Atlantic past Rockport Harbor. Take the first right onto Mount Pleasant Street.

On Tuna Wharf to the right, you may find painters capturing the harbor or Motif #1 on Bearskin Neck, the quaint wooden fishing shack whose name refers to its prominence in many works of art.

24. A right turn onto South Road leads to the narrow peninsula **Bearskin Neck**, formerly a fishing and lobstering port.

Its fishing shacks and commercial buildings, tastefully renovated to retain the charm of a bygone era, now function as specialty shops, galleries, and restaurants.

25. From the Neck, turn right onto Main Street.

To view examples of local artwork, stop at the **Old Tavern**, at 12 Main Street, which houses the Rockport Art Association. The original tavern was built in 1787. A ballroom was added in 1838.

26. Continue straight on Beach Street as Main (Route 127) heads off to the left.

Beach Street runs by two small sandy beaches, Front Beach and Back Beach. Between the two, on the opposite side of the street, lies the **Old Parish Burying Ground**, containing graves of Rockport's earliest settlers.

After passing Gull Cove, don't miss Rockport's abandoned granite quarries on the left. Surrounded by chiseled granite ledges, these isolated, water-filled quarries present a stark, picturesque scene. Granite was loaded on flatcars that traveled on a path under the road to the pier. From there the stone was shipped all over the United States.

27. From the quarry, remain on Granite Street (the new name for the coastal road which is now also Route 127) for 1.4 miles, passing Pigeon Cove, until you reach Gott Avenue and the sign for Halibut Point Reservation. Turn right on Gott Avenue and park your bike in the rack near the lot. (Again cyclists avoid the parking fee.)

Do not miss the view from the 50-foot bluff on the northernmost tip of Cape Ann. On a clear day you can see New Hampshire and Maine. The 66-acre **Halibut Point State Park and Halibut Point Reservation** are managed jointly by the Massachusetts Department of Environmental Management (DEM) and the Trustees of Reservations. Walking trails curve around tidal pools, past bayberry thickets and wind-blasted scrub-oak trees. Ask one of the rangers for the self-guided trail map of the Babson Farm Quarry that occupied this site until 1929.

28. Return to and turn right on Granite Street (Route 127). From Halibut Point, cycle uphill and downhill 3 miles past a succession of coves and small villages until you reach the turnoff to Annisquam.

29. To enter Annisquam Village, turn right on Leonard Street.

The white **Annisquam Village Church** sits at the head of Lobster Cove and welcomes visitors to what was once a thriving port. Annisquam's protected harbor fostered its early settlement in 1631 and contributed to the village's prosperity, which is reflected in the stately old homes that line the narrow twisting streets.

Continue down Leonard Street for a half-mile, passing many of the historic homes built at the beginning of the 18th century.

Surrounding the small village green sits the Annisquam Exchange and Art Gallery; the Village Hall, containing the library and post office; and the Annisquam Historical Society, housed in a former firehouse.

30. Follow Leonard to River Road. Turn left and walk your bike. (River Road is a one-way street.)

31. River Road leads to the Lobster Cove Bridge. Turn right and cross the bridge.

In 1847, Lobster Cove Bridge was constructed originally as a draw-bridge. Fares were charged to all who crossed, from a penny for pedestrians to twelve cents for horse-drawn wagons.

32. Now back on Route 127 (Washington Street), turn right and cross the stone bridge and causeway over Goose Cove on your return to Gloucester Center.

33. Proceed on Washington Street for 2.6 miles. Turn left on Poplar Street just before the rotary.

On the corner of Washington and Poplar Streets stands Gloucester's oldest dwelling, the **White Ellery House**, built in 1650. When located in Gloucester Center, it was owned by Reverend John White, followed by William Ellery who transformed it into a tavern. When the Cape Ann Historical Association purchased the building in 1947, it was moved to its present site.

34. After 0.4 mile, turn right on Maplewood Avenue (Texaco station on the corner).

35. Follow Maplewood 0.6 mile to Railroad Avenue. Turn right to return to the railroad station and parking lot.

6

NEWTON

BROOKLINE

 Distance and Difficulty: 17 miles of relatively easy biking—one steep incline. Depending on the time of day, you may encounter short sections of heavy traffic.

This surprisingly scenic tour through Newton and Brookline avoids the heavy traffic, commercialism, and highways that defeat most urban bike routes. The ride begins in Newton, where it follows the Charles River as it winds through the densely wooded Hemlock Gorge Reservation. It passes three large parks, vast landscaped expanses within four golf courses and three college campuses, and tree-lined streets bordered by meticulously manicured lawns surrounding slate-roofed brick mansions.

The second half of the tour circles Chestnut Hill Reservoir before ascending a steep incline, the back slope of the infamous "Heartbreak Hill" at mile 21 of the Boston Marathon. The ride continues along four more miles of the marathon course via the uncrowded access road next to Commonwealth Avenue.

Transportation: By automobile: From Routes 128/95, take Exit 24, Route 30 east. Turn right at the light at the end of the entrance ramp onto Route 30. Turn right at the next traffic light onto Auburn Street. Follow Auburn until you reach the train station on the right. You can park in the lot or along Auburn Street.

By commuter rail: From Back Bay or South Station take the Framingham Line to Auburndale. The ride begins at the Auburndale station on Auburn Street.

If biking from Boston, follow the Emerald Necklace bike ride (chapter 1) until the Perkins Street/Jamaicaway intersection, just before Jamaica Pond. Turn right on Perkins and follow it past Jamaica Pond to the junction with Cottage and Goddard Streets. Bear right on Cottage, which becomes Warren. Remain on Warren until you reach Heath. Turn right. Take your first left on Reservoir and pick up the directions for this chapter at #20.

Food and Drink: Pockets of commercial activity exist at the beginning and end of the ride: Near the train station in the Auburndale section of Newton are the Bread Song Bakery, 349 Auburn Street; the Ice Cream Man, 419 Lexington Street; Bruegger's Bagel Bakery, 2050 Commonwealth Avenue; and Coffee Cafe, 2096 Commonwealth Avenue. Fast-food shops also are located around the Boston College campus at the east end of Commonwealth Avenue, including Box Lunch at #11 and White Mountain Creamery at #19. Farther down Commonwealth Avenue, at #549 and #551, are Provizers' Delicatessen and Tuler's Bakery.

Restrooms: Echo Bridge Service Station, 1010 Chestnut Street (4 miles into the ride) also provides a water fountain and tissues. Near the end of the ride is a cluster of eating establishments, some with restrooms: Bruegger's Bagels, 2050 Commonwealth Avenue, and the Coffee Cafe, 2096 Commonwealth Avenue.

Fees: Museum of Transportation, 15 Newton Street. Open Wednesday through Sunday 10:00 A.M. to 5:00 P.M. (617-522-6140).

Recreational Options: In-line skating along 4.5 miles of service road that parallels Commonwealth Avenue, walking around Chestnut Hill Reservoir or Hemlock Gorge, off-road biking in Nahanton Park.

Background: When the English colonists landed in Boston in the 1630s, they settled in and around the city's port. As the population increased, some moved to outlying areas where land was more plentiful. By 1638, settlers were farming in Newton and Brookline.

On a map, the town of Brookline looks like a peninsula extending into Boston. Brookline's proximity and the wealth of many if its inhabitants inspired Boston to try to annex the town five times. Each time Brookline residents successfully resisted the attempt. Formerly characterized by affluent aristocrats and restricted golf and tennis clubs, Brookline is known now for its variety of nationalities drawn to the town's fine school system and its location close to Boston's universities and hospitals.

Newton was settled originally as 14 villages, each with its own distinctive identity. Individual characteristics continue to define these small communities. The villages of Auburndale and Newton Upper and Lower Falls, all situated on the Charles River, became mill towns and produced textiles. Though no longer manufacturing centers, they still resemble small New England mill towns. Others, like Oak Hill, Thomsonville, and Chestnut Hill, abut Brookline and are more upscale.

THE RIDE

1.   From the railroad station, turn left on Auburn Street.

2.   Take the first left on Woodland Road.

3.   Proceed 0.25 mile, while crossing over the Massachusetts Turnpike, to the stop sign at the intersection with Hancock Street. Turn right.

4.   Hancock merges with Grove Street. Remain on Grove for 1.2 miles as it passes the large parking area for the Riverside Station, the last stop of the MBTA Green Line, and Woodland Golf Course, the first of five on the route. Grove crosses Route 128/95 and enters the village of Newton Lower Falls.

5.   At the **T** intersection, turn left, remaining on Grove Street.

6.   After biking a total of 1.6 miles, turn left on Route 16, a busy commercial street. A wide sidewalk offers a safe refuge from the traffic as well as a great view of the Charles River, which runs alongside the road.

7.   This next sequence of turns can be confusing. At the traffic light turn right onto the entrance ramp to Route 128/95. Do *not* take a sharp right onto Wales Street. Follow the entrance ramp past the Pillar House restaurant on the left. Bear left on Quinobequin Road. A sign reads For Pleasure Vehicles Only (that's you). *Do not miss this left turn and end up on Route 128/95.*

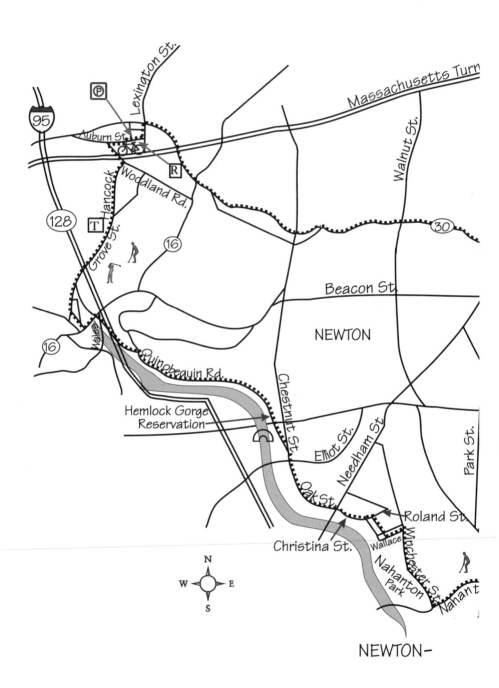

NEWTON–

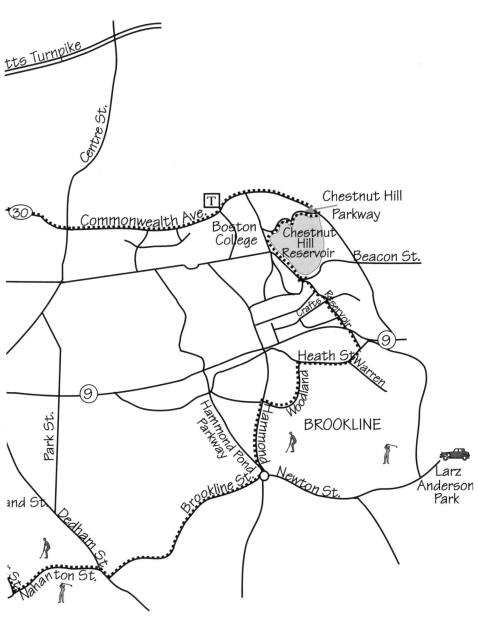

tts Turnpike

Centre St.

30

Commonwealth Ave.

T

Boston College

Chestnut Hill Reservoir

Chestnut Hill Parkway

Beacon St.

Crafts Reservoir

9

Heath St.

Warren

Woodland

BROOKLINE

9

Park St.

Hammond Pond Parkway

Hammond

Brookline St.

Newton St.

Larz Anderson Park

and St.

Dedham St.

Nahanton St.

-BROOKLINE

Is it worth the trouble to access this road? Yes! For 1.5 miles a dense woodland separates Quinobequin (the Native American word for "river") Road from the Charles River. Occasional openings reveal picturesque vistas of the river.

After 1.6 miles on Quinobequin (3.7 miles total), just as the road starts to ascend and go under a bridge, pull off to the right.

> A narrow footpath leads to **Hemlock Gorge** and **Echo Bridge**. A steep river gorge dominates the 23-acre reservation, acquired in 1895 by the Metropolitan District Commission, which oversees a system of parks throughout the Boston area. Most visitors feel compelled to yodel or shout beneath Echo Bridge, the massive granite and brick structure that spans the river and gorge. The Boston Water Works built the bridge in 1877 to bring in water for Newton residents. Because of its size, age, and triple-arch construction, Echo Bridge is designated as a National Historic Landmark.

8. Continue the short ascent through the stop sign intersection (home to the hospitable Echo Bridge Service Station, which has clean restrooms and a water fountain) and bear right on Chestnut Street. You are now in Newton Upper Falls.

9. At the traffic light (4.4 miles), turn right on Oak Street.

10. At 4.7 miles, cross busy Needham Street onto Christina Street, which quickly changes from a commercial to a quiet residential road.

11. Remain on Christina until it ends at Wallace Street. The stockade fence on the south side of Wallace Street protects the community gardens in Nahanton Park. Turn left and pedal alongside the fence.

12. Take the next right onto Winchester Street.

> One of the entrances to 57-acre **Nahanton Park** is off Winchester Street. Opportunities for off-road biking exist on trails that lead to a nature center, gardens, pond, wetlands, and boat dock on the Charles River.

13. Turn left onto Nahanton Street (6 miles).

> The Charles River Country Club occupies both sides of the street. You are now in the village of Oak Hill.

14. Remain on Nahanton for 0.6 mile until the traffic light at Dedham Street. Turn right.

15. At the next traffic light turn left onto Brookline Street.

The well-manicured grounds on the left belong to Mount Ida College.

16. Not surprisingly, Brookline Street leads to the town of Brookline. Remain on Brookline Street until you reach one of Boston's famous (or infamous) rotaries (8.2 miles). You may have to dismount in order to circle around to the left onto Hammond Street, with Putterham Meadows Country Club on the right.

To visit the **Museum of Transportation**, turn right onto Newton Street and continue 1.5 miles until you reach Larz Anderson Park. The museum is located in the park.

17. From the rotary, follow Hammond for 0.6 mile to Woodland Street. Turn right.

In this elegant section of Brookline, beautifully landscaped lawns enhance grand old mansions. Open space is guaranteed because much of the land is occupied by schools, parks, and private country clubs. Beaver Country Day School sits on the left and Dane Park on the right, followed by the gorgeous campus of Pine Manor Junior College. Behind the college sits yet another golf course, which belongs to the venerable Country Club. Established in 1882, the Country Club claims to be the oldest course in the United States. Here prosperous Bostonians play tennis, golf, and the ancient sport of curling.

18. At the **T** intersection, turn right onto Heath Street.

19. Remain on Heath 0.8 mile (10 miles total). Don't miss the left turn on Reservoir Road. Start looking for Reservoir on the left after you pass Warren on the right.

20. Reservoir Road leads to Route 9. To proceed across this busy highway, push the traffic signal on the left side of Reservoir Road. After crossing, turn left on Route 9, pass the fire station, and turn right to pick up the continuation of Reservoir Road.

Boston College's Gasson Hall as viewed from Commonwealth Avenue.
(Photo by Katharine Allan Zobel)

21. Follow Reservoir through the intersection with Crafts Road. Reservoir Road appears to dead-end at the Ⓣ tracks. It does, *but* a pedestrian (and bike) walkway crosses the tracks.

22. At 10.9 miles you reach Beacon Street, another busy thoroughfare. Turn right and make a quick left to enter the unpaved path that circles **Chestnut Hill Reservoir**. This maneuver avoids the traffic on Beacon Street.

23. Proceed left around the reservoir until the path bears to the right. You now have the option of biking on Chestnut Hill Parkway or on the path above the reservoir. The low footpath next to the water is reserved for pedestrians. Go halfway around the reservoir until reaching Commonwealth Avenue. Dismount to cross at the intersection—a killer combination of trolley tracks, trolleys, automobiles, and pedestrians.

24. Turn left on Commonwealth Avenue and attempt to navigate this busy stretch. Walking your bike along the wide sidewalk is one alternative. After you pass the Ⓣ station, a service road appears on the right and continues for 4.5 miles.

   The MBTA station provides transportation to students of **Boston College**, which occupies many of the buildings on the left side of the avenue. A Jesuit school founded in 1863, BC educates 14,500 students in its undergraduate and graduate schools.

   As you ascend the back slope of **"Heartbreak Hill"** and then experience an exhilarating downhill run, be aware that Boston Marathon runners climb this steep incline after the 21-mile journey east from Hopkinton.

25. Aside from occasional stop signs and traffic lights, the service road provides delightful, relaxed riding. It functions much like an urban alley, allowing residents and delivery people safe access to the elegant homes that overlook Commonwealth Avenue.

26. After pedaling 4 of the marathon miles, take the first left after crossing over the Massachusetts Turnpike, onto Lexington Street toward Auburndale.

   Several food shops on Commonwealth Avenue are located just west of this intersection.

27. Take the second right onto Auburn Street to return to the starting point.

7

Minute Man
Commuter
Bikeway

Cambridge to Bedford

Distance and Difficulty: 24 miles of easy riding.

On sunny Sunday afternoons recreation seekers flock to the Minute Man Commuter Bikeway. A recent addition to the local landscape, this 11-mile trail, favored by bikers, in-line skaters, dog-walkers, parents pushing baby carriages, and toddlers on tricycles, has been an unqualified success. Its fans praise its smooth asphalt surface, the scenic and varied landscape, and the many options available en route.

Beginning in Davis Square in Somerville, where nearby Tufts University has inspired a number of restaurants and nightspots, the bikeway travels through Cambridge, accessing side streets and passing ball fields before circling around the mammoth Alewife MBTA Station. A tricky maneuver near the Route 2 overpass leads to the main bike path, which extends more or less continuously for the next 10.5 miles through the suburbs of Arlington, Lexington, and Bedford. The ride returns along the same path, so it can be as long as 24 miles or as short as you choose.

The Minute Man Bikeway has been thoughtfully designed. Fieldstones set in concrete serve as advance warning of road crossings. Roman numerals, etched on both sides of granite mile markers, display the distance from the end point in Bedford on one side and from the eastern terminus in Arlington on the other. Distances from Davis Square and Bedford are painted on the asphalt.

Some bikeway diversions involve picnicking beside scenic Spy Pond, visiting historic sites along the way, off-road biking in the adjoining meadows, or stopping at the ice cream stands and shops that have sprung up along the path. If you have an aversion to crowds, ride during the week when the traffic diminishes.

Bikers have the option of linking with the Lexington-Concord Historical Tour (chapter 8) or connecting with the Cambridge-Boston Charles River Loop (chapter 2). Direct links to both the Charles River Bike Path and the Minute Man National Historical Park Trail are being discussed and may be in place by the time you take this ride. If you seek off-road biking, you can continue past the terminus in Bedford and follow the old rail beds to either Concord (see chapter 19) or Billerica. Directions to Billerica appear at the end of this chapter.

Transportation: By automobile: The Minute Man Bikeway runs east and west, paralleling Route 2. The eastern terminus of the expressway section of Route 2 is at the Fresh Pond rotary near the Alewife MBTA parking garage where parking is available (daily fee) and where you can pick up the bike path (see direction #6). Exit 59 (Route 60) off Route 2 leads to Arlington Center (direction #12). You can also take Exit 54 (Waltham Street) to Lexington Center (direction #15). Both Arlington and Lexington have large municipal parking lots north of Massachusetts Avenue that are free on weekends. Free parking is also available at the western terminus of the bike path at the Bikeway Source, a bike and in-line skate shop on Loomis Street, off Routes 4/225 in Bedford.

By commuter rail: You can enter the Minute Man Bikeway from the Porter Square Station, served by the Fitchburg Line which departs from North Station. From Porter Square pedal west on Massachusetts Avenue for 1 mile. You can pick up the bike path on the left side of Massachusetts Avenue at Cameron Avenue in Cambridge (direction #4). Or you can get on the Davis Square extension of the path by exiting the Porter Square Station on the Elm Street side and traveling six blocks north. Cedar Street leads to the starting point of the path. Cedar Street works best on the return because certain blocks are one-way traveling south.

By rapid transit: With a Ⓣ bike pass (available Sundays only), take the Red Line and exit at either Davis or Alewife.

Food and Drink: You will not lack for food and drink on this trip. In Davis Square, Au Bon Pain and other fast-food shops are near the Ⓣ station. Between the two Ⓣ station entrances, on Holland Street and College Avenue, lies a plaza where you will find Dave's Yogurt Bar, which serves great ice cream and frozen yogurt. Within the Alewife MBTA Station are a number of fast-food purveyors, among them Bertucci's, which also has a pizza restaurant in Lexington Center. In Arlington Center, the bikeway passes near a Ben & Jerry's Ice Cream shop, located at 451 Massachusetts Avenue. Scoops, Starbucks, Aesop's Bagels, the Gingerbread Construction Co., and Via Lago (which prepares superb sandwiches and pasta salads), are among the shops in Lexington Center. Water fountains sit on the plaza next to the Davis Square station and next to the former Lexington Depot in Lexington Center.

Restrooms: Davis Square MBTA station; Alewife MBTA station; Bertucci's in Alewife Station and Lexington Center; Bikeway Cycle on the bikeway at the Arlington-Lexington town line; Museum of Our National Heritage in Lexington; The Bikeway Source, the bike shop at the end of the bike path in Bedford; and outdoor portable bathrooms at the Bedford terminus.

Fees: Munroe Tavern, Buckman Tavern, and Hancock-Clarke House. All are open from mid-April through October, Monday to Saturday 10:00 A.M. to 5:00 P.M. and Sunday 1:00 to 5:00 P.M. The admission charge includes a guided tour.

Recreational Options: In-line skating, walking, cross-country skiing, off-road biking.

Background: Following an old rail bed that was built in 1846 to provide rail service between North Cambridge and Lexington Center, the Minute Man Commuter Bikeway became America's 500th rail-trail conversion in 1992.

The last 150 years witnessed first the railroad's popularity and then its slow demise. In 1874, increased usage convinced the Boston and Lowell Railroad to extend the railway line to Bedford. One hundred years later local residents' devotion to their automobiles and expanded highway construction greatly reduced the number of train riders, and in 1980 the Boston & Maine Railroad discontinued rail service on its Cambridge-Bedford line. For the next 11 years a committed group of Arlington and Lexington residents promoted the idea of a commuter bike path. Finally, in 1991 the commonwealth of Massachusetts agreed to the plans and funded the bikeway.

THE RIDE

Because the bikeway is so popular, cyclists should be aware of its guidelines:

- ☛ Keep to the right, except to pass.
- ☛ Pass on the left, and only when clear of oncoming traffic. Inform the passee that you are passing on the left.
- ☛ Come to a complete stop at all intersections. Sometimes oncoming traffic will stop at the crosswalk; other times it will not.
- ☛ When stopping on the bikeway, move off the pavement.
- ☛ Carefully enter and exit the bikeway only at designated locations.
- ☛ Bicyclists may ride two abreast only when the bikeway is uncrowded.
- ☛ Bicyclists must yield to pedestrians and in-line skaters.

1. The ride begins at the Davis Square Ⓣ station, which is surrounded by engaging sculpture.

   When the Ⓣ stations were refurbished in the early 1980s, money was set aside for public art. A triangular plaza that links the Holland Street and College Avenue entrances holds a water fountain, park benches, and cast cement groupings of a family, an elderly couple, street entertainers, and sightseers, all modeled from local residents. The figures represent types of people that sculptor James Tyler had spotted in the square.

   The bike path also extends a half-mile east of Davis Square. To enter it, cut through the plaza, cross College Avenue, and bike down the one-way road next to the Ⓣ station. After pedaling for a block and cutting through a parking lot, you'll reach the continuation of the bike path. Future plans are for the path to follow an unused rail bed into Boston.

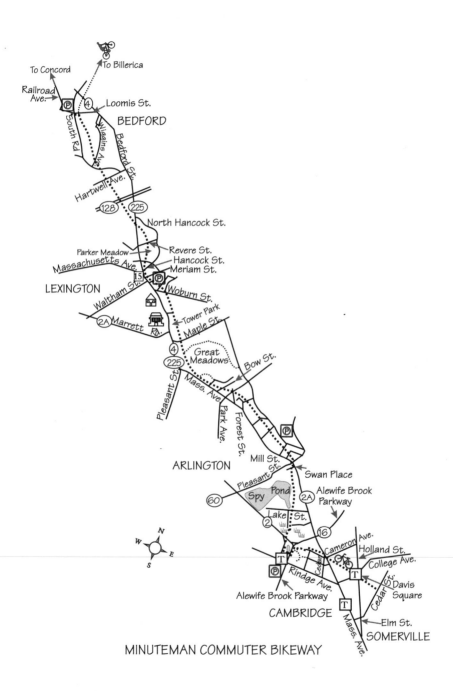

To Concord

To Billerica

Railroad Ave.

South Rd

Wiggins Ave.

④ Loomis St.

BEDFORD

Bedford St.

Hartwell Ave.

128 225

North Hancock St.

Parker Meadow

Revere St.
Hancock St.
Meriam St.

Massachusetts Ave.

15

LEXINGTON

Waltham St.

Woburn St.

2A Marrett Rd.

Tower Park
Maple St.

④ 225

Great Meadows

Bow St.

Pleasant St.

Mass. Ave.

Park Ave.

Forest St.

Mill St.

Pleasant St.

ARLINGTON

Swan Place

60

Spy Pond

2A

Alewife Brook Parkway

Lake St.

2

16

Cameron Ave.

Holland St.

College Ave.

T

Rindge Ave.

Cedar St.

Davis Square

Alewife Brook Parkway

CAMBRIDGE

Cedar St.

T

Elm St.

Mass. Ave.

SOMERVILLE

N
W   E
S

MINUTEMAN COMMUTER BIKEWAY

2. From the Davis Square Ⓣ station on Holland Street, head west. The path passes **Seven Hills Park**, a collection of six sculptures and a clock that tower above brick bases.

    These "environmental graphics," created by Clifford Selbert, a graphic designer and landscape architect, commemorate the seven hills on which Somerville was built. The pieces depict two historic houses, a fort, cow, tree, and fish—specifically an alewife, the name-sake of the nearby brook and parkway.

3. Continue on the bike path until reaching Cedar Street. Cross the street, dismount, and turn left on Cedar to cross busy Massachusetts Avenue.

4. Turn right on Massachusetts Avenue, cross Cameron Avenue, and pick up the continuation of the bikeway, distinguished by brick pillars and brick sidewalk.

5. Remain on the bike path for 0.3 mile until it ends on a side street. This section becomes a little tricky because there are no signs to guide you. Go directly across the street and follow the path through the opening in the fence as it skirts the edge of a playing field and passes behind bleachers.

6. Just after the bleachers, turn right onto the paved walkway that leads to a large concrete structure, the Alewife MBTA station, which is 1 mile from the Davis Square Station.

7. Pass by the north entrance to the station and continue toward the main building. Upon reaching the concrete facade, turn right, passing a playground on your left, toward the parking garage exit road.

8. Upon reaching the road, turn right onto the continuation of the bike path. The path crosses a small bridge and runs under the Route 2 overpass.

9. Follow the path as it bends left, passing a ball field and parking lot. Begin the main section of the Minute Man Commuter Bikeway.

10. After cycling for 1 mile (2 miles from Davis Square), you'll see **Spy Pond** on the left.

    Stairs descend to a playground and picnic tables near this picturesque pond. Spring-fed and carved by a glacier 16,000 years ago, the pond reaches depths up to 250 feet. Once used for ice harvesting, Spy Pond now offers sailing and windsurfing but, alas, no swimming.

The bikeway pauses at Swan Place in Arlington Center, requiring another tricky maneuver. Turn right at Swan Place and then left onto the brick sidewalk along Massachusetts Avenue.

11. Cross Massachusetts Avenue at the traffic light at the Route 60 (Pleasant Street) intersection. Follow Pleasant Street for about 50 feet and turn left onto the continuation of the bikeway, protected by a statue of Samuel Wilson, one of Arlington's native sons. Again, brickwork defines bikeway access.

12. For the next 8 miles the only interruptions in the Minute Man Bikeway are stop signs at intersecting streets.

    Four miles from the Alewife station is Bikeway Cycle on Bow Street in Lexington, where bikes can be rented or repaired and soft drinks are sold.

    Soon after Bikeway Cycle and 6 miles from Davis Square, 180 acres of open meadows appear on the right. **Great Meadows** contains trails through wetland, forest, and meadow. Hiking and bird-watching are encouraged; off-road biking is acceptable if bikers dismount in environmentally sensitive areas such as wetlands and before ascending and descending steep inclines.

13. At the next stop sign at Seasons Four Garden Center, after biking 6.3 miles from Davis Square (5.3 from Alewife), turn left if you wish to visit the Museum of Our National Heritage and the Munroe Tavern.

    To reach the museum, head up the Seasons Four entrance road and turn left on the paved path that runs east through Tower Park. At the end of the park, pedal along the sidewalk to the crosswalk at the intersection of Massachusetts Avenue and Marrett Road. The **Museum of Our National Heritage** is the modern brick building dominating the hill. Cross Massachusetts Avenue and head up Marrett Road to the entrance.

    This handsome museum, which has no entrance fee, displays changing exhibits on American history and popular culture. On weekends the museum often offers concerts, lectures, and children's workshops, for which fees are charged. The museum is open from 10:00 A.M. to 5:00 P.M. Monday to Saturday and from noon to 5:00 P.M. on Sunday. To hear a recorded message of exhibits and events, call 781-861-9638.

To reach **Munroe Tavern**, retrace your route to Tower Park and go 0.2 mile west past the park. Munroe Tavern is the barn-red clapboard structure on the left.

The 300-year-old tavern became historically significant when British General Earl Percy commandeered it for 1,000 British soldiers on the afternoon of April 19, 1775. Suffering greatly after their grueling march from Boston and the bloody running retreat from Concord, the hungry troops consumed much of the tavern's food and drink, while the wounded were treated in the tavern's dining room.

The tavern displays many 18th-century articles from the period when William Munroe served as tavern proprietor. Upstairs, documents relating to President Washington's visit in 1789 are exhibited.

Return to the bikeway via the Seasons Four entrance road.

14. After cycling west on the bikeway for another mile, you'll reach quaint Lexington Center.

Stately churches and dignified old homes border the famous Battle Green. Here you have the option of expanding your knowledge of the events that precipitated the American Revolution by visiting the town's historic buildings. See chapter 8 for details.

The Lexington Visitor Center sits next to the bikeway just west of the Meriam Street intersection. **Buckman Tavern**, where the Lexington Minute Men gathered to await the arrival of the British soldiers, sits next to the visitor center. The famous Minute Man statue stands in front of the historic **Battle Green**, where the skirmish between the Minute Men and the British took place. The green lies directly across Massachusetts Avenue from the visitor center. The **Hancock-Clarke House**, where Paul Revere stopped during his midnight ride to alert the patriots that the British were marching to Concord, is located 0.2 mile north of the bikeway on Hancock Street.

15. The bikeway passes the old Lexington Railway Depot and water fountain before it crosses busy Hancock Street.

Another opportunity for off-path recreation is available at **Parker Meadow**, a conservation area west of the Hancock Street intersection 0.5 mile on the right.

To cross busy Bedford Street (8.5 total miles), push the button on the traffic light and wait for the signal to cross.

After pedaling on the bridge over Route 128/95 you will next reach the intersection with Hartwell Avenue, where there is a push-button traffic control. The Minute Man Commuter Bikeway then travels through a quiet wooded section and ends 1.3 miles ahead in Bedford.

If you wish to extend your ride, you have the option of following the directions in the Lexington-Concord chapter to Carlisle and Bedford. If you are interested in off-road riding, you can follow an old rail bed west through the Great Meadows National Wildlife Refuge to Concord (see chapter 19).

Another unused rail bed (thankfully, minus the railroad ties) travels 3 miles north through Bedford to the town of Billerica. To enter the rail bed north from the western terminus of the bikeway, turn right on South Road. Take an immediate right onto Loomis Street. The path begins 0.1 mile on the left side of Loomis Street, between a fire hydrant and two granite posts. The width and composition of this level trail change often during the ride, from a narrow single track to smooth wide sections covered with stone dust.

For the first 0.3 mile the narrow path runs by a brook on the left side and a playing field on the right. During the next 0.6 mile the path crosses Great Road, Hillside Avenue, and Pine Hill Road. Along the next mile, the trail skirts the edge of a VA hospital, York Conservation Area, and the large campus of Middlesex Community College.

At 2 miles, the trail reaches Fawn Lake, a carefully landscaped and well-tended recreation area and a great place for a picnic. A paved path heads down to the water, passing rhododendron and mountain laurel bushes.

After another mile, the trail ends at Spring Street in Billerica.

8

HISTORICAL

TOUR

Lexington—Concord—Carlisle—Bedford

 Distance and Difficulty: 20 miles of moderate riding. A few hills and sections where traffic may be heavy.

Curious about our nation's past? Would you like to step back in time and visit the sites where the American Revolution began? This historical tour covers 20 picturesque miles through four western suburbs: Lexington, Concord, Carlisle, and Bedford.

These towns have taken great care to conserve their centers and surrounding countryside. Carefully restored taverns, farmhouses and barns and acres of open farmland rimmed by antique stone walls serve as constant reminders of our country's past. In addition, Minute Man National Historical Park has set aside 875 acres within Lexington and Concord to further protect and highlight sites associated with the events that precipitated the American Revolution.

Grassy horse pastures grace the rolling hills around Concord and Carlisle.

The first half of this tour follows the Battle Road, the route marched by British troops on April 19, 1775, from Lexington's Battle Green to Concord's North Bridge. In Minute Man National Historical Park, you'll find guided walks, movies, and a new 5.5-mile Battle Road Trail that connects important historic sites. Along the trail, you'll find 26 Wayside Exhibits which chronicle the events that took place on April 19, 1775. After leaving the trail, you can visit several historic sites, some from the Revolutionary War era and others that housed such 19th-century writers as Louisa May Alcott, Nathaniel Hawthorne, and Ralph Waldo Emerson. Because many of these sites are open to the public and offer tours, this section of the ride can take an hour or several days, depending on how many places interest you.

The second half of the ride balances the heavy dose of history. Pure scenic pleasure awaits you on country roads that wind through Concord, Carlisle, and Bedford. The last three miles return you to Lexington via the Minute Man Bikeway.

For children who are experienced cyclists, this tour offers a great opportunity to combine history with recreation. When possible the route bypasses the most heavily traveled areas, but some sections do require riding with traffic.

Transportation: By automobile: From Boston follow Storrow Drive west to Route 2. In Cambridge, Memorial Drive follows Route 2. Remain on Route 2 around the rotaries in Cambridge, continuing west as Route 2 becomes an expressway. From the expressway, take Exit 56, Routes 4/225, toward Lexington. Turn right at the exit ramp and follow the road to the junction with Massachusetts Avenue. Turn left to follow Routes 4/225 for 2.5 miles to Lexington Center. Continue through the traffic light in the center and take the first right into Depot Square. Continue straight to enter the large municipal parking lot. (A nominal fee is charged during the week; no fee on weekends).

From Routes 95/128, take Exit 31, Routes 4/225 east toward Lexington. Follow Routes 4/225 for 2 miles to Lexington Center. After passing Lexington Green on the right, take the third left into Depot Square (the second left into Depot Square is one-way) and proceed straight to the parking lot.

By the Minute Man Bikeway: From Alewife Station, travel 6.5 miles to Meriam Street in Lexington Center.

By commuter rail: From North Station or Porter Square take the Fitchburg Line to Concord. From Concord Station, turn left on Thoreau Street. Turn right at the traffic light onto Sudbury Road. Follow Sudbury Road for a half-mile as it merges with Main Street to the rotary in Concord Center. Pick up the directions at #19.

Food and Drink: Both Lexington and Concord offer a wide range of places to eat. At the beginning of the ride in Lexington, Via Lago at 1845 Massachusetts Avenue creates great sandwiches and salads and sells drinks and pastry. You can pick up provisions at the tiny Concord Hill Market on the crest of the hill at 2219 Massachusetts Avenue. Bedford Farms, at the 14-mile mark on the right side of Route 225, provides a convenient snack stop.

Restrooms: Lexington Visitor Center across from Lexington Green, Battle Road Visitor Center, North Bridge Visitor Center, on the left side just after you enter the Minute Man Bikeway in Bedford.

Fees: Lexington: Buckman Tavern, Hancock-Clarke House; Concord: the Wayside, Orchard House, Emerson House, Concord Museum, the Old Manse. Most of these historic buildings are open from mid-April through October 31, 10:00 A.M. to 5:00 P.M. (Sunday 1:00 P.M. to 5:00 P.M.).

Background: During our country's first 130 years, Britain was too busy trying to wrest control of France's North American holdings to be bothered with the expatriates who had settled in the new land. By 1763, Britain had the time and energy to devote to its new colony. In an attempt to exercise control, the British shipped an army to America. How would Britain pay for the troops' weapons, clothes, and food? Impose duties and taxes on the colonists.

Over the next 10 years, the British continued to increase the number of taxable items and to impose more regulations. They ordered the colonists to buy tax stamps for their newspapers, playing cards, and legal documents; provide room and board for British soldiers; and pay duty on molasses, paper, and lead. The more taxes and regulations the British government demanded, the angrier the colonists became. A tax on British tea in 1773 precipitated a memorable protest: A band of colonists, disguised in Indian garb, boarded British ships laden with tea and dumped the cargo into Boston Harbor. The British government punished its charges by closing the harbor with the Intolerable Acts in 1774.

Rumors of colonists stockpiling arms and supplies in Concord convinced Lieutenant General Thomas Gage, the British North American commander-in-chief, to send troops to find and destroy the cache of supplies and arrest the patriot leaders. On the night of April 18, 1775, Gage dispatched 700 troops to Concord.

When Dr. Joseph Warren, a patriot leader who organized the militia, heard of the British plans, he dispatched Paul Revere and William Dawes to alert the colonists. In order to ensure that the colonists would be notified of the impending advance, Warren had Revere and Dawes take two separate routes in case one of them could not elude British troops. If both messengers were captured, two lights from the steeple of the Old North Church also would warn the countryside that the British were preparing to row across the Charles River before they began their 16-mile march.

THE RIDE

1. Begin on the Minute Man Bikeway between Depot Square and the municipal parking lot. Follow the bike path west past the intersection with Meriam Street.

    The ride begins at the back entrance to the **Lexington Visitor Center** (#1 on the map), just west of the starting point on Meriam Street. Inside, you'll find a diorama of the British attack on the Battle Green.

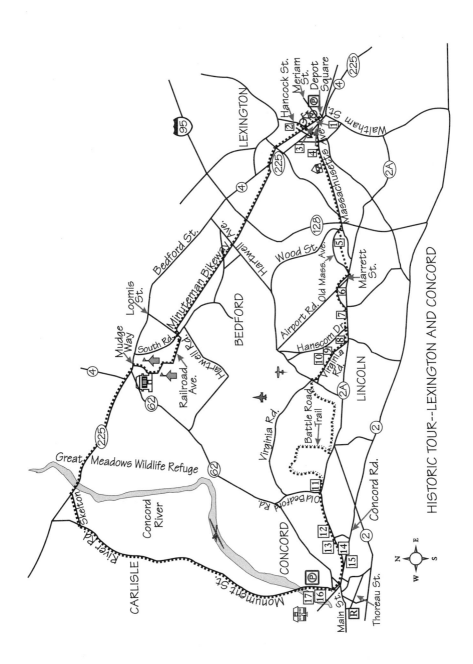

HISTORIC TOUR--LEXINGTON AND CONCORD

2.   If you wish to visit the **Hancock-Clarke House** (2), pedal west one block on the bike path, turn right on Hancock Street, and proceed 0.2 mile.

   Both Paul Revere and William Dawes successfully evaded the British and arrived here on horseback late in the evening of April 18, 1775. They awoke John Hancock and Samuel Adams, guests of the owner, Reverend Jonas Clarke, and warned them that the British regulars were on their way. (The British arrived five hours later.)

   Inside you'll find furnishings and portraits owned by the Clarke and Hancock families, who occupied the house before Reverend Clarke and his 12 children. In the entrance hall, cases display items, such as the drum used to summon the Minute Men—the name for the colonists who fought against the British—and a musket used in the skirmish between the Lexington Minute Men and British regulars on the Battle Green. A 30-minute guided tour of the house is offered on the hour.

3.   To visit **Buckman Tavern** (3), retrace your route down Hancock Street. At the stop sign, turn left. The tavern is set back from the road just ahead on the left.

   Buckman Tavern was built in 1710 and soon became one of Lexington's busiest hostelries. The Minute Men gathered here on April 19 to await the British. One of the items on display is the old front door, which was pierced by a British musket ball during the battle on the green.

4.   Cross Bedford Street to the **Lexington Battle Green** (4), often referred to as the "birthplace of American liberty."

   At the east end of this triangular grassy expanse stands a bronze replica of a young Minute Man sculpted by Henry Hudson Kitson.

   Here on the green at 5:00 A.M. on Patriots Day, the third Monday in April, a group of residents don Minute Man and British Redcoat garb and reenact the battle of April 19, 1775. Neither Redcoats nor Minute Men admitted firing the single shot that started the skirmish. Although Captain John Parker lined up his Minute Men on Lexington Green, he wished only to emphasize their resolve. Parker was not naive; he knew his 77 men could not stop the advance of 700 British soldiers.

By the time the inexperienced British soldiers arrived in Lexington, they were exhausted. They had departed from Boston Common in the middle of the night, jumped in their boats at high tide, and rowed through the swampy Back Bay to Lechmere Point to pick up their firearms. Weighed down by 13-pound muskets and lead bullets, the Redcoats marched 14 miles to Lexington Green to face a motley group of Minute Men. An unexpected shot may have spooked the fatigued British troops, who were oblivious to Major John Pitcairn's orders to stop shooting. They continued to fire, killing eight of the fleeing Minute Men.

Perched in the center of the green, a boulder marks the grave of one of the Minute Men, inscribed with Captain Parker's command, "Don't fire unless fired on, but if they mean to have a war, let it begin here."

5. Walk your bike across the green and proceed west on Massachusetts Avenue, away from Lexington Center, to follow the path of the British troops as they trudged along the Battle Road toward Concord.

6. Pass through the traffic-light intersection and climb Massachusetts Avenue, passing the tiny stone Concord Hill Market on your right. Proceed a total of 1.4 miles from the Battle Green to Wood Street (just after you cross a bridge over Route 128). Turn right.

7. You can either immediately turn left onto a foot path leading to Fiske Hall or take the first left onto Old Massachusetts Avenue and access the Battle Road Trail, located on the right of Old Massachusetts Avenue.

8. There may be no sign designating **Fiske Hill** (5), because you are entering through the back door. The main entrance and parking lot are on the opposite side. No riding is allowed on this historic property, so dismount and walk your bike.

9. Pass the old foundation of the home of Ebenezer Fiske, a wealthy Lexington farmer whose family farmed 116 acres of land from the 17th through the 19th centuries. Ebenezer accumulated his wealth both by farming and by selling refreshment from the popular taproom in his parlor. Bear right at the fork.

    Climb the hill on the path that parallels the route the British confidently marched after their early-morning rout of the Minute Men.

Marching and dodging musket fire on the return from Concord, the physically and emotionally exhausted British troops broke ranks and ran down Fiske Hill. Their officers fired in an attempt to stop the troops' retreat. When Ebenezer Fiske returned home that evening, he found the bodies of five British soldiers lying on his doorstep.

10. At the #2 stake, marking the stone wall that defined Fiske's pastures, bear right and cross the wooden bridge to exit.

11. Pedal through the parking lot to Old Massachusetts Avenue.

12. Cross Old Massachusetts Avenue and turn right onto the Battle Road Trail.

13. Follow the trail, which leads to the main entrance of the **Minute Man National Historical Park**. To reach the **Minute Man Visitor Center** (6), follow the signs and turn left onto a long walkway.

    Open in spring, summer, and fall, the Minute Man Visitor Center offers restrooms and water as well as a 22-minute film that gives the background of events leading up to the fight between the Minute Men and the British. Fifteen-minute talks by the park rangers are offered every two hours.

    Inquire at the information desk for Park Service maps and materials.

14. Upon leaving the visitor center, return to the parking area, turn left onto Nelson Road, and continue on the Battle Road Trail.

    Minute Man Rock, the large boulder on the right behind the #3 marker, protected Captain William Thorning as he shot and killed two British soldiers.

15. Follow Nelson Road to the **Paul Revere Commemorative Site** (7) (2.6 total miles total).

    On this spot at 2:00 A.M. on April 19, 1775, British patrols captured Paul Revere as he rode into Concord to warn the colonists of the Redcoats' advance. Revere's companions, William Dawes and Dr. Samuel Prescott, escaped. Dawes turned back, but Prescott, who had joined Revere and Dawes in Lexington, eluded the patrols by jumping over a stone wall and traveling over back roads to carry the warning into Concord.

16. Continue on the trail to the underpass below Hanscom Drive.

17. Follow the trail to the next historic site, the **William Smith House** (8).

Once the home of the captain of the Lincoln Minute Men, the Smith House's modest wooden, unpainted exterior typifies dwellings of that time. The interior of this "saltbox" is dominated by a massive central fireplace used for cooking and heating. Its low ceilings and southern exposure helped retain the heat.

Proceed 0.2 mile to **Samuel Hartwell House Site** (9), the foundation and fireplace in what remains of the home of Sergeant Samuel Hartwell, also a Lincoln Minute Man. A closer inspection of the site reveals how chimneys and fireplaces were designed to heat homes more than 200 years ago.

Next door is the **Ephraim Hartwell Tavern** (10), a popular country inn built in 1754. On weekends, guides lead tours of the tavern, furnished in the style of the period.

18. Make a sharp right at the **Bloody Angle**, the spot where Minute Men ambushed the British and killed eight Redcoats.

The trail now continues for 2 miles through historic farming fields and on boardwalks over wetlands. Please do not ride your bike on the boardwalks.

19. The trail crosses a parking lot before it ends at **Meriam's Corner** (11). This junction of Old Bedford Road with Route 2A was formerly known as the "Bloody Curve." When the Redcoats returned to Boston, the Concord Minute Men hid behind the Meriam house, now the oldest home in Concord, and opened fire, wounding and killing many British troops.

20. Turn right onto Route 2A. The **Wayside** (12) sits on the right, 0.5 mile from Meriam's Corner (6 total miles).

Home of Samuel Whitney, the captain of the Concord Minute Men, and storage place for their weapons, the Wayside later housed the Nathaniel Hawthorne family, who were preceded by the Alcotts before they moved across the road to Orchard House. The National Park Service now owns the Wayside, which is open to the public. For a nominal fee, you can join a ranger-led tour.

Just ahead, also on the right, sits the **Orchard House** (13), home of the Alcott family from 1858 to 1877, where Louisa May Alcott wrote

Little Women. The admission fee includes a guided tour of the home. Fans of *Little Women* enjoy viewing Louisa's bedroom, Amy's wall drawings, and the children's play costumes and furniture.

A half-mile down the road on the left is the **Concord Museum** (14). Inside you'll find 15 furnished rooms, each reflecting a specific period during the last three centuries. The museum also holds artifacts from the battle at North Bridge, a collection of Henry David Thoreau's belongings, and one of the lanterns from the steeple of Boston's Old North Church.

Across Concord Road stands the **Emerson House** (15), home of Ralph Waldo Emerson from 1835 to 1882. The house contains his books, personal effects, and furniture.

If you are interested in more information on Concord, stop at the tourist information booth on the corner of Heywood Street and Route 2A, 0.2 mile west of the Emerson House.

21. Proceed into Concord Center. At the rotary, bear right and head toward the Colonial Inn, following signs to the Old North Bridge.

    The first right leads to Sleepy Hollow Cemetery, where many of the town's authors are buried.

22. Now facing the Colonial Inn, take the second right onto Monument Street.

23. Remain on Monument Street for 0.6 mile (7.5 total miles) to the parking lot for the Old North Bridge and Minute Man National Historical Park. The bike rack is on the left side of the road.

    To reach the **Old Manse** (16), backtrack 200 yards south of the park.

    Ralph Waldo Emerson lived in the weathered gray house, a National Historic Landmark, while he wrote his first book of essays, *Nature*. Later, newly married Nathaniel Hawthorne moved here with his bride and was inspired to write *Mosses from an Old Manse*. The house now contains 18th- and 19th-century furnishings.

24. To visit the **Old North Bridge** (17) from the Old Manse, walk through the meadow and turn left on the path that runs through the park.

    By the time the British reached Concord, patriots had learned of the skirmish on Lexington Green. As the Redcoats began to search for and destroy the colonists' arms, militiamen gathered in Concord. When a mass of militiamen advanced over North Bridge, British troops, who had stayed behind to guard the bridge, retreated while firing their muskets. After the British shot two patriots, Major Buttrick of Concord ordered, "Fire, fellow soldiers, for God's sake, fire!" Ralph Waldo Emerson memorialized this moment with his description: "The shot heard round the world."

The outnumbered British retreated to the center of town, regrouped, and began the long march back to Boston. Patriots poured in from outlying communities, stationed themselves along the Redcoats' route, and fired continuously on the retreating British. By the time the troops returned to Boston, the British counted 73 dead, 174 wounded, and 26 missing.

The bronze statue of the Minute Man on the entrance path marks the spot where the colonists opened fire. Ralph Waldo Emerson secured the commission of this work for Daniel Chester French, then a young, inexperienced sculptor who had studied drawing with May Alcott, Louisa's sister. French later became one of the most sought after sculptors in the Northeast, creating many pieces in and

"Here once the embattled farmers stood"—the Old North Bridge in Concord.

around Boston. He is best known for creating the bronze entrance doors to the Boston Public Library.

25. Cross the Old North Bridge on the way to the former Buttrick Mansion, which serves as the Old North Bridge Visitor Center.

The bridge's high arch was not designed just for aesthetic reasons. It both strengthens the structure and places the bridge high enough above the river so flood waters will not damage it.

The visitor center contains exhibits, a video, and a small shop. Rangers offer informative tours of the park.

26. To proceed to the scenic, nonhistoric second half of the tour, leave the park and turn left onto Monument Street.

After crossing the Concord River on foot, you will now cycle over it. This picturesque 3-mile stretch is one of my favorites. I love the narrow, curving road lined with tall trees and crumbling stone walls, the landscape dotted with old farmhouses next to wide open pastures. Now horses have replaced the cows, sheep, and goats that once grazed on the land.

27. Bike 3.3 miles and turn right onto Skelton Road (11 total miles).

28. Follow Skelton to the **T** intersection with Route 225. Turn right.

The road crosses the Concord River as it passes through the Great Meadows Wildlife Refuge.

29. Remain on Route 225, bearing left at the fork into Bedford Center as Route 225 merges with Routes 4 and 62.

Bedford Farms Ice Cream is on the right just after the junction with Route 4.

30. After the merge, take the first right onto Mudge Way, while following the signs to the high school and library (13.3 miles).

31. Remain on the roadway as it passes the library on the right and the playing field on the left, and head toward the tennis courts. Keep the tennis courts on your left as you follow the roadway to the bike path wedged between two fences.

32. The bike path leads to a road and a school. Turn left.

33. Follow the road as it curves around and ends at Railroad Avenue. Turn left.

34. Proceed a short distance on Railroad Avenue until the intersection with Loomis Street. Turn right.

The bike and in-line skate shop, the Bikeway Source, is on the right corner.

35. Take an immediate left onto the Minute Man Bikeway. Remain on the trail for 3.5 miles to the intersection with Meriam Street.

The **Bedford Depot** sits on the left side at the beginning of the bikeway. More than 100 years ago, it serviced two railroad lines that intersected in Bedford: the Boston and Lowell Railroad, now the bikeway, and the first two-foot-gauge railroad in the country, which extended north to Billerica.

For further information on the Minute Man Bikeway, see chapter 7.

9

LINCOLN—WESTON

WAYLAND—SUDBURY

 Distance and Difficulty: 25 miles on easy to moderate terrain; several hills.

Cycling through the picturesque, well-preserved and -conserved suburbs of Lincoln, Weston, Wayland, and Sudbury offers relaxed biking along shaded, narrow, winding back roads bordered by antique stone walls. Two- and three-acre residential zoning guarantees well-manicured expanses surrounding 18th-century farmhouses and modern mansions.

The route passes the Case Estates, an offshoot of Harvard University's Arnold Arboretum, with trails leading to perennial, wildflower, and rhododendron gardens among 110 acres of woodlands. A section of the ride runs for seven miles in and around the scenic Great Meadows National Wildlife Refuge, where the Sudbury River, marsh, woods, and meadows provide protected habitats for waterfowl.

Transportation: From Routes 128/95 take Exit 28 west on Trapelo Road toward Lincoln. Remain on Trapelo Road for 2.5 miles to the stop-sign intersection with Lincoln Road (marked by a traffic island with plantings). Turn left on Lincoln Road. Drive 1 mile to the Lincoln Guide Service parking lot on the left side. The owner has given permission to park here during your bike ride. Rental bikes are available (781-259-1111).

By commuter rail: From North Station or Porter Square in Cambridge, take the Fitchburg Line to Lincoln.

Food and Drink: Across from Lincoln Guide Service and the train station lies Lincoln Mall, which contains the Whistlestop, a small coffee shop, and Donalon's, a food market that sells sandwiches and drinks. Halfway into the ride, the AAA Market stands on the corner of Route 27 and Pelham Island Road in Wayland, and farther along is the Letteri Farm Stand on Landham Road in Sudbury.

Restrooms: Lincoln Guide Service, 152 Lincoln Road, where the trip begins; the Mobil service station, just past the Lincoln train station; Great Meadows Wildlife Refuge Visitor Center, Weir Hill Road, Sudbury, open 8:00 A.M. to 4:00 P.M. weekdays (in May and October, open weekends as well).

Fees: Drumlin Farm Wildlife Sanctuary, adults $5.00, children and seniors $3.50. Open 9:00 A.M. to 5:00 P.M., closed Mondays (781-259-9807).

Recreational Options: Hiking around Great Meadows National Wildlife Refuge.

Background: As you ride on back roads in undeveloped areas, common topographical features emerge: wetlands, ponds, rolling hills, stone walls, and woodlands. The first three characteristics were created by the most recent glacier as it inched its way southward 16,000 years ago, gouging out ponds and valleys and then depositing the ground-up rock and gravel to form these hills and ridges. The rustic stone walls were constructed by colonists who supplanted the Native Americans. In order to provide shelter for their families, the colonists chopped down the abundant trees and constructed dwellings which they heated by burning logs. Woodlands were transformed to open fields studded with stones the glacier had ripped from ridges or unearthed from bedrock. Families gathered the stones and piled them into walls to contain livestock, demarcate their land, and make some sections plowable.

By the 19th century, settlers had transformed wood lots and pastures into vegetable gardens and hayfields. They dammed wetlands to create sufficient water flow to power mills. By 1840, two-thirds of the land had been deforested. Not until the end of the 19th century, with the arrival of the railroad and the increased use of coal and gas for fuel, were the forests allowed to regrow. The stately oaks and pines that now shade the road and enhance the landscape are less than 100 years old. Many of the stone walls that run through Lincoln and Weston are relics of the farming era and predate the trees by more than 100 years.

Crossing the Sudbury River in the Great Meadows National Wildlife Refuge.

THE RIDE

1. With your back to Lincoln Guide Service and the train station, turn left on Lincoln Road.

2. Take the first left onto Codman Road.

3. After biking for 0.6 mile, bear left at a stop sign onto Route 117. The numerous bird feeders on the property on the right belong to Drumlin Farm Wildlife Sanctuary.

4. At 1.3 miles turn right on Tower Road, a narrow, winding, wooded country road lined with old stone walls.

5. At. 2.7 miles, bear left at the stop sign.

   The large brick complex on the left is the Campion Center, a Jesuit residence and renewal center.

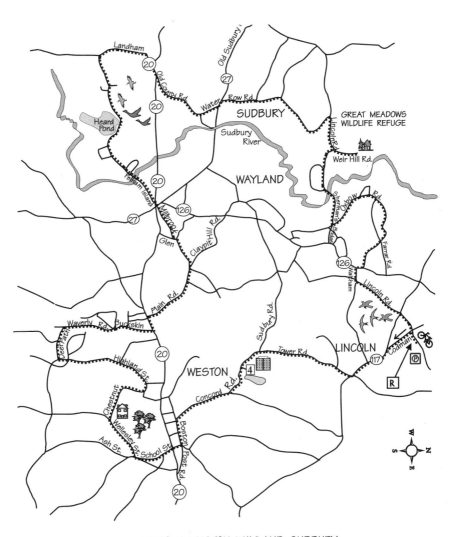

LINCOLN–WESTON–WAYLAND–SUDBURY

Just past the Campion Center is the entrance road to the College Conservation Area, where the off-road ride in Weston Woodlands begins (see chapter 18).

6. A great downhill run on Concord Road leads to Weston Center. At the stop sign, turn left on Boston Post Road (4.3 miles).

7. Travel through Weston Center, passing the impressive Weston Town Hall and the unique stone First Parish Church on the left. Turn right on School Street (4.7 miles).

8. Proceed through the intersection with Route 20 (stoplight), following the sign to Regis College and Route 30. Continue on School Street as it passes the new Weston Public Library and Weston elementary schools and then merges with Wellesley Street. Remain on Wellesley as it bears to the right.

   The **Case Estates** appears on the right (5.6 miles). Owned by Harvard University, this 112-acre property is used as an adjunct to Arnold Arboretum (chapter 24). Unlike the meticulously landscaped arboretum, the Case Estates has remained unmanicured. Here, horticulturists grow plants in a natural setting in order to determine which plants thrive under certain controlled conditions.

   Case Estates continues an 80-year horticultural tradition. For 33 years the property's previous owner, Marian Case, established and conducted a school for gardening, called Hillcrest Gardens. The students, local boys who worked on her estate, earned a minimal wage but were entitled to bring home some of the produce they grew in the gardens.

   There is no entrance fee. Visitors can stroll around the grounds or walk on trails through woods filled with wildflowers, many planted by Marian Case.

9. Take your next right onto Chestnut Street, passing on the corner the oldest residence in Weston.

   Cycle along the narrow winding road enhanced by several large old farmhouses that have expanded considerably from the two-room structures built 200 years ago.

10. Follow Chestnut to the stop sign (6.8 miles). Turn left, remaining on Chestnut.

11. Follow Chestnut to the **T** intersection with Highland. Turn left (7 miles).

12. Remain on Highland for 1.5 miles (8.5 miles total) and turn right onto Deer Path Lane.

13. Deer Path bends to the right into Waverly Road, a wide tree-lined street flanked by large impressive homes.

14. Remain on Waverly until it ends at Buckskin Drive (9.9 miles). Turn right.

15. At the junction with Route 20 (Boston Post Road, at 10.4 miles), turn left.

16. Make your first right onto Plain Road. You are now in the town of Wayland, an upscale suburb similar to Lincoln and Weston.

17. Follow Plain for 0.9 mile as it forks left and continues for another 0.4 mile (12 miles total).

18. Bear left onto Glen.

19. Take an immediate right onto Millbrook.

20. Continue straight, crossing two busy thoroughfares, Route 27 and Route 20 (12.4 miles), onto Pelham Island Road, which winds in and out of the **Great Meadows National Wildlife Refuge**. The Great Meadows Visitor Center is located 7 miles ahead. The large body of water coming up on the left is Heard Pond.

> Great Meadows consists of 3,400 acres of woods and wetlands that border the Sudbury and Concord Rivers. Managed by the U.S. Fish and Wildlife Service, the property functions as a habitat for wildlife, particularly migratory birds. The Sudbury River section is one of two refuges; the other extends through the suburbs of Concord, Bedford, and Carlisle.
>
> The name was shortened from Great River Meadows, referring to the grasslands that remained during dry summers when the river did not spill over into the flood plain. Native Americans and colonists grew and harvested hay here until the early 19th century, when a new milldam caused the water level to rise and flood the meadows. Waterfowl soon replaced hay; hunters and fishermen replaced farmers.

21. At the T intersection (15.1 miles), turn right on Landham Road.

22. At the stop-sign (15.7 miles), turn right at the junction with Route 20 (Boston Post Road).

23. Proceed 0.4 mile (16.1 total miles) on this busy stretch, and take the second left onto Old Country Road (*before* you reach Sky Restaurant).

24. Take your first left onto Water Row Road. At 17.2 miles, proceed through the stop sign intersection with Old Sudbury Road, remaining on Water Row as it skirts the western edge of Great Meadows in the town of Sudbury. A sign announces the refuge headquarters 2.5 miles ahead.

25. Remain on Water Row for 2 more miles until it ends at Lincoln Road. Turn right (19.1 miles total).

    To visit the Great Meadows National Wildlife Refuge Visitor Center and Weir Hill, continue on Lincoln for a half-mile and turn left onto Weir Hill Road. The center and trails are a half-mile down bumpy Weir Hill Road.

    > Weir Hill, a drumlin formed from debris piled up by glacial movement 16,000 years ago, was named for the fences (weirs) that Native Americans used to trap fish in the Sudbury River. Trails from the visitor center lead through woods and fields to the river and marsh.

    > The visitor center contains exhibits on the refuge and its wildlife, habitat, and endangered species. A one-mile trail climbs the hill, skirts the marsh, crosses through a red-maple swamp, and circles a small pond.

26. Return to Lincoln Street and turn left (20.6 miles).

27. Follow Lincoln for 1.0 mile and turn left on Oxbow Road (21.6 total miles).

28. After pedaling for 1.3 miles on Oxbow, you'll come to a tricky spot where Oxbow bears to the right. (If you continue straight, you'll end up on Farrar Road.) Remain on Oxbow until the stop sign at Route 126 (23.4 total miles).

29. Turn right on Route 126 and make an immediate left onto Waltham Road.

30. Take the first left onto Lincoln Road. After pedaling for 0.2 mile, you can enter a bike path on the right.

31. At 24.5 miles, you reach the stop-sign intersection with Route 27. Proceed through the intersection and remain on Lincoln Road back to the starting point.

Children adore **Drumlin Farm Wildlife Sanctuary**, which occupies 180 acres adjacent to the bike path. Operated by the Massachusetts Audubon Society, Drumlin Farm functions as both a farm and a wildlife sanctuary. Barns house farm animals and pens contain animals (who were injured and would not survive in the wild) native to the New England countryside.

10

WELLESLEY

NEEDHAM

DOVER

 Distance and Difficulty: 23 miles of moderate biking; a few rolling hills.

Escape the hubbub of congested streets and pedal along quiet wooded back roads. Beginning in the college town of Wellesley, one of Boston's loveliest suburbs, the ride runs through the campus of Wellesley College, Hillary Rodham Clinton's alma mater and one of the most picturesque in the country. The ride then parallels the Charles River as it flows through Needham and Dover. Needham's large modern dwellings provide a visual contrast with the horse farms and quaint old farmhouses in the bucolic suburb of Dover, whose tiny town center resembles a stage set from an earlier era.

Transportation: By automobile: To the starting point at the Wellesley Center train station and Tailby Parking Lot, take Exit 21B, Route 16 west, off Routes 128/95. Follow Route 16 for 3 miles into Wellesley Center, past the town-office complex on the right to the traffic light at Grove Street. Turn right at the light into the large parking area. Metered long-term parking is free on weekends. If the parking lot is full, park at Saint Moritz Sports, a bike shop half a mile east at 475 Washington Street.

By commuter rail: From Back Bay or South Station, take the Framingham Line to Wellesley Square. From the station, head toward the post office and then pedal down the roadway to the traffic light.

Food and Drink: At the beginning of the ride, Truly Yogurt sits on the corner of Grove and Washington Streets. Farther east on Washington Street are White Mountain Creamery, Bruegger's Bagel Bakery and Au Bon Pain. In the middle of the ride, the Dover Market, Mobil gas station, and Dover Pharmacy in Dover Center sell food and drink.

Restrooms: In Wellesley Center, the library and police station at 530 and 535 Washington Street have public restrooms. In Dover Center a restroom is located in the Mobil gas station on the corner of Walpole and Centre Streets.

Recreational Options: Off-road biking or hiking in Noanet Reservation (see chapter 17), walking around Wellesley College and Lake Waban (see chapter 34).

Background: Although Wellesley is now an affluent community enhanced by two fine colleges, private schools, country clubs, and large homes, it was not always so blessed. Settled in 1660 by farmers who cultivated tiny tracts of land and depended on the sale of wood products for income, Wellesley did not join the ranks of well-to-do suburbs until the mid-19th century.

The town was named for one of its colonial occupants, Samuel Welles, who moved there in 1763. In 1881, the year of the town's incorporation, Welles's grandson-in-law, H. Hollis Hunnewell, bought the large Welles estate and named it Wellesley. Because Hunnewell was one of the town's main benefactors, his name is attached to several of the town's buildings.

Wellesley's development and prestige improved when Wellesley College opened in 1875. Its founder, Henry Durant, transformed his country estate overlooking Lake Waban into one of the first institutions to offer young women opportunities for education. He hired a talented architect and landscape designer and ordered them to create the most beautiful women's college in the world.

When biking through Wellesley, you undoubtedly will notice numerous lovely, large homes. All were built within the last 100 years, in contrast to Dover, which has many grand antique farmhouses. Dover began as a wealthy farming community, with a small number of farms owning vast acreage.

Later, affluent Boston Brahmins bought the farms and spent summers riding their horses over the rolling hills. Their descendants winterized the estates and remained year-round when the invention of the automobile and development of expressways allowed them to commute to their jobs in Boston. Much of Dover's considerable charm results from how little it has changed over the last 200 years. Its conservation-minded citizens have rejected any attempts at development, so it continues to have more open space than any other Boston suburb.

THE RIDE

1. From the Tailby Parking Lot and Wellesley Square train station, head for the traffic light and turn right to follow Route 135 (Central Street) 0.8 mile through Wellesley Center to **Wellesley College**.

2. Turn left at the traffic light at the Wellesley College entrance sign and follow the main road as it cuts through the 500-acre campus.

    Remain on the road as it ascends and passes on the right the Jewett Arts Center and the Academic Quad, whose red-brick Gothic-style buildings are the focal point of the campus. Beyond the quad lies Lake Waban. The "form follows function" design of the modern Science Center on the right side deliberately contrasts with the college's more-traditional buildings.

3. Continue on College Road until it reaches Route 16 (Washington Street). Turn left (1.6 miles).

4. Take the first right onto Dover Road.

5. Remain on Dover as it merges with Grove Street, enters the suburb of Dover, and ends at Charles River Street. Turn left (3.2 miles).

6. Upon entering the suburb of Needham and passing Ridge Hill Reservation on the left, remain on Charles River for 1.4 miles (4.6 total miles) until reaching South Street. Turn left.

    Charles River Street and South Street parallel the Charles River, hidden by the woods on the right side. On this trip we follow a western section of the Charles River. Chapter 2 explores the eastern end, which flows through Watertown, Cambridge, and Boston.

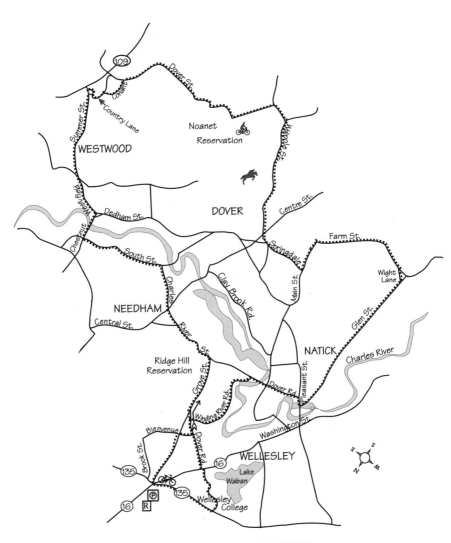

WELLESLEY–NEEDHAM–DOVER

7. Remain on South Street until the blinking traffic light at the intersection with Chestnut Street. Turn right and cross the Charles River.

8. Take the next left onto Westfield Street.

9. Follow Westfield for 0.5 mile into the suburb of Westwood and bear right onto Summer Street.

10. After pedaling for 1.0 mile on Summer Street, turn right onto Country Lane, a side road that escapes the congestion on Route 109. If you come to a **T** intersection at Route 109 you've gone too far.

11. After a great downhill ride on Country Lane, turn right on Conant Road for another descent.

12. Follow Conant to the stop sign at Dover Street. Turn right.

13. As you might expect, Dover Street runs into the suburb of Dover, where its name changes to Powisset Street.

    Antique farmhouses hug the road. Their age is revealed by stone foundations common to homes built several hundred years ago. Colonists gathered stones that had littered the landscape since the latest glacial recession 12,000 to 16,000 years ago, and put them to good use as foundations for their houses and walls to contain their livestock.

    After biking for 1.5 miles on Dover/Powisset Street (11.1 miles total), **Noanet Reservation** appears on the right. Owned by the Trustees of Reservations, Noanet, which offers great off-road biking and hiking, is explored in chapter 17.

14. At 12.8 miles Powisset ends at Walpole Street. Turn right.

    Walpole Street runs by the western section of Noanet Reservation, where horse jumps reflect the community's preferred mode of recreation.

15. After cycling for 0.5 mile (13.3 miles total), you reach a traffic light in bustling Dover Center, which consists of a church, town hall, gas station, pharmacy, and market. Proceed through the intersection, pedal 1 mile, and turn left on Farm Street.

16. Remain on Farm for 1.5 miles (15.8 miles total) and turn right onto Wight Lane, a tiny cutoff that connects with Glen Street, which runs into the town of Natick.

17. Remain on Glen for 2 miles to the T intersection with Pleasant Street. Turn right (16.8 miles total) and cross the Charles River.

18. Take the second left onto Dover Road.

19. Remain on Dover for 1 mile, cross another section of the Charles River, and turn left onto Winding River Road (19.9 miles). This street does just what its name implies, curves around and follows the path of the Charles River.

20. At the T intersection, turn left on Dover (20.3 miles).

21. Take the first right onto Bienvenue, opposite a golf course.

22. Take the first left onto Grove. Follow Grove as it passes elegant homes and Dana Hall School, a private girls' secondary school, on the return to the parking lot and train station.

11

HINGHAM

COHASSET

 Distance and Difficulty: 21 miles of easy biking.

This ride has everything! The tour begins on a paved bike path through the Wompatuck State Forest, skirts the salt marshes of Scituate and Cohasset, and explores quaint Cohasset Common, so picturesque it was featured in a movie. Continuing along one of Massachusetts' most scenic coastal roads, the tour travels to Hingham to view its historic churches and elegant old homes, occupied by our country's early settlers.

Hot and sticky? No problem, stop for a swim at one of the three beaches en route. Interested in off-road biking? Wompatuck State Park and Cohasset Town Forest offer challenging opportunities. Hungry? Both towns boast many fast-food shops and restaurants. A history buff? Numerous well-maintained historic buildings line the roads. Enjoy riding along the ocean? The two-mile stretch along Cohasset's craggy coast offers unsurpassed scenery. Allow a full day to experience all this area has to offer.

Transportation: By automobile: Take Route 93 south to Route 3 south toward Cape Cod. From Route 3 take Exit 14, Route 228 north, toward Hingham. Remain on Route 228 for 4 miles and turn right onto Free Street, following the signs for Womapatuck State Park, where the bike ride begins. Remain on

Free Street until the **T** intersection with Lazell Street. Turn left. Take your next right onto Union Street and head into the park. The large parking area is on your right.

By public transportation: At the time of publication, no rail line serviced the South Shore. However, the MBTA is trying to reinstate the Old Colony Rail Line from Boston to Hingham.

Bikes are allowed on commuter boats that run during the week from Rowe's Wharf in Boston to Hingham Harbor. Most boats run early in the morning and late in the afternoon. If taking the commuter boat, exit and head up Shipyard Drive to Route 3A (Lincoln Street) and turn right. At the intersection with Beal Street (traffic light), turn left. Remain on Beal Street for 1.4 miles until the intersection with Fort Hill Street. Turn right and follow the trip directions starting with #25 to get to Wompatuck, where the chapter begins.

Food and Drink: Soft drink and juice machines are located in the Wompatuck State Park Visitor Center. Brewed Awakenings on Central Avenue in Hingham Center; Village Gourmet and French Memories on Main Street in Cohasset Village.

Restrooms: Wompatuck State Park Visitor Center; bathhouse at Sandy Beach, Cohasset.

Fees: Maritime Museum, Historic House, and Independence Gown Museum, all in Cohasset and open seasonally; Old Ordinary in Hingham, open seasonally.

Recreational Options: Wompatuck State Park offers mountain biking, hiking, cross-country skiing, in-line skating on its paved bike trails, horseback riding, and camping (781-749-7160); swimming at Cohasset beaches.

Background: When 28 settlers from the English town of Hingham landed on Boston's south coast in 1635, they encountered the friendly but diminished Massachuset tribe, which had lost many members to a deadly plague. Peter Hobart, a Puritan minister and the colonists' *de facto* leader, negotiated with Chief Sachem Wompatuck to parcel off land and build a village. The colonists named the town Hingham after their English home. By 1639, Hingham's population had swelled to 200. One hundred years later, its thriving fishing, shipbuilding, and trading industries contributed to another tenfold increase in population. During the 19th century, Hingham's port

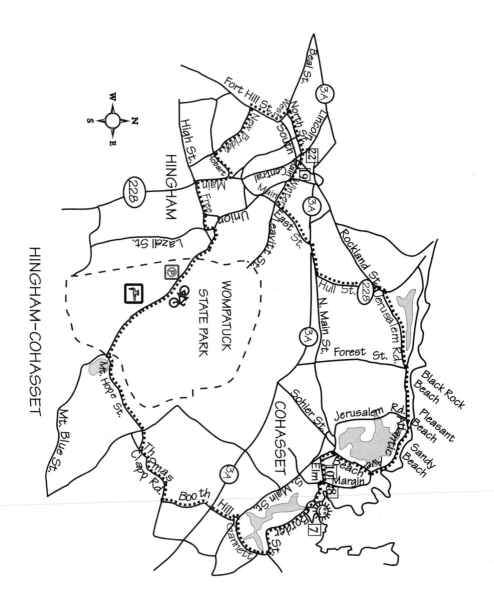

bustled, as many ships unloaded their cargo at its convenient harbor. Steamboats and trains then transported the cargo into Boston.

Cohasset and Hingham were a single community until 1717, when Cohasset, after a long battle, succeeded in breaking away to form a separate precinct. As in Hingham, Cohasset residents successfully fished, traded, and built ships. The gracious old homes of these two communities attest to the prosperity of their former inhabitants.

When the Industrial Revolution led to the decline of the fishing and shipbuilding industries, the towns focused on the newly constructed South Shore Railroad. The rail line drew wealthy Bostonians who built summer estates along the scenic coast. By the turn of the century, these summer estates were sold to families who lived there year-round. With no real industries to sustain them, Hingham and Cohasset evolved into affluent Boston suburbs.

THE RIDE

1. From the parking lot in **Wompatuck State Park,** turn right onto the main road that bisects the reservation. If you are interested in exploring the park, you can obtain maps in the visitor center.

    Named for Sachem Wompatuck, this 3,500-acre park was used mainly for pasture and wood lots until 1941, when the U.S. Navy took over the land. The navy built massive bunkers to store missiles and shells, as well as roads and railroad tracks to move the equipment to the naval yard near Hingham Harbor. In 1967 the navy donated the property to the state, which converted the former rail beds into 15 miles of paved bike paths.

    Pedal on the road for 2.2 miles as it climbs a hill and then pass on the right first the campground and then Mount Blue Spring, a natural water source where you can replenish your water supply.

2. After exiting from the park, turn left onto Mount Hope Street.

3. Remain on Mount Hope for 2.6 miles (total of 4.8), passing over Aaron River, then marshland, and crossing the intersection with Summer Street. Turn left on Booth Hill Road.

4. Proceed on Booth Hill, crossing Route 3A, for 1.1 miles (5.9 total miles) until reaching Gannett's Corner, marked by a plaque stating that Matthew Gannett settled there in 1651. Turn left.

5. At the stoplight, turn right onto Gannett Street.

6. Pedal through this commercial section and by a wide marsh. After riding for 6.8 miles total, look on your left for a grassy triangle and a sign advertising the Golden Rooster. Turn left at the triangle onto Border Street, which borders the east side of the marsh.

7. Follow Border as it leaves the town of Scituate and enters Cohasset. An inlet from Cohasset Bay parallels the road.

    After traveling 2 miles on Border Road (8.8 miles total), look on your right for a gigantic granite ledge that forms part of **Government Island**, a small peninsula jutting into Cohasset Harbor. If you pull into the parking area, you can see the copper-covered dome and bell from the original lighthouse built on Minot's Ledge on Government Island.

    Constructed in 1850 to protect vessels from running aground on Cohasset's craggy coast, **Minot's Light** functioned for only a year before a tropical storm toppled it into the sea. Determined that the second Minot's Light last longer than the first, the designer supervised the carving of 3,514 tons of granite into 1,079 dovetailed blocks. The bottom layer had to be constructed precisely to adhere to the tiny sheer ledge and yet provide enough stability to allow the structure to rise 114 feet. Minot's Light was completed in 1860 and has withstood wind blasts and stormy seas for nearly 140 years.

    On the ledge that overlooks the exhibit, a path climbs 80 feet to the top of Beacon Rock. Here, a panoramic view includes the road already traveled as well as a preview of what is yet to come.

8. Cross the bridge and turn right onto Margin Street for a short loop to view the impressive Georgian-style brick Cox mansion built by Clarence Barron, former publisher of the *Wall Street Journal*.

9. From Margin Street take the second left onto Stockbridge Road, which loops back to Margin.

10. Turn right on Margin, which becomes Elm Street as it merges with North Main Street and enters Cohasset Village.

The **Maritime Museum** at 4 Elm Street contains a myriad of relics including scrimshaw, ship models, weights and measures, paintings, and whaling implements.

Next-door to the Maritime Museum stands the gray clapboard **Historic House**, managed by the Cohasset Historical Society. The house was built in 1810 for Captain John Wilson, who sailed his schooners around the world and operated a ship's chandlery on the first floor of his house when he wasn't at sea. His family lived upstairs, which is now decorated with furnishings from that era.

The **Independence Gown Museum** sits on the corner of Elm and South Main Streets. The museum houses a collection of elegant historic gowns, modeled by mannequins adorned with fans and parasols.

11. Continue on North Main Street as it borders **Cohasset Common**, the broad green expanse surrounded by three glistening white churches, the stately town hall, and fine old homes. After viewing the historic buildings on North Main, turn right on the street that flanks the common.

Saint Stephen's Episcopal Church sits on the corner of Main Street across from the common. The granite Gothic-style church contains a 51-bell carillon donated by Clarence Barron's daughter in memory of her mother, Jessie. If you are cycling on a Sunday morning, you may hear the array of bells that range from the five-and-a-half-ton bourdon bell to a 12-pound ship bell.

One of the oldest structures, the **Unitarian Parish House** at 19 North Main Street, was built in 1722 by Reverend Nehemiah Hobart, a descendant of Peter Hobart, the leader of Hingham's first colonists.

The gracious old homes that border the common were built from the mid-18th to the mid-19th century. At first glance the white clapboard homes, adorned by black or green shutters, appear to be similar. A closer inspection reveals a variety of designs which reflect the periods in which they were built, from the early, simple Federal-style homes to the later, more-ornate Georgian and Greek Revival styles.

12. Turn left on Highland Avenue.

Following Cohasset's separation from Hingham, the residents built the **First Parish Meetinghouse** in 1747. Its soaring steeple was added in 1799 and its clock appeared in 1846.

A religious disagreement led to the formation of the **Second Congregational Church**, built on Highland Avenue in 1824. To the right of the church stands the large Cohasset Town Hall. Behind the hall lies **Cohasset Town Forest**, containing trails and bridle paths that lead to the harbor.

13. Continue down Highland Avenue and turn right onto Beach Street.

14. After passing Little Harbor, turn left onto Atlantic Avenue. Be prepared for magnificent scenery along this 2-mile stretch—spectacular enough to require a rest stop.

    You have three opportunities to swim, picnic, or linger on the granite ledges. Tucked between massive granite outcroppings, **Sandy Beach** offers both a bike rack and bathhouse. Farther ahead, where Jerusalem Road merges with Atlantic Avenue, sits **Moors Rock Reservation** and Pleasant Beach. Walk onto Moors Rock for a panoramic view of the Boston skyline, lighthouses, harbor islands, and, on a clear day, north to Cape Ann. **Black Rock Beach**, a sometimes sandy, sometimes pebbly beach, lies at the end of the coastal road where Atlantic Avenue veers to the right and Jerusalem Road continues straight.

15. At the intersection where Forest Road comes in on the left and Atlantic Avenue splits to the right, continue straight on Jerusalem Road as it skirts the edge of Straits Pond on the right. There may not be a Jerusalem Road sign (12.7 miles total).

16. Remain on Jerusalem Road for 1 mile until you reach a stop sign at Route 228. Turn left toward Hingham.

17. Proceed on Route 228 for 2.5 miles as you pedal through the traffic-light intersection with Route 3A. Pass the town offices on the left and take the next right onto Winter Street (16.2 miles total).

18. At the T intersection, bear right onto Main Street, lined with elegant old white clapboard homes.

    After passing Water Street, look to your right for the **Old Ship Church**, the oldest church in the United States continuously to hold Sunday services. Look above the entrance door for the date of its construction, 1681, carved in Roman numerals. Constructed by shipbuilders, its unusually shaped roof resembles the inverted hull of a boat.

On the hill behind the church rests the Hingham Cemetery, formerly the site of the Old Fort. Granite slabs and statues mark the graves of Hingham's founding fathers.

Farther down Main Street sits the stately **Old Derby Academy,** founded in 1784 by Sarah Derby, who at the age of 69 realized her dream of establishing the first coeducational school in the country. The school now has moved to another location, and the Hingham Historical Society rents the building for events and meetings.

19. Follow Main Street to the T intersection with North Street.

20. Turn left on North Street. On the right side of this block sit five structures built during the 17th and 18th centuries. The Norton and Gay Houses belonged to the respective ministers, while the Nye and Waters Taverns served food and drink to residents and visitors.

21. Continue on North to Lincoln Street. A statue of Abraham Lincoln sits on a wedge of land at the junction of the two roads. Bear right and pedal to 21 Lincoln Street if you wish to visit the **Old Ordinary.**

Once a tavern, now a beautifully preserved reminder of life hundreds of years ago, Old Ordinary is furnished with outstanding period pieces, including paintings, clocks, hand tools, and collections of china, glass, and pewter. It was built in 1680 as a two-room house, one room up and one down. Twenty years later Thomas Andrews, son of the original owner, was granted a license "to sell strong waters provided he send his customers home at reasonable hours with ability to keep their legs." The Ordinary functioned as a tavern until the 20th century, when it became the home of Dr. and Mrs. Wilmon Brewer, who later donated it to the Hingham Historical Society. The Hingham Garden Club maintains the prize-winning colonial garden, designed by Frederick Law Olmsted.

22. Return down Lincoln Street to the statue and bear right on North Street.

This section, home to the Lincoln family for more than 300 years, is designated as the **Lincoln Historic District.** The private homes, clustered around the Lincoln statue at numbers 181, 182, and 172 North Street, belonged to General Benjamin Lincoln and Samuel Lincoln, ancestors of Abraham.

23. Continue on North Street until the **T** intersection with Beal Street. Turn left.

24. Take the next right onto Fort Hill Street. The total distance is approximately 18 miles.

25. Pedal 0.4 mile and turn left on New Bridge Street.

26. After 0.8 mile (19.2 total miles), turn left on Hobart Street.

27. At the **T** intersection with Main, turn right. Additional historic homes, some constructed in the mid-1600s, border the road.

28. Following the signs to Wompatuck State Park, turn left on Free Street.

29. Proceed on Free until the **T** intersection with Lazell Street. Turn left.

30. Take the next right on Union to return to the parking lot at Wompatuck State Park.

12

MIDDLESEX FELLS

RESERVATION

Western Section

Distance and Difficulty: 7.2 miles of varied terrain and moderate difficulty.

One of my favorite places and an incredible resource close to Boston is the spectacular Middlesex Fells. Divided into western and eastern sections by Route 93, the densely wooded Fells encompasses more than two thousand acres within the towns of Winchester, Medford, Melrose, Stoneham, and Malden.

In the western section, woodlands surround three reservoirs that supply water to the town of Winchester. The 7-mile loop around the reservoirs provides a great mountain-biking experience. It offers diverse terrain, from wide carriage roads to steep, rocky single-track trails, and plenty of hills to raise your pulse rate. The view from the top of the observation tower on Bear Hill encompasses the skyline of Boston and mountains in southern New Hampshire. If you are a foliage fanatic, visit the Fells in mid-October, when the woods are ablaze with color.

The wide carriage roads crisscrossing the western Fells are perfect for cross-country skiing and relaxed dog walking, whereas the narrow footpaths that wind up hills and through wetlands afford challenging hiking.

Transportation: By automobile: From Route 93 take Exit 33, following signs for Route 28, Fellsway West, and Winchester. If traveling north on Route 93 from Boston, exit the expressway, turn left over Route 93 toward Winchester, and then turn right onto South Border Road. If traveling south on Route 93, from Exit 33 take your first right onto South Border Road. Follow South Border Road for 2 miles until you reach the Long Pond Parking Lot on the right.

By train: From North Station, take the Lowell Line to Winchester Center. The distance from the Winchester train station to the Long Pond Parking Lot is a little more than half a mile. From the station, go right on Skillings Road. Make a 90° left turn onto Mount Vernon. Follow Mount Vernon straight through the set of lights. Here the name of the road changes to South Border Road (which borders Middlesex Fells). Long Pond Parking Lot is just ahead on the left (a paved parking area with a posted Long Pond sign).

Food and Drink: The nearest stores are on Main Street in Winchester Center, a half-mile from the reservation. Among the offerings are Yankee Yogurt, 527 Main Street; Bagel Works, 538 Main Street; and Starbucks, 542 Main Street.

The reservoirs of Middlesex Fells are peaceful and protected
by woods from the urban landscape just a few miles away.

Restrooms: Located in the three establishments listed above.

Recreational Options: Cross-country skiing, hiking, horseback riding.

Background: One of the Boston area's oldest parks, Middlesex Fells Reservation has been parkland since 1894, when the Metropolitan District Commission (MDC) took possession. Before then, the Fells's valuable timber was used to build ships and heat homes. The rocky land also supplied granite and gravel for construction. Remnants of these quarries lie in the southern section of the Fells.

Because the western section of the Fells contains Winchester's water supply, the town is very protective of the trails near the reservoirs and has ruled them off-limits. In order to accommodate off-road bikers, the MDC has established a route around the reservoirs that does not encroach on Winchester's water supply nor does it place bikers on trails that are susceptible to erosion. The route described here is marked by red discs attached to trees. In time the discs often become dislodged, so I have included other landmarks to guide you. The Fells's policy toward mountain bikers is under review, so be alert to posted signs.

This route uses sections of four trail systems that have colored blazes painted on trees. The white blazes signify the Skyline Trail, a challenging route that circles the reservoirs. The Reservoir Trail, blazed with orange circles, also loops around the Fells but stays closer to the water on easier trails. The blue blazes are for the Cross Fells Trail which runs east-west and links the eastern and western sections of the Fells. The pink-blazed trail makes a short loop to Long Pond.

Please do not ride on the trails posted with the white plastic No Mt. Biking discs. Biking in the Middlesex Fells is prohibited between January 1 and April 15.

Although the directions refer to names of roads, do not expect to find signs on the trails themselves; use the names as reference points when reading the map.

THE RIDE

1. From the west side of the Long Pond Parking Lot on South Border Road, ride (or walk) up the incline near the stairs and head up the paved trail.

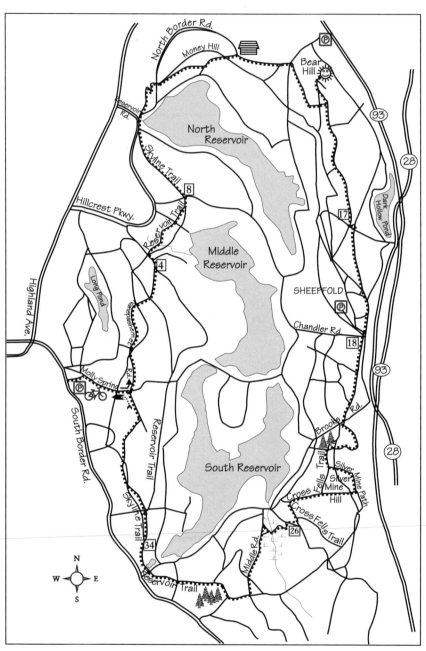

MIDDLESEX FELLS RESERVATION--WESTERN SECTION

2. Bear right onto Molly Spring Road.

3. Remain on Molly Spring for 0.2 mile and take the second left onto a carriage road (Nanepashemet Road).

4. Climb and then descend Nanepashemet Road for 0.5 mile (0.7 total) until you reach a **T** intersection. Bear left onto the orange-blazed Reservoir Trail.

5. Follow the orange-blazed trail as it leaves the carriage path, heads off to the right (just after the intersection with the white-blazed trail), and becomes a narrow single-track trail with steep and rocky sections. Be prepared for an initial plunging descent, followed by a stream crossing over a narrow wooden bridge, and then a steep ascent.

On a carriage road in Middlesex Fells

6. After traveling through this precipitous rocky section for 0.2 mile (0.9 total), watch for a fork in the path. Bear right and continue to follow the orange-blazed trail. (If you miss this turn, you'll remain on the path with the white blazes and you'll have to haul your bike over rock outcroppings!)

7. After biking for 0.1 mile (1.0 mile total), cross another carriage road and look for a trail hidden between two large stones. Again, the trail is marked by orange blazes on the trees. In order to prevent erosion, remain on the narrow plank bridge when riding over the stream bed.

8. After 0.1 mile (1.1 miles total), the path intersects with a carriage road. Turn right, then make a quick left onto another carriage road blazed in both orange and white (the merging of the Reservoir and Skyline Trails). This section may be undergoing construction, as the Winchester Water Resources Department will be installing water pipes under the trail. The path approaches Hillcrest Parkway and then parallels Reservoir Road.

9. Go right onto the paved road and head toward the old firehouse (built in 1898) on your right, passing by the western tip of North Reservoir. The trailhead resumes on the right between the firehouse and an old garage. Look for two boulders and orange and white blazes on the trees lining this single-track trail.

10. At 1.5 miles, begin your descent on this rocky trail marked by two steep switchbacks.

11. Cross a wooden bridge, ascend a steep incline, and cross a carriage road. At the fork, bear right on the orange-blazed trail.

12. A steep descent down Money Hill leads to a carriage road (1.9 miles). Bear left.

13. After 0.1 mile (2 miles total) you meet a large granite outcropping. Leave the orange-blazed trail and remain on the carriage road as it heads toward a building with a corrugated steel roof.

14. At the intersection with another carriage road, bear right, keeping the building with the distinctive roof on your left.

15. Go through the next intersection and head right, up the steep trail that climbs 317 feet to the top of Bear Hill, the highest point in the Fells.

16. Ignore all narrow hiking trails on your left that lead to Bear Hill Tower, until at 2.5 miles you reach the double-track fire road open to cyclists. Turn left. You have completed the strenuous section of the climb; now it's an easy ride to the tower.

    At the top you'll see a mammoth reservoir tank. Behind it stands the observation tower.

    At the top of the tower you'll have a splendid view of the Boston skyline and Tobin Bridge to the southeast, Mount Wachusett to the west, and Mount Monadnock to the northwest. If you look to the northeast, you may be able to spot the peninsula of Nahant, explored in chapter 3.

17. Return to the same carriage road (Bear Hill Road). Enjoy the long downhill ride until after 0.6 mile you reach a five-corner intersection (3.3 miles total). Bear left for a few feet.

18. Quickly turn right onto the gravel-covered road which parallels the highway.

    The Sheepfold, containing 10 acres of open fields, on the right is a popular picnic and recreation area. The occasional wooden slats are reminders of the trolley that carried passengers over this route.

19. Immediately after you cross the bridge over Chandler Road, leave the trolley route, make a wide-angle right turn, and then an immediate left onto a carriage road.

20. At 4.2 miles, continue on the carriage road as it crosses Brooks Road (another carriage road) and then ascends.

21. At 4.4 miles (having traveled 0.7 mile from Chandler Road) pass the intersection with the Skyline Trail and turn left at a clearing with a stand of pine trees. Look for blue blazes on the trees, indicating that you are now on the Cross Fells Trail.

22. Remain on the carriage road (Silver Mine Path) for 0.1 mile, leaving the blue-blazed trail, which bears right.

23. Proceed 0.2 mile. At the next intersection, Silver Mine Path heads off to the left (a posted Silver Mine Path sign here). *Turn right* onto another carriage road that soon rejoins the Cross Fells Trail at the base of Silver Mine Hill.

24. Pedal 0.1 mile and bear left, remaining on a carriage road. Continue 0.2 mile and take the next left, continuing on the blue-blazed Cross Fells Trail.

25. At the point where the Cross Fells Trail heads off to the left, leave the blue-blazed trail and continue straight on the carriage road.

26. Proceed approximately 300 feet and turn right onto a narrow path. Cross the carriage road and pick up the path that runs through the wetland (5.1 miles).

27. In 0.2 mile you can test your balance by attempting to pedal over several narrow wooden bridges. The sweet fragrance of the wetland-loving **sweet pepperbush** permeates the air. Unfortunately, *your* sweet fragrance will attract the mosquitoes that breed in the marsh.

28. At 5.4 miles (0.1 mile from the bridges), the path forks. Bear right and attempt to pedal up this steep stretch.

29. Take the next left onto the carriage road (Middle Road).

30. Remain on Middle Road for 0.4 mile (5.8 miles). Turn right onto a blue-blazed carriage road.

31. Keep to the right on the carriage road as the Cross Fells Trail veers left.

32. The road enters a pine forest and is joined by both the Skyline and Reservoir Trails. (Trees are now marked by orange and white blazes.)

33. After crossing two carriage roads, the trail appears to head out of the Fells onto South Border Road (6.3 miles). The large building on the right is the Winchester Filtration Plant. Continue on the orange- and white-blazed trail while passing a tiny pond on the right.

34. At 6.4 miles, remain on the carriage path as the Skyline and Reservoir Trails bend left. You'll see a green water tank on your right.

35. Proceed on the carriage road, ascending and descending two hills. Several carriage roads join on the right. Continue to bear left and then turn left at an intersection with another carriage road onto Molly Spring Road, where an island of trees separates two paths, after having pedaled north on the carriage road for 0.8 mile (7.2 miles total).

36. Just before you reach a small field, bear left up a hill. The trail meets a paved walkway that leads back to the parking lot.

13

LYNN

WOODS

 Distance and Difficulty: 5 miles of moderate difficulty, with steep grades and loose gravel.

"Lynn, Lynn, city of sin," a ditty locals use to describe this community, is one reason why bikers and hikers hesitate to explore Lynn Woods, one of the most fascinating, scenic, and accessible parks in the Boston area. Until recently, frequent fires and general neglect had blemished Lynn Woods's reputation as well. In 1990, the Friends of Lynn Woods, a group of Lynn residents, united to protect and rejuvenate this magnificent property. Unlike most reservations, Lynn Woods welcomes bikers, and several mountain-biking races are held here. The Friends believe that the property's 30 miles of trails can support a variety of recreational pursuits and that regular use will provide a safer environment.

This 2,200-acre reservation is chock-full of historic sites, hills with sweeping vistas, man-made lakes, and challenging terrain. The 5-mile tour circles the western section of the woods and visits noteworthy sites: Dungeon Rock, with its subterranean tunnel and rumor of buried treasure; a medieval-style stone tower atop Burrill Hill; and rose and perennial gardens, lovingly landscaped by the Friends. The ride, for the most part, stays on wide carriage roads. Those seeking more challenging terrain can tackle the rocky outcroppings in the interior sections or ride the trails east of Walden Pond.

Transportation: By automobile: From Boston, take Route 1 north and exit onto Routes 129 east toward Lynn. (This exit is just before the junction with Route 95/128.) Remain on Route 129 for 2 miles and turn right on Great Woods Road. Pass between two stone pillars into the large parking lot. A playing field is on the right, and the entrance to Lynn Woods is at the far end of the lot.

From Routes 95/128, take Exit 44B onto Route 129 east toward Lynn and follow the above directions.

By commuter rail: From North Station, take the Rockport Line and exit at Lynn Station. The station is about 3 miles from Lynn Woods. From the station, turn left on Washington Street and proceed for just under a mile until it ends at Boston Street. Lynn Hospital sits on the right corner. Turn right on Boston, passing Pine Grove Cemetery on your left. At the **T** intersection, turn left on Chestnut Street (Route 129). Remain on Chestnut for 0.8 mile until the road forks. Bear left onto Great Woods Road and continue straight into the parking lot.

Food and Drink: A snack bar is in the golf clubhouse in the Gannon Municipal Golf Course, down the road to the left of the parking lot.

Restrooms: In the golf clubhouse. Directions above.

Recreational Options: Hiking, cross-country skiing, horseback riding.

Background: Situated 11 miles northeast of Boston, Lynn was one of the earliest European settlements. In 1629, Europeans claimed the Pawtucket Indians' hunting grounds in Lynn Woods and chopped down trees for fuel and shelter. Fifty-seven years later, the settlers officially purchased the land for $75. Throughout the 18th and early 19th centuries residents grazed their livestock in Lynn Woods and cut down trees to heat their homes.

In 1850, the Exploring Circle was formed to explore and record the area's plants, animals, and geology. The group shared information on the woods's remote swampy, rocky interior.

Inadequate fire-prevention capability contributed to fires that ravaged several factories in 1869. The city responded by developing additional water sources. Its first purchase was Breed's Pond, an abandoned millpond in the southeast corner of Lynn Woods. Four brooks within the woods were then dammed to create four artificial ponds to store water. Roads were built to augment ancient cart paths. This increased use of the property drew the attention of developers. In response, the Trustees of the Free Public Forest, led by conservationist Cyrus Tracy, was established to guarantee the preservation of Lynn Woods.

During the late 19th century, the nationwide park movement also was claiming land to ensure open spaces for hard-working city dwellers. Increased financial support allowed the trustees to improve roads, provide signs, and raise money to buy surrounding land. The trustees consulted with Frederick Law Olmsted, the landscape architect who designed New York's Central Park and Boston's Emerald Necklace. He convinced the Lynn Park Commission to enhance the natural features of this "rugged and wild forest." By 1891 the park commission, which had increased its holdings to 1,600 acres, followed Olmsted's advice. They protected its special features, added fire towers, and installed a trolley line to carry city residents to the park.

THE RIDE

1. From the far end of the parking lot, head through the eastern gate onto the wide carriage trail, Great Woods Road, that runs to the left of Walden Pond.

2. Proceed 0.2 mile. Bear right at the fork and remain on the path as it runs above Walden Pond.

   This reservoir was excavated in 1871 in response to the city's need for additional water. This Walden Pond has no connection with the body of water made famous by Henry Thoreau; it was named after Edwin Walden, the first chairman of the Lynn Public Water Board.

3. Remain on Great Woods Road as it bends around to the left. At 1.9 miles, just after another carriage path merges from the left, the trail crosses Penny Bridge and reaches a **T** intersection marked by an island of three cedar trees. Bear left past the cedars onto Pennybrook Road.

   Penny Bridge crosses Penny Brook, which flows from Tomlins Swamp into Walden Pond. Early settlers named the bridge after the penny toll charged to anyone who carried out timber.

4. Continue straight on Pennybrook Road toward the western entrance to Lynn Woods. Pass by the barrier and take the next right up the paved road that leads to Camp Kiwanis, a school and camp for Lynn special-needs students.

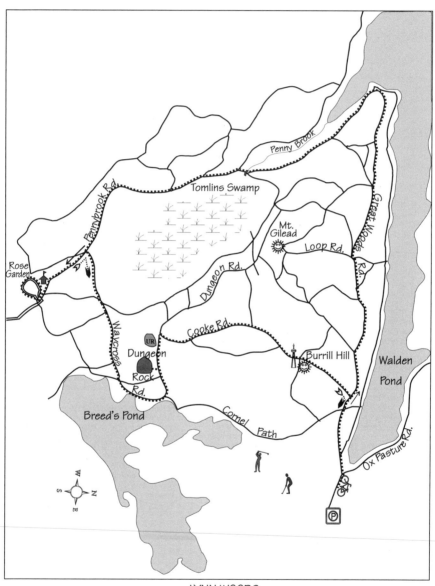

LYNN WOODS

5. Pass to the left of the school building and up the drive on your way to see the **Rose Garden**. Follow the gravel path to the flower beds, meticulously maintained by the Friends of Lynn Woods.

6. Return by the same route. Bear right at the fork onto Waycross Road to complete the loop around the reservation. Follow Waycross past the shore of Breed's Pond to famous Dungeon Rock.

7. At the 4-mile mark, after struggling up the steep rocky hill, dismount and head left, down the rock-lined path to **Dungeon Rock**.

   The tale involving the rock begins in the 17th century, when four pirates rowed ashore from the Saugus River to secretly purchase handcuffs and leg irons at the Saugus Iron Works. They returned a few months later, snuck into a remote section of Lynn Woods, and reputedly buried treasure inside a stone cave within the granite outcroppings. Word of their hiding place spread, and three of the pirates were captured and eventually hanged. The fourth pirate, Thomas Veal, escaped and hid in the cave where the treasure was buried. Veal remained there, mending shoes to earn money, until 1658, when an earthquake sealed the cave, entombing him forever.

   Almost 200 years later, a spiritualist named Hiram Marble purchased the rock plus five surrounding acres. Believing that Thomas Veal's spirit would communicate where the treasure was buried, Marble spent his life and all his money seeking the stash. He often contacted mediums who, after consulting with spirits, directed him where to dig. Marble built a house for his family near the rock and included his son, Edwin, in a lifelong search for the treasure. Turning to dynamite to speed their search, they spent decades blasting out a 174-foot-long circular tunnel. The rocks scattered along the hillside are testimony to the Marbles' single-minded search. The only money they reaped from this long endeavor was the 25¢ fee they charged tourists who entered their tunnel. If you enter the opening in the cave and look to the right, you'll spot the opening that leads to Marble's tunnel.

8. Return to Dungeon Road and go left.

    Union Rock stands on the left side before the junction with Cooke Road. The initials U. R. are carved into the lower section of this huge bicolored boulder, which served as a meeting place for Hiram Marble and his fellow spiritualists.

9. Take the first right onto Cooke Road on the way to the Stone Tower on Burrill Hill.

    This picturesque path offers gigantic stone formations on the left and vistas of Breed's Pond below on the right.

10. After riding for 4.7 miles, you will reach the summit of 286-foot **Burrill Hill**.

Burrill Hill's Stone Tower offers a fine lookout over the Boston area.
(Photograph by Mark McInerney)

You may climb even higher by trudging to the top of the recently restored medieval-style **Stone Tower.** It was built in 1936 as a project of the Works Progress Administration to serve as a fire lookout. The 360° view from the top encompasses Breed's Pond, the coast of Lynn, and the peninsula of Nahant to the south; Boston skyline and Logan Airport to the southwest; Mount Monadnock in southern New Hampshire to the northwest; and Mount Wachusett to the west. A close view within the reservation reveals Walden Pond and the steel tower on Mount Gilead.

11. From Burrill Hill, continue on Cooke Road for 0.2 mile until returning to Great Woods Road, where you turn right. The eastern gate lies ahead.

Waycross Road winds through Lynn Woods. (Photograph by Mark McInerney)

If you seek a short challenging ride, take the first right after returning to Great Woods Road onto narrow, rocky Cornel Path. This half-mile trail runs past the golf course and Breed's Pond. Cornel Path ends at Dungeon Road. To return, you can either follow Cornel Path or pick up the directions at #7.

14

HAROLD PARKER

STATE FOREST

 Distance and Difficulty: 6 miles of easy biking; 1.5 miles of challenging, rocky single-track trails.

A wedge of land here and a few hundred acres there eventually add up. Over the last 80 years, Harold Parker State Forest has accumulated more than 3,000 acres of woodland, 11 ponds, 15 dams, seven streams, and 130 campsites. Paved streets and carriage roads link the parcels within the towns of Andover, North Andover, Middleton, and North Reading.

Harold Parker offers a myriad of recreational opportunities: trout fishing and canoeing in the ponds, as well as hiking, biking, horseback riding, and cross-country skiing on 36 miles of trails. This 7.5-mile tour of the northeastern section of the forest consists of five short loops of varying difficulty. While trails in this reservation are not well marked, paved roads and civilization are never far away.

Transportation: By automobile: Follow Route 93 north to Exit 41, Route 125 north, toward Andover. Follow Route 125 for 2.5 miles. Turn right onto Harold Parker Road and follow it until it ends at Jenkins Road. Turn left on Jenkins and proceed to a stop sign at the intersection with Salem Street/Middleton Road. Turn right. Continue for 1.5 miles until you reach the headquarters parking lot.

By commuter rail: Harold Parker is 5 miles from the Andover railroad station. From North Station take the Haverhill Line and exit at Andover. From the station, turn right on Ridge Street and then left on School Street. Follow School to Main Street (Route 28), pass Phillips Academy, and take your third left onto Salem Street. Follow Salem, crossing Route 125, for 4 miles to the reservation headquarters.

Food and Drink: In downtown Andover, 5 miles from the forest.

Restrooms: Located near the contact station in the southwest corner of the forest.

Recreational Options: Cross-country skiing, hiking, horseback riding, fishing, camping (from the Friday before Patriots Day through Columbus Day; to reserve, call 978-686-3391).

Background: Farmers settled in Andover and surrounding towns in 1650. They attempted to farm the rocky, marshy land until manufacturing jobs became available in the mid-1800s. Quarries and logging camps replaced farms until 1916, when conservationist Harold Parker, the first chairman of the state forest commission, convinced the legislature to appropriate money for the purchase of available property. Much of the land in this forest, priced at $5 an acre, was the first in a series of state aquisitions that now total more than 270,000 acres.

The land remained undeveloped until 1933, when the Civilian Conservation Corps (CCC), conceived by President Franklin D. Roosevelt to provide jobs during the Depression, arrived to rework the land. During their digging, the CCC discovered Native American artifacts as well as remnants from sawmills and quarries that had supplied granite and soapstone to surrounding communities two hundred years ago. The CCC built fire roads, created nine ponds, and constructed recreation and administration facilities. They planted pine groves to replace trees that had fallen victim to fires or sawmills.

Lack of state funding has closed the swimming area and reduced the number of interpretive programs. Without strong community support, many of the state forests that offer unlimited recreational potential have languished.

If you ride in November and December when deer hunting is allowed, wear bright orange clothing.

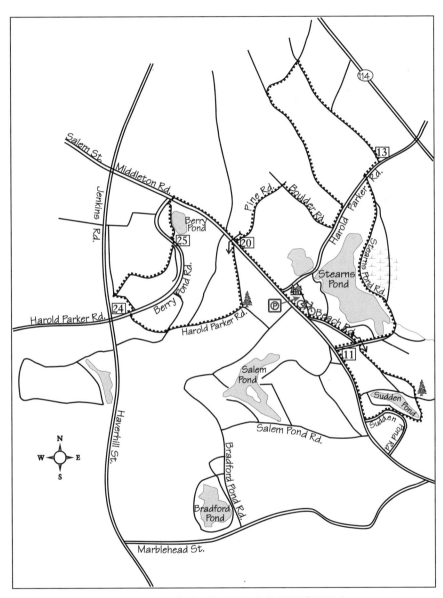

HAROLD PARKER STATE FOREST

THE RIDE

Sudden Pond Loop

1. With your back to the headquarters building, pedal to the left end of the parking lot. Pass through a metal gate. Remain on paved Beach Road, following the sign to the beach.

2. Bear right at the fork and continue straight through the beach parking lot.

3. Turn left at the T intersection. Pass through another gate and the continuation of the beach parking area to Stearns Pond Road.

4. Turn left onto paved Stearns Pond Road (there should be a road sign attached to a tree) and continue for about 100 feet.

5. Bear right onto a wide trail heading toward Sudden Pond.

6. At the first fork, bear left. You'll spot a tiny body of water to your left that is not Sudden Pond.

7. At 0.9 mile, the trail forks. A large pine tree is perched between the two paths. Bear right. In 0.1 mile (1 mile total), you'll spot Sudden Pond on the right and large granite boulders on the left.

8. Cross over the dam at the head of Sudden Pond via the small stone bridge, both constructed by the CCC. Turn right and hug the pond. The path disappears as it winds through a pine forest, also a CCC contribution.

9. Continue through the forest until you reach Sudden Pond Road, an access road for a campground formerly located on the left side of the road. Turn right onto Sudden Pond Road and follow it until you reach Middleton Road (also called Salem Street) another paved road.

10. Turn right onto Middleton Road (at 1.5 miles) and continue until you reach the next paved road on your right, Stearns Pond Road.

Stearns Pond Ride

11. At 1.9 miles, turn right onto Stearns Pond Road (street sign on tree). The paved road turns to gravel as it winds around Stearns Pond, which, before the CCC excavation, consisted of a brook winding through a red-maple swamp.

This loop dazzles in autumn when the orange, yellow, and red foliage on the **beech**, **birch**, and **maple** trees reflects off the water. Snapping turtles crossing from wetland to water are the only obstacles on this easy-cruising carriage trail.

Beech

12. Turn right onto Harold Parker Road, the paved road that divides the east and west sections of the park.

Challenging Loop

13. Take the second left into a clearing large enough to hold a couple of cars and head onto the fire road, protected from automobile access by a wire cable and several boulders.

    Although this loop begins benignly, it soon becomes a steep, rocky single-track trail.

14. Continue past the path that goes off to the right. At the next fork turn left (at 3.5 miles). White blazes are painted on the trees on both sides of the path. Shift into low gear in preparation for a steep ascent.

    If you are biking during the summer, you can use the bountiful **blue-berry** bushes lining the trail as an excuse to dismount and gather a blueberry energy boost.

15. Turn left at the **T** intersection.

    Huge granite boulders, dropped by the receding glacier 10,000 to 15,000 years ago, are scattered through the woods.

16. After cyling on this loop for 0.8 mile (4.3 total), the trail returns to Harold Parker Road. Turn right.

Boulder Road Loop

17. Take your first right onto Boulder Road

18. Take the next right through a small parking area, past the boulders and wire cable blocking the entrance to the trail. The Boulder Road sign should be posted on a tree just past the stakes that hold the cable.

19. Continue to bear left until you reach Pine Road, at 5.3 miles, where you turn left.

20. Follow Pine Road until it meets Middleton Road. Turn right.

Berry Pond Loop

21. Travel about 50 feet and take the next left onto a carriage road marked by a boulder with blue writing on it and a gate with a chain across it.

22. Proceed 0.2 mile (5.7 miles) and turn right past a **pine tree** sitting in the middle of the intersection onto another wide carriage path.

23. Continue on this unpaved section of Harold Parker Road for 0.8 mile (6.5 miles total), pedaling through a wide open area that was once a parking lot. Bear right onto Berry Pond Road and pass though the gate.

24. After pedaling 0.1 mile, you have the option of leaving the paved road and turning left onto a challenging red-blazed, single-track trail. The trail ascends steeply and descends equally steeply for a half-mile before it returns to Berry Pond Road, where you turn left. (If you do not wish to be challenged, continue on Berry Pond Road and pick up the directions at #27.)

25. Just after returning to the road, turn right onto the path that follows Berry Pond, a scenic area often filled with fishermen reeling in trout from the state-stocked pond.

26. Turn left at the end of the path and go through the barrier. Turn right onto Berry Pond Road.

27. Turn right again onto Middleton Road and head back to the parking lot and reservation headquarters.

15

BRADLEY PALMER

STATE PARK

Distance and Difficulty: 4 miles of varying difficulty. Most of the ride is on wide grassy bridle paths. Because many equestrians ride on the trails, be prepared for ruts. The scenic river trail is narrow, tree-rooted, and often muddy, and has one abrupt descent and ascent.

Visitors enter Bradley Palmer State Park on an impressively landscaped entrance road that leads to wide grassy expanses dotted with numerous horse jumps. A natural reaction may be, "Oops, I made a wrong turn and landed in a fancy hunt club!" A reasonable response, considering the property belonged formerly to Bradley Palmer, a wealthy equestrian who purchased thousands of acres so he and his friends could ride and hunt. Palmer built an elegant mansion and then carved bridle trails through 3,000 acres that also encompass the neighboring Willowdale State Forest.

At 720 acres, Bradley Palmer is a relatively small park, but, combined with Willowdale State Forest, more than 40 miles of trails are open to cyclists. Unfortunately, many of the trails are not marked, so it is easy to lose your way, especially when surrounded by a number of similar-looking open fields. But the park's small size works to its advantage: A lost biker is never very far from either of the two entrances.

This 4-mile tour, though short in distance, takes more time than you might expect. The route passes by Palmer's former mansion via a nature trail on the way to a scenic, challenging path by the Ipswich River. It crosses through fields and climbs the two highest points in the park. If you wish to supplement the ride, you can pedal across Ipswich Road into the larger, more remote but less scenic Willowdale State Forest. A Willowdale map is available at Bradley Palmer headquarters.

Transportation: By automobile: From Route 95, take Exit 50 onto Route 1 north, or from Boston, follow Route 1 north. From the junction of Route 95 and Route 1, proceed 4 miles on Route 1 until you reach the intersection with Ipswich Road (traffic light). Turn right toward the town of Ipswich, following the sign to Bradley Palmer State Park. Remain on Ipswich Road for 1.2 miles and then turn right on Asbury Street. After 0.2 mile, turn left into the park. Continue straight on the entrance road to the park headquarters. If there's space, park near the headquarters; otherwise, turn right toward a second parking lot.

By commuter rail: From North Station, take the Ipswich Line to the Hamilton/Wenham station. The distance from the station to the park is 2.6 miles. From the station on Main Street turn right, and then turn left on Asbury Street. Remain on Asbury for 1 mile to the blinking light at the intersection with Highland Street. Turn right. Remain on Highland, bear right at the fork, and ignore the signs for Bradley Palmer State Park that direct you to the main entrance. The right at the fork guides you to the picnic/pool entrance that cuts through the park and decreases the distance to the main entrance. After remaining on Highland for 1.3 miles and passing the Pingree School on the right, turn left at the second sign for Bradley Palmer State Park; marked by a stone building in front and a metal entrance gate (the first sign is for the parking lot). Turn left into the park and follow the paved road for 1.3 miles to park headquarters (978-887-5931).

Food and Drink: In Hamilton on Railroad Avenue across from the train station are the Black Cow and the Weathervane. In the shopping center adjacent to the station is the Coffee Table. To reach Topsfield Center, which is 2 miles from the park, follow Ipswich Road 1 mile west of the Route 1 intersection. The popular Topsfield Bagel Company and Coffee House offers sandwiches, pastry, bagels, and coffee.

Restrooms: An outdoor portable toilet is located at the edge of the parking lot near park headquarters. Restrooms and bathhouse, located near the wading pool and picnic area at the south entrance, are open seasonally.

Recreational Options: Hiking, in-line skating, cross-country skiing, horseback riding, fishing, canoeing, and dunking (you can't actually swim in the wading pool but you can change into a bathing suit in the bathhouse and cool off).

Background: At the beginning of the 20th century, monied men often displayed their wealth by purchasing vast tracts of land within commuting distance of Boston, and then spared no expense creating monuments to themselves. Thomas Proctor's former estate at Ipswich River Wildlife Sanctuary (see chapter 31) is one example. Bradley Palmer, a Boston lawyer, accumulated thousands of acres that included what are now Willowdale State Forest and Bradley Palmer State Park. He laid out and constructed a formal entrance road and many miles of bridle trails. Palmer lavishly decorated and landscaped his estate, which he named Willow Dale.

Palmer grew up in Pennsylvania but remained in Massachusetts after graduating from Harvard University and Harvard Law School. A sociable fellow who became a respected attorney, he entertained at Willow Dale such dignitaries as President William Taft, General George Patton, and the Prince of Wales, who often went horseback riding around the property. Palmer was chosen to represent President Wilson at the peace conference following World War I.

Construction of the stone mansion, located in back of park headquarters near the Nature Trail, began in 1902. Craftsmen were transported from Italy to sculpt marble, lay stones, and carve exotic woods. Influenced by the variety of plantings in Boston's Arnold Arboretum, Palmer ordered fruit trees, evergreens, and freight-car loads of flowering shrubs from nurseries all over the United States and from as far away as Scotland.

Since Palmer had no heirs, he willed his 3,000-acre estate to the commonwealth of Massachusetts in 1944 and then leased back the 107 acres that surrounded his mansion, coach house, garage, and superintendent's cottage.

THE RIDE

1. Facing the park headquarters, pedal down the driveway to the right of the building, heading toward the Nature Trail.

2. To see Palmer's monastery-like stone mansion (visitors are not allowed inside), bear to the left, passing behind the headquarters building.

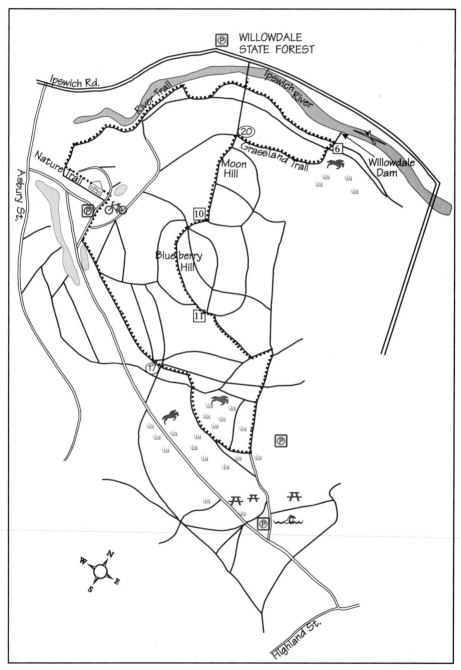

BRADLEY PALMER STATE PARK

Offices now occupy the luxurious interior containing a once magnificent ballroom, complete with balcony designed to hold an orchestra, a shower cut from a solid block of marble, stained-glass windows, inlaid tile mosaics, and hand-carved mantels and moldings.

3. Return down the same route to enter the narrow Nature Trail, marked by numbered signs, which begins to the left of the tiny pond.

Rhododendron

The Nature Trail runs through what was left of Palmer's beloved conservatory. Over the years, he planted hundreds of hardy **mountain laurel** and **rhododendron** bushes. Both of these large evergreen shrubs have broad leaves with a waxy coating that serves as protection from frigid temperatures as well as arid conditions. Although both mountain laurel and rhododendron are members of the heath family and bloom in late spring, their blossoms and leaves differ considerably. Mountain laurel sports clusters of small white flowers surrounded by long, pointed elliptical leaves, whereas the rhododendron boasts larger pink flowers and more oblong-shaped leaves.

4. Continue straight and follow the signs to the River Trail. At the intersection with the River Trail, leave the Nature Trail and turn right. The River Trail is blazed with small blue discs displaying paw prints.

The trail, shaded by pine trees whose shallow roots obstruct the path, follows the course of the Ipswich River. Tiny streams 15 miles southwest merge to form the Ipswich River. It empties into the ocean about 6 miles east in the town of Ipswich.

Mountain laurel

5. After you've cycled for 0.6 mile, the path leaves the riverbanks and heads inland onto a wider carriage road. Continue left on the trail for 0.1 mile until the River Trail resumes, unless

you prefer to remain on the smoother carriage road. Both trails rejoin about a half-mile ahead.

The trail passes the footbridge that crosses the river and leads to Willowdale State Forest. The scenery in the next section of the trail is spectacular. Unfortunately, the path is often muddy. Beaver dams have disrupted the river's flow, so it often spills over its banks. Be prepared to dismount.

Continue to follow the blue paw print as the trail abruptly descends and steeply ascends into a grove of hemlocks and pines on a ridge over-looking the river.

Remain on the trail until you reach a turnoff to the river, marked by the Willowdale Dam.

During the 19th century a textile mill powered by the river's swift current occupied this site. Now fishermen and a canoe-rental concession share the spot.

6. From the dam, at 1.3 miles, turn right, shift into low gear, and pedal up the steep narrow incline that opens into a field. Turn right, passing several horse jumps.

Trail etiquette states that horses have the right of way. If you encounter a horse and rider, step off the trail on the uphill side and stand motionless.

7. After pedaling for 1.5 miles, follow the Grassland Trail as it bends to the right through the field.

8. At 1.8 miles, when you reach the intersection with the path leading to the river and footbridge near a brown stake with the number 20 marking the Discover Hamilton (DH) trail, turn left (away from the river) to begin your climb to the highest point in the park, Moon Hill.

The Hamilton Conservation Commission marked the Discover Hamilton Trail with brown stakes with arrows pointing in the direction of the trail. Stakes at major intersections are labeled with numbers. The DH Trail runs for 9.9 miles from Hamilton Center through Harvard Forest, Bradford conservation land, the Pingree Reservation, Bradley Palmer, Willowdale, and Appleton Farms Grass Rides.

9. Follow the path to the top of Moon Hill. Turn left onto the grassy path and then make an immediate right to the crest of the hill. A DH Trail stake designates the trail.

10. Continue straight until you reach a carriage path. Proceed straight on the path as it ascends Blueberry Hill.

11. To descend from Blueberry Hill amidst the maze of paths, first bear left, then follow the wide path as it winds down the hill.

12. From the **T** intersection at the base of the hill, go straight across the field to the dirt trail.

13. Turn left, heading toward the picnic area and pool at the south entrance. Horse jumps dot the fields.

14. Remain on the dirt road to the paved parking lot. If you wish, you can explore this area or use the facilities.

15. To return to the main entrance, turn right at the paved area and head toward the woods. A double-track trail parallels Palmer's paved estate road and returns to the headquarters, parking lots, and main entrance to the park. Finding and following this trail may be confusing, as it runs through open fields amidst several converging trails and few landmarks. You are on the correct path and are less than a half-mile from the parking area if you spot a granite stone boundary marker and a #17 DH Trail marker at the intersection of several trails. Bearing right at the markers onto any of the three trails will return you to the starting point. If you find yourself totally confused, you can always bail out and follow the paved road back to headquarters.

16

Dogtown

 Distance and Difficulty: 5.5 miles of varying difficulty, from the easy, practically paved 2-mile loop around Goose Cove Reservoir to the narrow, steep, and very rocky Babson Boulder Trail.

Sitting in the center of the coastal community of Gloucester, desolate Dogtown appears to be light-years away from the bustling harbor. Within this 3,000-acre property, eerie rock formations embellish a landscape of old cellar holes, reservoirs, and woodlands. Many of these massive granite boulders are etched with such maxims as KEEP OUT OF DEBT or NEVER TRY, NEVER WIN.

Dogtown, at first glance, resembles a vast wasteland. Because no state agency or private organization oversees the land, it has sustained much fire damage; yet it remains extraordinarily picturesque. It attracts not only bikers and hikers who attempt to tackle its tough terrain, but also naturalists to track birds and other wildlife.

Geologists come to view one of the finest examples of terminal moraine in the country. In this section of Cape Ann, about 15,000 years ago, the great ice sheet stopped moving forward and began to melt, depositing huge boulders torn from the earth's bedrock. These moraines, or extensive accumulations of boulders, are piled on top of each other and often stretch for a half-mile.

This 5.5-mile tour of Dogtown begins benignly on the main road and then offers a slight challenge on a side road that cuts through the moor to

Goose Cove Reservoir. The relaxing ride on the semipaved road that circles the reservoir contrasts with the enervating experience of maneuvering over rocky terrain on Babson Boulder Trail. A reward for such exertion may be the discovery of IF WORK STOPS, VALUES DECAY etched on a mammoth boulder amidst a remarkable rockscape.

Transportation: By automobile: Take Route 128 north to Exit 11 in Gloucester. Go three-quarters of the way around the rotary and turn right onto Route 127 north (Washington Street). Immediately turn right on Poplar Street. Take your first left onto Cherry Street. Follow Cherry for 0.7 mile, passing a school on your left and a sign for the Cape Ann Sportsman's Club on the right. Turn right onto a road where there may be a sign reading Welcome to Historic Dogtown. Travel down the entrance road for 0.2 mile. Park on the side of the road just before the barrier to the entrance. (The sportsman's club is on the right.)

Cape Ann's Dogtown is dotted with uplifting messages carved in granite boulders.

By commuter rail: From North Station, take the Rockport Line to Gloucester (not West Gloucester). The distance from the Gloucester station to Dogtown is less than 2 miles. Take Railroad Avenue to Maplewood Avenue. Turn left on Maplewood and follow it as it crosses Route 128 and ends at Poplar Street. Turn left on Poplar Street and take your first right on Cherry Street. Pedal for 0.7 mile and turn right into the entrance road to Dogtown. Remain on the road and travel past the barrier.

Food and Drink: Most of the restaurants are near the harbor, about three blocks south of the railroad station (right on Maplewood, right on Dale, and right on Prospect). From the Grant Circle rotary (Exit 11 off Route 128), turn right on Washington Street, which leads to Main Street and the waterfront. Two good places for seafood and sandwiches are Cameron's restaurant, 206 Main Street, and Captain Carlo's Seafood, Harbor Loop.

Restrooms: Cape Ann Visitor Information Center, near the harbor at the intersection of Washington Street and Western Avenue.

Recreational Options: Cross-country skiing and great hiking.

Background: The history of this fascinating spot has been well chronicled. Its development began around 1633 when settlers landed on Cape Ann. Colonists probably chose this location because of its close proximity to the Annisquam River and its several feeder brooks that would supply water for crops and livestock and power for mills. They also felt protected from pirates and Native Americans in an area several miles from the harbor that was fortified by large boulders.

During Dogtown's first hundred years, 80 prominent families built small walled-in farms along Dogtown and Common Roads and formed a thriving community. These families also obtained numbered "cow rights" or "wood lots," where they cut wood and grazed their animals in an area known as Common Pastures.

Dogtown began to decline around 1750, when pirates no longer plied the waters and settlers were finally free to fish and trade. Thirty-three years later, the Revolutionary War ended. Families settled near the coast with no fear of English warship or pirate attacks. The children of Dogtown's original settlers gratefully ceased trying to farm the rocky, arid land and moved closer to the ocean.

Another of Roger Babson's moral lessons carved in a Dogtown boulder.

After the grand exodus, Dogtown homes were rented to people who could not afford other lodging. Many occupants were widows of men killed in the Revolutionary War, who kept dogs for companionship and protection. The dogs roamed, bred, and soon outnumbered the inhabitants. During this declining era, residents of Cape Ann named the development Dogtown, in reference to both its impoverished inhabitants and its numerous mangy, starving dogs. By 1830, the last inhabitant, an old servant with frozen toes, was removed from the cellar of his house and carried to the poorhouse. Five years later all dwellings were razed, leaving only the cellar holes that now line what were the two main roads.

Although the property was neglected for the next hundred years, it did provide a spooky summer playground for local youngsters, among them Roger Babson. An astute businessman, Babson made a bundle by predicting accurately when the booming stock market of the 1920s would crash. His address to the Gloucester Rotary Club in 1927 counseled its members, "When things look rosy, is the time to sell; while when things look bad is the time to buy." Babson, eager to preserve land he regarded as historically and geologically significant, purchased more than 1,000 acres, which he donated immediately to the town of Gloucester.

During the Depression, Babson hired unemployed stonecutters to chisel numbers on stones at specified spots along Dogtown and Common Roads. In order to highlight his beloved boulders, Babson carefully chose large smooth granite slabs, which he had carved with moral lessons for his fellow citizens, such as HELP MOTHER, PROSPERITY FOLLOWS SERVICE, and GET A JOB.

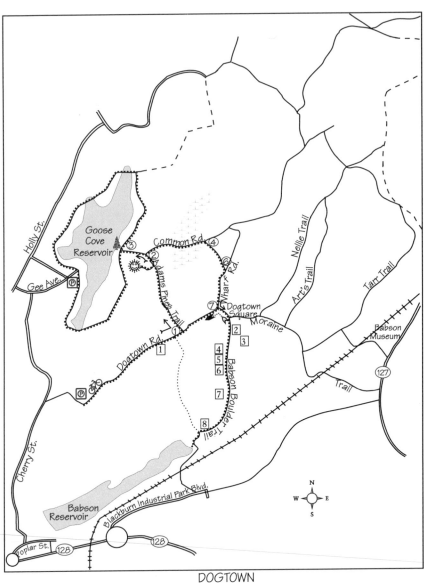

DOGTOWN

THE RIDE

The numbered intersection markers on the map originally corresponded to numbered stakes installed by the Dogtown Advisory Committee in 1987. Some, none, or all may be in place at the time of your ride. The directions refer only to the numbered stakes that I observed when laying out the route.

1. Begin at the barrier prohibiting cars from entering Dogtown. Cycle down this wide carriage road, a continuation of the paved entrance road that once was the main street in the village, for 0.6 mile.

    If you're interested in investigating old cellar holes, look carefully on the side of the road for rocks etched with numbers and follow the footpaths that branch off from the main road.

    At 0.4 mile, just off the right side of the road, sits a boulder inscribed NEVER TRY, NEVER WIN.

2. Turn left onto the well-worn single-track Adams Pines Trail, where you will pass through a stand of conifers, an open meadow, and heathland.

    After 0.4 mile on this trail, look to your left for a narrow path at the southwesterly corner of a grassy clearing. Follow the path up a steep incline for a panorama of Ipswich Bay, Wingaersheek Beach, and the soon-to-be-visited Goose Cove Reservoir.

Sweet pepperbush

3. After pedaling for a little more than one mile, turn left at the junction with Common Road.

4. Common Road leads to an eroded asphalt road that circles Goose Cove Reservoir. Turn either left or right on the reservoir road.

    This scenic stretch, shaded by cherry, birch, and pine trees interspersed with water vistas, passes the Gee Avenue reservoir entrance and parking area.

5. After completing the 2-mile loop (watch for a pine tree in the corner next to the turnoff), return on rocky Common Road.

   Proceed on Common Road, past Adams Pines Trail, passing such wetland- and moisture-loving shrubs as **sweet pepperbush, spicebush, greenbrier, highbush blueberry**, and **sheep laurel**. Stone walls that delineated the boundaries of the earliest settlers' homes and pastureland line the road.

6. After traveling 1 mile on Common Road, turn right at the #4 intersection.

7. At the next intersection, with Wharf Road, turn right.

8. Remain on Wharf Road until the next major intersection, Dogtown Square. Look in the corner for the letters DT SQ incised in a rock. Turn right onto Dogtown Road.

9. Take your next right onto Babson Boulder Trail that extends for 0.6 mile, 0.2 of which is challenging cycling.

   Discovering the inscribed rocks requires dismounting and hunting a little, as they are rarely next to the trail. Look for cleared areas and paths off the main trail.

   Immediately after entering the trail, keep your eyes open for INDUSTRY, located just off the path on the left side. Behind INDUSTRY sits a mammoth boulder displaying SPIRITUAL POWER. Ahead on the right is INTEGRITY, followed by INITIATIVE. In between a small and a large boulder sits a rock etched with IDEAS.

   Proceed 0.2 mile from IDEAS past a broad expanse of jumbled rocks. KINDNESS sits on the right.

10. Babson Boulder Trail leads to Babson Reservoir. A short steep path climbs to a water overlook.

11. The return to Dogtown Road is via the same route. However, the landscape looks quite different on the return trip. At the beginning of the return trip watch for STUDY inscribed on one side of a boulder and BE ON TIME on the other.

12. After cycling for 0.6 mile, bear left at the intersection and proceed back to Dogtown Square.

13. Bear left onto Dogtown Road and proceed 0.8 mile to the entrance.

17

NOANET

WOODLANDS

RESERVATION

 Distance and Difficulty: 5 miles of easy to moderate riding.

Noanet is just what one would expect in the refined wooded suburb of Dover—a tranquil, tidy, bucolic reservation that also has the necessary attributes for a great ride. Within Noanet's 695 acres are 10 miles of wide, well-marked trails surrounded by splendid scenery that includes a meandering brook and four ponds. A peak with a view of the Boston skyline is especially dramatic when framed by dazzling fall foliage. Noanet is the place for cyclists who seek relaxed riding rather than technical challenge.

Because Noanet has become so popular with bikers, the Trustees of Reservations, which manages the property, requires riders to purchase a season permit from the ranger stationed at the entrance. On weekends and holidays, cyclists are not permitted on the trails before 11:00 A.M.

Transportation: By automobile: From Routes 95/128, take Exit 17 onto Route 135 west. Remain on Route 135 for 0.7 mile and turn left on South Street (just after the road crosses the Charles River). After traveling 1 mile, turn left on Chestnut Street. Remain on Chestnut until the road forks and bear right on Dedham Street (after another crossing of the Charles River). Remain on Dedham Street for 1.5 miles and turn left into Caryl Park in Dover, the location of the parking lot and entrance to Noanet Woodlands Reservation.

By commuter rail: From South Station or Back Bay Station take the Needham Line and exit at Needham Junction. Noanet Woodlands Reservation is 2.5 miles from the station. From the Needham Junction Station, go south on Chestnut Street for a half-mile. Turn right on Dedham Street. Follow Dedham Street for 2 miles to the reservation.

Food and Drink: The closest food purveyors are in Dover Center, 0.6 mile east on Dedham Street. The Mobil gas station on the corner of Walpole and Dedham Streets sells ice cream, drinks, and snacks. Dover Market sells pastries, drinks, salads, and sandwiches. Dover Pharmacy has a snack bar.

Restrooms: Located in the Mobil gas station on the corner of Walpole and Dedham Streets.

Fees: Seasonal biking permit is $15; members of Trustees of Reservations pay $5.

Recreational Options: Hiking, cross-country skiing, horseback riding, fishing.

Background: Now covered with trees, Noanet Woodlands Reservation once was cleared for farmland and pasture. Early settlers built stone walls to contain their cattle and sheep.

In the 19th century industry replaced farming. The Dover Union Iron Company dammed Noanet Brook in order to furnish enough power to run their ironworks. After manufacturing iron products for 60 years, the company closed when a flood destroyed the dam in 1876.

Amelia Peabody eventually purchased the land. An environmentalist who realized the scenic potential of her property, she promptly rebuilt the dam in order to alter the flow of the Noanet Brook and fill three small ponds. Ms. Peabody improved the ancient Peabody Trail in order to connect her horse farm at the north end of the property with her beef and pig farm at the south end.

For years Amelia Peabody generously allowed her neighbors to hike, ski, and ride horses on her land. To perpetuate that tradition she bequeathed her property to the Trustees of Reservations in 1984. Olivia and Henry Cabot contributed additional parcels.

The Trustees of Reservations, founded by Charles Eliot (who also established Boston's metropolitan park system), is the oldest private land trust in the world. During the past hundred years the Trustees have acquired 73 properties in Massachusetts, totaling more than 18,000 acres.

THE RIDE

Of the many trails that run through Noanet, three are marked and color coded. You will be following two of them, the blue-blazed Peabody Trail and the yellow-blazed Caryl Trail. Major intersections are numbered, a great help to us mountain bikers who become so focused on negotiating the trail that we often lose our way.

1. Begin at the trailhead, located south of the tennis courts and parking lot and behind the ranger station. The Caryl Trail, marked by round yellow discs attached to trees, begins on a trail cushioned with pine needles and turns right onto a gravel-covered carriage path.

Shagbark hickory

2. After pedaling for 0.1 mile, bear left onto a trail covered with wood chips. The trail to the right leads to another parking area.

    The trail, often studded with tree roots, meanders first through a pine grove and then a woodland filled with oaks, maples, and a few **shagbark hickories**, with their distinctive shaggy gray bark, and crosses a culvert directing water from Noanet Brook.

3. Soon after pedaling up a slight incline and passing a large glacial erratic behind an ash tree, look for a "3" posted to a tree and signs for the red and blue trails (0.5 mile). Turn left, heading for the blue-blazed Peabody Trail. Be prepared for a short climb over a path dotted with tree roots.

4. At the intersection marked by a "4," bear right onto the blue-blazed trail. Three horse jumps appear on the right.

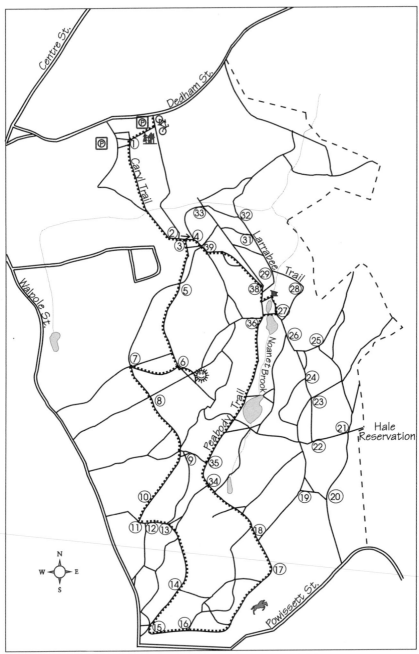

NOANET WOODLANDS RESERVATION

5. At 0.7 mile the trail runs through an open field, splits, and then merges. Bear left onto the carriage road.

6. After riding for 0.9 mile, turn left toward the pond and old mill site. Remnants of the ironworks sit on the left.

7. Cross the bridge over the dam and turn right onto the path that hugs the shore.

> Moisture-loving **sweet pepperbush** and **elderberry** hang over the water. Recognizing these two bushes is easier in autumn when dry, gray fruiting capsules extend from the tips of branches on the sweet pepperbush and clumps of purplish black berries hang from the elderberry.

8. Turn right onto the next bridge and return to the blue-blazed trail. If you search, you may find "36" tacked to a tree, facing in the opposite direction.

9. Turn left onto the blue-blazed Peabody Trail, passing a series of ponds on your left.

10. At 1.6 miles, you'll reach an intersection with three paths. Proceed up the center path, passing on your left the highest and largest of the ponds. Climb the steep gravelly hill while paralleling the stone wall to your right.

11. At intersection 18 (1.8 miles), the Peabody, Caryl, and Larrabee Trails merge. Continue straight, heading toward the boundary gate until you spot a "17" posted on a tree and the yellow-blazed Caryl Trail bending to the right. Turn right and follow the yellow blazes for the return leg of the loop.

12. At the next fork, bear left on the yellow-blazed trail. A horse farm lies to the left of the trail.

Maple-leaf viburnum

> **Maple-leaf viburnum** bushes grow alongside the path. The shrub is easily distinguished by its three-lobed leaves that resemble those on maple trees. In spring, it sends out small white clusters of flowers that turn to purplish black berries in the fall.

13. At 2.4 miles and intersection 15 (facing in the opposite direction), turn right. The trail borders Walpole Street.

14. At 2.8 miles, bear left while continuing to watch for the yellow blazes. Number 13 is posted on the tree just ahead.

A cluster of **sassafras** seedlings grows near the turn. Note the three distinct leaf shapes: three-lobed, two-lobed, and single-lobed.

15. When you reach "13," bear left onto a carriage trail.

16. At 2.9 miles and intersection 11, bear right. Continue straight over the cleared gas-line path.

17. At 3.2 miles, bear left onto the only path of the five that has yellow blazes.

18. At 3.5 and intersection 7, make a sharp right turn.

19. At the next intersection, "6," turn right and leave the Caryl Trail to ascend Noanet Peak. Or try to ascend—the trail is rocky and very steep. Biking is allowed only to a certain point and then you must walk the remaining 100 feet.

On the summit, look to the northeast for a view of the Boston skyline. A visit in mid-October yields a dazzling view of foliage at its peak. You may even meet a TV crew that makes an annual pilgrimage to film the colorful display.

20. Descend to intersection 6. Turn right, returning to the yellow-blazed trail. Prepare to be challenged. This section is steep with rocks and tree roots obstructing the trail.

21. At intersection 3, the Caryl Trail returns over the initial route. If you wish to ride farther, turn right onto the red-blazed Larrabee Trail, which runs along the eastern edge of the reservation. It offers more challenging riding than the Caryl and Peabody Trails.

18

WESTON

WOODLANDS

Distance and Difficulty: Three connecting loops of 3, 2.3, and 1.5 miles, for a total of 6.8 miles of easy riding with several stream crossings.

Quiet, litter-free, well marked and well maintained, the 65 miles of trails running through conservation land in the town of Weston offer some of the mellowest riding around. A combination of wide carriage roads and single-track trails run past Weston's characteristic stone walls within pine forests and wetlands. Despite occasional stream crossings and pine tree roots that protrude on the paths, most of the riding is quite tame.

The tour consists of three interconnected loops mainly on single-track trails and, when possible, avoids marshy areas. Weston Forest and Trail Association has done a terrific job of marking and maintaining trails. Their insignias indicate the direction of the trail and are attached to trees at most intersections. Numbers or letters mark major intersections.

Transportation: By automobile: Take Routes 128/95 to Exit 26 (Route 20) west toward Weston. Remain on Route 20 for 1 mile. Turn right onto Boston Post Road (which is opposite the left turn toward Regis College and Wellesley). Remain on Boston Post Road for 0.7 mile, passing through Weston Center to Concord Road. Turn right on Concord Road, following the signs to Weston

Observatory and the Campion Center. Proceed on Concord Road, bearing left at the fork to the College Conservation Area on the right (1.3 miles from Boston Post Road). The turn is just after you pass a pond and just before a yellow road sign and the main entrance to Campion Center. A "Soccer" sign is posted to a tree. Turn right on the road that leads to the College Conservation Area and then fork right into the parking lot adjacent to the tennis courts.

By commuter rail: From North Station take the Fitchburg Line to the Kendal Green Station. The distance between the station and the beginning of the ride at the College Conservation Area parking lot is 2.7 miles. From the station, turn right onto Church Street. Follow Church for 1.1 miles to Weston Center. Cycle past the wide town green through the small town center to Concord Road. Turn right and follow the above directions.

Food and Drink: In Weston Center are the 4-5-6 Cafe, Bruegger's Bagel Bakery, and Omni Food Market.

Restrooms: Weston Town Hall on the north side of the green in Weston Center.

Recreational Options: Hiking, cross-country skiing.

Background: The numerous stone walls throughout Weston conservation land reveal the town's agrarian past. Settlers dragged the rocks from their fields and put them to good use—defining boundaries and containing livestock. Just as the town has cared for its conservation land, so too has it carefully conserved its antique stone walls.

How has Weston, a desirable community in a convenient location, managed to preserve 2,200 acres of land? Approximately half the acreage is comprised of individual gifts; the other half was accumulated through town acquisitions. In 1972, when developers were eyeing tracts of land, several prominent Weston citizens convinced residents to appropriate town money to conserve the land. They argued that the money should be spent now for land rather than later for additional schools and services for families in the new developments.

The Weston Forest and Trail Association was formed in 1955 to maintain and mark the trails. The association has designed clear, accurate maps which are sold at Weston Town Hall.

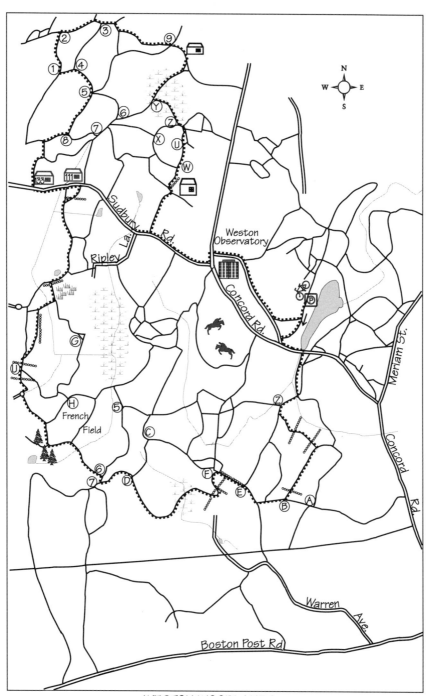

WESTON WOODLANDS

THE RIDE

Cyclists must ride respectfully in order to guarantee continued access to Weston's terrific trails. If you encounter a horse and rider, dismount immediately and stand to the side of the trail. Give walkers the right of way. Walk through muddy areas to prevent trail erosion.

1. From the parking lot, return to Concord Road and turn left. Travel 0.1 mile and turn right onto the narrow path directly across from the southern tip of the pond. Look for the Weston Forest and Trail insignia posted to a tree. Carry your bike down several steps and then begin the ride in a picturesque pine forest carpeted with **Canada mayflower**. In May, clusters of tiny white star-shaped flowers peek out above broad leaves.

Canada mayflower

2. Ride 0.1 mile. The path meets a wide carriage road. Turn right.

3. After passing the Z intersection on the right, take the next left (0.3 total trail miles).

Many, but not all, intersections are marked with numbers or letters placed between the tree insignias and attached high on a tree. Sometimes you may have to hunt to find the marker and confirm your location. Don't assume, however, that because you cannot find the marker, you have made a wrong turn. Keep going and look for other landmarks. For example, in this section, you will go through a break in a stone wall before passing through a pine forest with an undercover of Canada mayflower.

Partridgeberry, another variety of ground cover, also grows here. It is distinguished by round, bright red berries above small, shiny green leaves with white veins.

4. The trail cuts through another stone wall and meets a **T** intersection. Turn right.

5. After a great run on a shady, scenic, and tree-rooted trail, you pass through another stone wall and meet a carriage road at B. Turn right (0.6 mile total).

6. Travel 0.1 mile to a **T** intersection. Turn left.

7. At the next intersection with a wide carriage road, turn right.

8. Pass the E intersection and pedal parallel with a stone wall to the F intersection (0.9 mile total). Turn left onto a narrower trail. The trail widens, then narrows, and at 1.1 miles cuts through one stone wall, bends right, and cuts through another.

Welcome to your first stream crossing! Dismount and pass to the left of the main trail, where the crossing is easier to negotiate. Your reward is an uninterrupted 0.4-mile run on a great single-track trail.

9. Turn right and enjoy the wide smooth carriage road.

While riding through swampy areas, you'll notice **skunk cabbage**, a low plant with wide, rough green leaves, similar in shape to those found on a cabbage. If the leaves are pulled away from the stem, a disagreeable odor is released, akin to the scent from a skunk. This odor may not attract humans, but it does lure insects that then pollinate the plant. Its flowers are among the first to appear in spring; however, it's hard to believe that the unusual red, green, or brown horns sticking up in the marsh are flowers. Skunk cabbage grows so quickly it gives off heat that melts the ice and snow around it.

The **sensitive fern** also thrives in moist places. This most unfernlike specimen has broad, almost triangular leaves and a thick center membrane. Its name refers to the fern's sensitivity to the cold; it dies at the first hint of frost.

10. Having traveled a total of 1.7 miles, you will reach intersection 6. Turn left onto a carriage road that leads to French Field. The path crosses the field and leads to a wide trail through a pine forest.

11. Now in the forest, take the first right.

12. Bear left at the fork. (The right fork heads back toward French Field.)

13. The path passes a house on the left and a stream on the right before reaching a road. Turn right and pick up another path on the opposite side of the stream (2 miles total).

14. The path runs beside the stream before turning left.

15. After cutting through openings in two stone walls, the path forks. Bear right onto a path that parallels a stone wall before it crosses a stream and heads into a field.

16. Upon entering the field, turn left. Pedal on the wood-chipped path that runs between the fenced-in field and stream.

17. Cut through the stone wall and turn right.

18. Remain on the path next to the wall, passing a tiny pond on the left, and turn left onto a narrow path. The path climbs a ridge, cuts through a wall, and meets a stream. Although the banks are slippery and steep, the stream is narrow enough to hop across. The path ends, after crossing yet another stone wall, on Sudbury Road across from house #111 (3 miles).

Sudbury Road Loop (2.3 miles)

19. Turn left on Sudbury Road.

20. Proceed 0.1 mile, while passing house #133, and turn right onto a narrow path protected by large boulders.

21. Proceed on the path 0.2 mile to a **T** intersection. Turn right.

22. Continue 0.1 mile to intersection 8 and turn left.

23. Turn left again at intersection 5 (0.6 mile total in Sudbury Road Loop).

24. Continue to bear left while passing intersection 4.

25. Turn right at intersection 1 onto a carriage road (0.8 mile).

    Wooden plaques explain the wood harvesting evident in the surrounding forest. By cutting trees selectively, Land Sakes, the company overseeing the operation, manages the forest in an ecologically sustainable manner.

26. Proceed straight until intersection 2. Turn right (0.9 mile).

27. In order to avoid a muddy section covered with narrow wooden planks, bear right onto a new path that runs beside the muddy old one.

28. Continue straight, passing "3," to the next fork. Bear right.

29. Pedal past intersection 9, then a house on the left, and take the next right onto a narrow path. If you miss the path, another entrance lies 20 yards ahead (1.5 miles).

30. Proceed on the path for 0.2 mile (beware—another stream crossing!) and bear left at the fork at the Y intersection.

31. After crossing still another stream (hint: go to the right of the tree for an easier passage), turn left at the Z intersection and then bear right at the fork.

32. Bear right at the U intersection (1.9 miles) and continue straight past "W," heading toward a stone wall and a huge house.

33. After passing the house, turn left at the next intersection. The path skirts a tennis court and meets a driveway. Cross the driveway and pick up the path that leads to Sudbury Road (2.3 miles).

34. Turn left on Sudbury Road and pedal for 0.2 mile to Concord Road.

35. Turn left and head down the entrance road to the Weston Observatory and the Campion Center.

    Weston Observatory, to the left of the entrance road, is used by the geology and geophysics departments at Boston College, a Jesuit institution. Campion Center, the huge brick building on the right, is a Jesuit renewal and retirement home.

36. Proceed to the parking lot in back of Campion Center and turn right. A trail at the far right end leads back to the parking lot where the ride began.

    Additional trails lie behind the College Conservation Area parking lot. A great 1.5-mile loop begins on the water side of the tennis courts, winds through woods, cuts through several fields, and ends in an apple orchard next to the pond off Concord Road. Be aware that although the trails are labeled with the Weston Forest and Trail insignia, the intersections here are not marked.

19

From Minuteman Bikeway through Great Meadows to Concord

 Distance and Difficulty: 10.5 miles of level riding with some sandy and muddy sections.

A bit of investigative mountain biking has revealed a terrific off-road route from the western end of the Minuteman Bikeway to Concord Center. A shaded, level dirt path offers a relaxing respite from the congested bikeway as it runs by streams through conservation land and follows the Concord River along the Great Meadows National Wildlife Refuge. The tour ends on a paved road that leads to Old South Burying Ground on Main Street in Concord. This tame 4.5-mile route into Concord can be cycled easily on a hybrid bike. Scenic and more-challenging digressions around the Mary Putnam Webber Wildlife Preserve in Bedford and the Great Meadows Refuge in Concord can add another 2 miles to the tour.

You can also begin the ride in Concord Center, a half-mile from the train station, or from the end of the bikeway.

Transportation: By automobile: If entering the path from the Minuteman Bikeway, see directions in chapter 7. To reach the Bedford terminus of the path, take Routes 128/95 to Exit 31B, Routes 4/225 west toward Bedford. Follow Routes 4/225 for 2 miles. Turn left on Loomis Street. Follow Loomis

0.3 mile through the intersection with South Road onto Railroad Avenue. A parking area is on the right side of the road.

A municipal parking lot is located on Keyes Road in Concord Center. To reach Concord, follow Route 2 west and take the Concord Center exit.

By commuter rail: From North Station or Porter Square, take the Fitchburg Line to Concord. From the Concord Depot, turn left on Thoreau Street. Turn right at the light onto Sudbury Road. Follow Sudbury Road for a half-mile as it merges with Main Street. Turn left on Keyes Street.

To reach the Great Meadows Wildlife Refuge, follow Routes 4/225 through Bedford Center and turn left on Route 62. Proceed south on Route 62 for 2.9 miles to Monsen Road. Turn right on Monsen and follow it for 0.3 mile to the refuge entrance on the left.

Food and Drink: Coggin's Bakery and Coffee Bar, two locations: next to the train station in Concord and near the bikeway on Loomis Street; Star Market, next to the bike path in Concord; Sally Ann Food Shop in Concord Center.

Restrooms: In the Bikeway Source, the bike and in-line skate shop, located at the corner of Loomis Street and Railroad Street at the western end of the bikeway in Bedford. Portable bathrooms are also located at the western end of the bikeway. Restrooms in the Great Meadows National Wildlife Refuge are open weekdays from 8:00 A.M. to 3:00 P.M. and sporadically on weekends, depending on staff availability.

Recreational Options: Hiking, cross-country skiing, and bird-watching around the Great Meadows National Wildlife Refuge, which is handicapped accessible.

Background: The 4.5-mile off-road trail that runs from Bedford to Concord is the continuation of a rail bed on which the Minuteman Bikeway now rests. Because Bedford and Concord did not want a bikeway running through their towns, they have left the trail unpaved. Fortunately, most of the wooden rail ties have been removed, but a few sections are bumpy reminders of the trail's original function.

Thousands of stone artifacts excavated along the Concord River in and around the Great Meadows have revealed that the area was occupied more than 7,500 years ago. The Native American occupants spent winters near the river and paddled to the sea in the spring. When the colonists arrived in this country, they too settled near the Musketahquid, the Indian name for the grassy banks of the Concord River.

In the early 19th century, a dam built to power mills in Billerica, a suburb north of Concord, caused a rise in the water level of the Concord River. The meadows near the river flooded, killing the hay that farmers grew in the flood plain. The flooded wetlands attracted waterfowl which, in turn, lured hunters and fishermen.

Seeking to preserve a favored hunting area, Samuel Hoar purchased a section of the Great Meadows in 1928. To ensure that the area would remain wet and continue to draw wildlife, he dammed and built earthern dikes around the marsh. In 1944, Hoar guaranteed preservation of the Great Meadows by donating 250 acres of land in Concord to the U.S. Fish and Wildlife Service, which has continued to manage the refuge and provide a freshwater wetland habitat for wildlife. Additional land has been purchased over the last 50 years, and now the two sections of the Great Meadows National Wildlife Refuge (the other is in Sudbury) encompass more than 3,000 acres.

THE RIDE

(If beginning on Keyes Road in Concord Center, pick up the directions at #18.)

1. From the end of the Minuteman Bikeway in Bedford, cross the road toward the Bikeway Source and continue on Railroad Avenue to the right of the store.

2. Follow Railroad Avenue for 0.3 mile until it bends right. Leave the road and continue straight into the dirt parking lot next to a playing field.

3. Pedal straight through the parking lot to the path that leads to Elm Brook Conservation Trail and runs alongside the Elm Brook.

4. Remain on the trail for 0.7 mile as it becomes a paved access road to the Bedford Well-Water Treatment Plant. Upon reaching the intersection with Hartwell Road, cross the road and pick up the trail directly across the street.

5. The trail travels through the Mary Putnam Webber Wildlife Preserve for 0.9 mile. The path widens and offers a lively roller-coaster ride before it turns sandy and becomes difficult to negotiate.

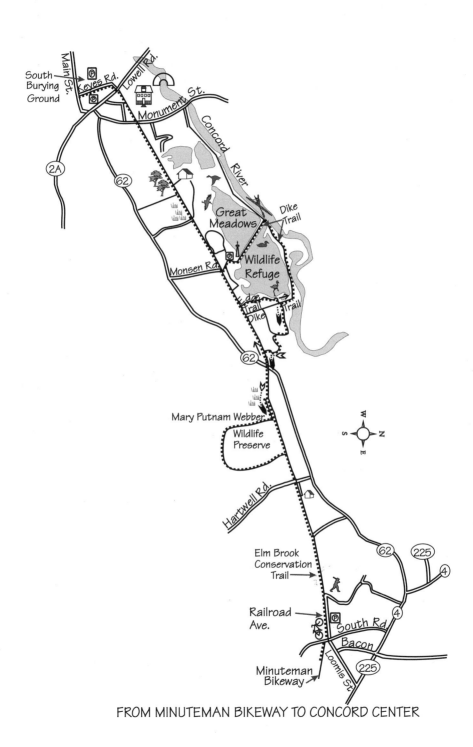

FROM MINUTEMAN BIKEWAY TO CONCORD CENTER

6. Upon reaching the road (Route 62), cross it and enter the narrow path hiding behind the metal barrier.

7. You are now in the **Great Meadows National Wildlife Refuge**. The wide path may occasionally become muddy. After traveling for 0.4 mile in the refuge (2.7 total), you will come to the broad Dike Trail on the right marked (but probably not named) by a wooden refuge sign. You can turn right, or continue straight for 0.1 mile and turn right on the narrow Edge Trail that meanders through the woods and over streams, and skirts the edge of the wetland. Be prepared to dismount when crossing the plank bridges.

Wood ducks

A photo blind along the Edge Trail offers the opportunity to view wildlife in and around the wetland. During one of my visits I watched a river otter swimming noisily among the reeds, a great blue heron standing at the edge of the water, colorful **wood ducks** paddling near their nesting boxes, and red-winged blackbirds foraging in the swamp.

A prime birding area, the Great Meadows boasts 221 species that have been spotted in and around the wetland. Other wildlife that frequent the area include white-tailed deer, muskrats, foxes, raccoons, rabbits, weasels, and, of course, the ubiquitous squirrel. Be careful not to cycle over a snake slithering across the path.

8. The Edge Trail returns to the main path. Turn left, passing over a dam that regulates the water for the holding area, and continue until reaching an intersection with another wide path (3.7 miles total). Turn left, with the wetland on the left and the Concord River on the right. If you are cycling on a warm weekend, you may spot canoeists paddling on the river.

9. Turn left onto the dike that divides the two holding areas of the Great Meadows. Benches near the water are perfect for resting and viewing the wildlife.

10. Follow the Dike Trail to the parking lot where the observation tower is located (4.2 miles).

11. Pedal through the parking lot to the entrance road. Follow the entrance road to the intersection with a wide dirt trail. Turn right to continue to Concord. In case you forget, the wooden ties will quickly remind you that you are traveling on an old rail bed.

12. Follow the trail for 0.5 mile. Turn left onto the paved road. Immediately turn right, pass through an opening in the metal fence (marked by a brown post), and go straight onto the path that skirts the edge of a wide field.

13. Continue straight for 0.2 mile on the path as it enters a woodland. (Do *not* turn left and follow the path around the field.)

14. After 0.1 mile the path emerges from the woods and meets another path. Turn left. (A right turn leads to a water treatment plant.)

15. After 0.6 mile (5.4 miles total), the trail intersects with Monument Street.

To visit the **Old Manse** and **Old North Bridge**, turn right.

16. Cross Monument Street and pick up the path behind two granite posts.

17. At 5.7 miles, cross Lowell Road onto Keyes Road, which leads to Main Street in Concord Center.

The **South Burying Ground** rests on the corner of Keyes Road and Main Street. Grave markers from as early as 1670 stand in a row. Our forebears did not bury their loved ones in such neat rows as the gravestones now indicate. This orderly arrangement replaced the original jumbled grouping.

18. The return (or the beginning, for those who are starting in Concord) travels down Keyes Road, passing the large municipal parking lot, and crosses Lowell Road.

19. Pick up the narrow path directly across from Keyes Road. The Concord Lumber Co. is on the left and a small park on the right. Pass the intersection of Bow and Lang Streets as you bear left and continue on the path.

20. At 0.6 mile, cross Monument Street and proceed past the large boulders onto the wide, but often muddy, trail.

21. Remain on the trail for another 0.6 mile (1.2 total on the return trip) until the intersection with another path. Bear right and head into the forest.

22. After emerging from the forest, continue straight on the path that skirts the edge of a wide field.

23. Upon reaching the road, turn left and make a quick right onto the trail (1.5 miles total) that leads to the Great Meadows National Wildlife Refuge. After a half-mile on the trail, you will reach an intersection with the entrance road to the refuge.

    You can either turn left toward the parking lot and public restroom (in the brown building to the left of the lot) and bike the 1.5-mile loop around the Great Meadows, or carefully cross the entrance road and continue straight on the old rail bed. If you choose to ride around the Great Meadows (highly recommended—look for wading birds such as the **great blue heron**), be alert for a side path on the return loop, on the left across from the Edge Trail. If on the side path, continue to bear left through a pine forest to merge with the old rail bed 0.3 mile from the Route 62 intersection.

    Great blue heron

24. If you choose to pedal straight from the Great Meadows entrance road, after 0.8 mile you will intersect with Route 62. Cross the road and pick up the trail behind the large boulders.

25. Now in the Mary Putnam Webber Wildlife Preserve, a path on the right runs through a meadow and then bends right into the forest. Continue to bear left to loop around the preserve and rejoin the main route.

26. At the next street intersection, cross the road and head onto the paved road to the Bedford Well-Water Treatment Plant. The dirt trail resumes after pedaling by four wooden posts.

27. The trail ends at a dirt parking lot. Continue straight through the lot onto Railroad Avenue. Proceed down Railroad Avenue to the next intersection.

28. To enter the Minuteman Bikeway, cross South Road and head toward the Bedford Depot Bakery. The Bikeway begins to the right of the parking lot (the site of the old train depot).

20

GREAT BROOK FARM
STATE PARK

 Distance and Difficulty: 4.7 miles of moderate biking; optional 1.5 miles of more-challenging terrain.

Care for a little farm with your forest? A working dairy farm containing cattle, hens, goats, pastures, and cornfields coexists with 15 miles of trails in this small but scenic reservation, situated in the bucolic suburb of Carlisle.

What draws bikers to Great Brook Farm State Park? They like the mix of wide-open pastureland, level carriage roads, and narrow single-track trails studded with tree roots that wind through this well-kept park. Its predominantly nonthreatening terrain provides a good introduction for novice off-road bikers, while several side trails challenge the more experienced riders. Take along insect repellent; the trails run near ponds and wetlands, so mosquitoes can be quite brutal in the summer.

Families as well as bikers are partial to this dairy-farm-within-a-park. Its wide, well-marked trails invite strolling and baby strollers. Young children delight in feeding the livestock along with the geese and ducks that paddle around the pond adjacent to the parking lot. Visits usually end at the cow barn, where the 120-head herd is milked twice daily and an ice cream concession dishes out rewards for physical exertion.

During winter, snow-covered fields are converted to 10 miles of cross-country ski trails, with rental skis and instruction available at the Great Brook Farm Ski Touring Center.

Transportation: By automobile: From Routes 128/95, take Exit 31B toward Bedford on Routes 4/225. Follow Route 225 west for 7 miles into Carlisle Center. Turn right on Lowell Street (at the traffic circle) and drive for 2 miles until you reach North Road and the Great Brook Farm State Park sign. Turn right on North Road. The parking lot is just past the large field on the left.

By commuter rail: From North Station, take the Lowell Line to North Billerica. The park is about 5 miles from the train station. Exit the station, pedal down Station Street, and turn right at the stop sign on Faulkner Street. Remain on Faulkner for 0.3 mile as you cross over the Concord River and pass several mills. Turn left onto Talbot Avenue (a wide street with a traffic island in the middle and no street sign). Remain on Talbot for 0.3 mile, passing the Talbot School and a church, until you reach a major intersection of six roads. Take a 90° right turn onto Sprague. Follow Sprague as it crosses Route 3A, becomes Rangeway Road, crosses Chelmsford Road, and crosses over Route 3 (expressway). Remain on Rangeway for 3 miles, passing a number of factories, until you reach North Road. Turn right. The park entrance is 0.7 mile on the left.

Food and Drink: Ice cream and drinks are sold in the cow barn. Kimball Farm, 0.6 mile east of Carlisle Center on Route 225, is famous for its homemade ice cream.

Restrooms: An outdoor portable toilet is located between the parking lot and the cow barn. A second, adjacent to the barn near Lowell Street, also services cross-country skiers.

Recreational Options: Cross-country skiing, snowshoeing, hiking, horseback riding.

Background: One of Massachusetts Department of Environmental Management's newest additions to its park system, 934-acre Great Brook Farm was purchased from a dairy farmer in 1974. To perpetuate the traditional New England farm, the state in 1987, leased barns, silos, and 90 acres of land to a farmer who maintains a 120-head dairy herd. The farmer and his wife live in the house next to the barn. Originally constructed in 1781 by Captain

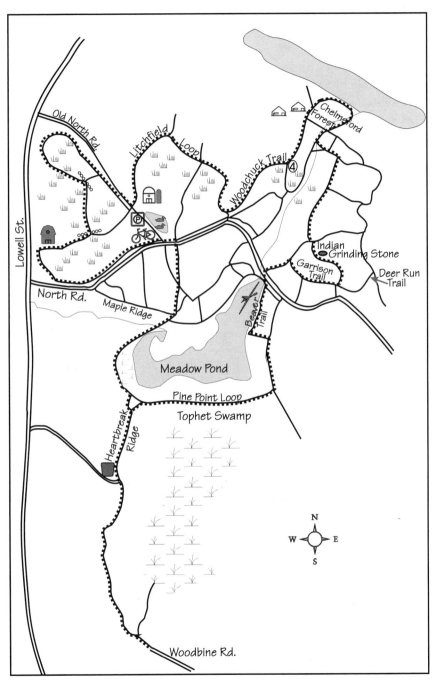

GREAT BROOK FARM STATE PARK

Timothy Ames (who fought in the Battle of Bunker Hill), the house has been added to over the years.

In the 18th century, gristmills and sawmills were built near the Great Brook in order to harness its water power. Remnants from that period can be found along the Garrison and Woodchuck Trails.

THE RIDE

Please remain on the trails when biking through the agricultural fields. Because families with small children and horseback riders share the trails, slow, cautious cycling is essential.

1. With your back to the duck pond, pedal across the parking lot and enter the pasture and mowed grassy trail on the left side. The trail circles the field as it passes Lowell Street, then a barn, portable restroom, and picnic tables where the ski-touring center is located.

2. After pedaling 0.3 mile, turn left through an opening in the stone wall to another field where the farmer grows hay to feed his cattle.

3. Remain on this path for 0.1 mile and then look carefully for a left turn onto a faint trail that cuts across the middle of the field. On the right side, just at the turn, is a trail coming through an opening in the stone wall. (If you end up back at the parking lot, you have missed the left turn.) The trail loops around the edge of the field as it borders Lowell Street and then Old North Road on the left.

4. At 1.1 miles turn left onto the path that cuts between the bushes toward Old North Road. Turn right onto Old North Road. You'll see an automobile barrier at the point where the paved road becomes gravel.

Phlox

5. At the next intersection (1.2 total miles), turn left onto the Litchfield Loop.

    If you're biking in the spring, you may notice at the intersection **wild blue phlox's** clusters of small

The duck pond at Great Brook Farm is a beautiful setting for a family picnic.

blue flowers and **jewelweed's** fragile yellow blooms brightening the side of the road.

6. At the fork, bear right and skirt the edge of the field to continue the Litchfield Loop. The trail leaves the field and enters the woods while passing several large glacial erratics, boulders deposited 10,000 to 15,000 years ago when the glacier began to melt and recede.

7. When you reach another field and a sign reading Stay on Marked Trails, fork right (1.5 miles). The path skirts a field and heads into another open area.

8. After pedaling for 0.3 mile (1.8 total), with the pasture on your right and the farm and silo at your back, leave the field and continue straight into the woods via the Woodchuck Trail.

Be prepared for a tough climb, as the Woodchuck Trail rises through a forest covered with more huge glacial erratics.

9. After 0.3 mile the trail emerges from the forest and comes to a **T** intersection and a #4 marker at the edge of yet another field. Turn left and leave Great Brook Farm to take a half-mile scenic jaunt through Chelmsford Forest.

The jaunt begins with a short, very steep descent, followed by a semi-steep ascent, and then passes a horse corral and several homes on the left.

10. After passing the homes and corral and pedaling for 0.3 mile in the forest, turn right at the fork. The trail passes more homes on the left, cuts through a stone wall, then ascends into a picturesque pine forest and runs along a pond.

11. After another steep decline and semi-steep ascent, bear left and continue to bike alongside the stream until you reach a wooden bridge. After 0.3 mile (2.7 total) turn left, cross the bridge, and turn right.

12. Proceed down this wide level road for 0.3 mile until you reach a **T** intersection. Turn left.

13. Take a quick right onto a narrow path with a wooden stake in front of it that marks the Indian Grinding Stone Trail.

14. After biking for 0.2 mile on the path, look to your left for the Indian Grinding Stone. Observe the boulder's hollow top, which reflects decades of corn grinding.

15. After passing the Deer Run sign, continue to bear right onto the Garrison Trail, crossing over a rocky section that once was a stone wall.

    The Garrison House soon appears on the right. Don't expect to find a house but rather a cellar hole filled with stones. According to local history, settlers fled to this cellar for protection from Indian attacks.

16. The trail descends and bears right before reaching a path covered with pine needles. Turn left and proceed 0.1 mile on the trail until you reach an automobile barricade.

17. Pedal past the barricade, cross North Road, and turn left onto the wide carriage road, passing the canoe launch on the right. The plastic discs covered with little pine trees indicate that you are now on the Pine Point Loop (3.5 miles).

18. Look to the right for a narrow path that runs for 0.2 mile next to Meadow Pond. This short section, named Beaver Trail, offers challenging riding and super scenery.

    Those who do not wish to be challenged can either continue to bike on the carriage road or walk their bikes over the difficult terrain.

19. Beaver Trail leads to a clearing for a scenic overlook and then turns sharply left and returns to the carriage road. Turn right to continue the Pine Point Loop.

    The trail, conveniently covered with pine needles to cushion the ride from tree roots, narrows as it travels over Tophet Swamp and then heads back into a pine forest.

20. A half-mile after the intersection of the Beaver Trail with the Pine Point loop (at 4.2 miles), the sign for Heartbreak Ridge appears on the left.

    This optional 1.5-mile ride begins with a steep climb up the ridge on a single-track trail until it reaches a huge boulder named Wolf Rock, rumored to have been a wolf rest stop. The path then widens and becomes quite tame. The trail ends at Woodbine Road, where you must turn around and retrace your route.

21. Upon returning to the Pine Point Trail, turn left and pedal past a swamp dotted with numerous dead tree trunks.

22. After crossing the Great Brook and passing the sign to Maple Ridge, take your next left onto a path that cuts across an open field.

23. Pedal through an opening in a fence onto North Road at the rear of the farm complex.

24. Turn left on North Road to return to the parking lot.

21

BLUE HILLS

RESERVATION

 Distance and Difficulty: 10 miles, including two 5-mile loops. Moderate difficulty with several steep ascents.

"Superlative" is the adjective that comes to mind when describing Blue Hills Reservation, the largest, highest, and most diverse recreational facility in and around Boston. Encompassing more than 7,000 acres within the towns of Milton, Randolph, Quincy, and Dedham, this Metropolitan District Commission (MDC) property boasts the most open land within 35 miles of Boston. At 635 feet, the Great Blue Hill is the highest point on the Atlantic coast south of Maine. The reservation's facilities offer the broadest range of activities: from hiking, downhill and cross-country skiing, horseback riding, and mountain biking on 125 miles of trails, to swimming and fishing in Houghtons Pond, ice-skating on the MDC rink, golfing at the Ponkapoag Golf Course, or viewing exhibits in the Trailside Museum.

A great way to explore the reservation's huge expanse and experience its varied terrain is via mountain bike. This introductory tour is divided into two 5-mile loops, one to the east of Hillside Street, the other on the trails to the west, or Houghtons Pond, side. The first loop ascends the summit of Blue Hill, where one can climb to the top of the observation tower for the panorama north to the Boston skyline and south along the shore. The route then winds through woodland and wetland, on wide, level carriage roads as well as narrow, hilly single-track trails. It circles Houghtons Pond, which sports a bathhouse and beach where hot, tired cyclists can end their ride with a swim.

While some trails, other than the ones included in this tour, are suitable for riding, many are not. Because of environmental or public safety concerns, certain trails are off-limits to cyclists and are posted with round white No Bicycle signs. Bikers are not allowed on any trails between January 1 and April 15.

Transportation: By automobile: From Routes 93/128 take Exit 3 and follow the signs toward Houghtons Pond. Turn right at the stop sign onto Hillside Street. The parking lot is on the right, next to Houghtons Pond.

By commuter rail: From South Station take the Attleboro Line to the Route 128 Station, which is approximately 4 miles from the starting point at the Houghtons Pond Parking Lot. From the station, go west on Green Lodge Street (also called Blue Hill Drive) for 2 miles to the T intersection at Washington Street (Route 138). Turn left, cross over the expressway, and after traveling 1 mile from Green Lodge Street, turn right at the stop sign onto Hillside Street. Pedal for another mile until you see Houghtons Pond on your right. The parking lot adjoins the pond.

Food and Drink: Concession stand and water fountain at Houghtons Pond, open from mid-April through mid-October.

Restrooms: Restrooms are open year-round in the Trailside Museum on Canton Avenue. Restrooms located in the Houghtons Pond Bathhouse are open from mid-May to mid-October.

Fees: Trailside Museum, 1904 Canton Avenue, Milton. Open daily 10:00 A.M. to 5:00 P.M. except Mondays (617-333-0690).

Recreational Options: Hiking, cross-country and downhill skiing, swimming, fishing, horseback riding, ice-skating.

Background: Blue Hills Reservation, located only 8 miles from Boston, belongs to a system of parks created by Frederick Law Olmsted and Charles Eliot in 1893 for the purpose of enriching the lives of city residents. Massachusetts established the Metropolitan Parks Commission to oversee this system, which at the turn of the century consisted of 9,177 acres of reservations, 13 miles of shoreline, 56 miles of riverbanks, and seven parkways. As part of this original parcel set aside for public use, the Blue Hills continues to offer many free facilities and programs. For program information call 617-698-1802.

Artifacts discovered in the reservation indicate that the land had been inhabited for at least 9,000 years. When the English colonists migrated southwest from Boston to the Blue Hills, they discovered the Machuseuck tribe, which means "people living near the great hills." Both the Native Americans and the colonists were drawn to this hilly location because of its close proximity to the Neponset River, high vantage points, and the granite that could be quarried below its ridges.

During the 1930s the Civilian Conservation Corps dug out miles of trails and constructed two stone observation towers. This tour stops at one of them, Eliot Tower, perched on the summit of Great Blue Hill.

THE RIDE

The Blue Hills system of marking intersections with numbered signs nailed to trees is a boon for mountain bikers, who often spend a lot of time riding in circles while trying to figure out where they are. My directions will use these numbers as reference points; this system, however, is not totally reliable, as occasionally the numbered signs disappear. Although the directions include trail names, don't expect to find signs on the trails themselves; use the names as reference points when reading the map.

1. From the parking lot, with your back to Houghtons Pond, turn right onto Headquarters Path, which parallels Hillside Street, for 0.2 mile. Cross Hillside Street and pedal past the state police station to the next driveway on the left, which leads to the Blue Hills Reservation headquarters.

2. Bike up to the far end of the driveway toward the tan shingled house where the rangers' offices are located. The trailhead is located behind a metal gate at the rear of the house.

3. Before you head onto the wide carriage road, shift into low gear, as the ascent up Wolcott Path is quite steep. Continue straight on the path for a half-mile, pedaling carefully over several bars used to divert streams of water from the trail. Go straight at the five-corners intersection, heading for the Blue Hills Tower.

4. At the T intersection (#1100) bear left, remaining on Wolcott Path.

5. At 1.3 miles, you will reach the paved road to the summit of Great Blue Hill. Turn left and be prepared to climb for 0.7 mile.

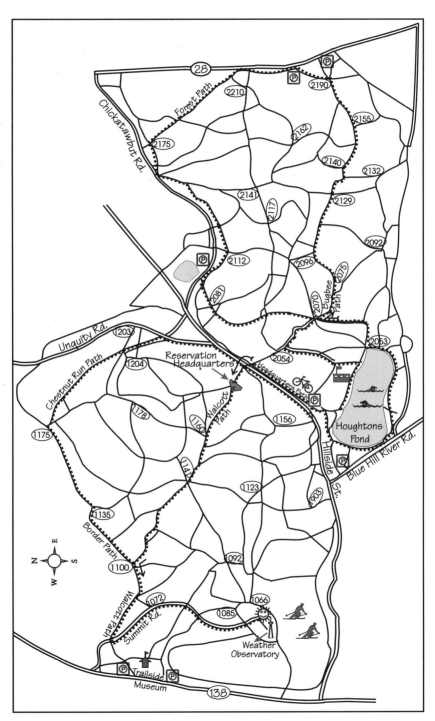

BLUE HILLS RESERVATION

6. At the summit, don't miss the 360° view from the top of the stone observation tower, built in the 1930s by the Civilian Conservation Corps.

> A view to the northeast reveals the Boston skyline and Boston Harbor and its islands. An eastern view includes the coastline of the towns of Quincy and Hingham. The sliver of land jutting into the ocean is Hull, where Nantasket Beach is located. On a clear day, you can see Mount Wachusett off to the west. Mount Monadnock lies north of Mount Wachusett. You also can look down at the ski slope, where you can practice parallel turns when the trails are covered with snow.
>
> Weather forecasting at the Blue Hill Meteorological Observatory, also located on this peak, has continued since 1880, when flying colored flags told the weather forecast. Weather has been monitored daily at the observatory longer than at any other station in the country. Guided tours of the observatory are available by reservation (617-696-1014).

7. Enjoy the downhill ride on the same paved road, but be alert for pedestrians.

> To visit the **Trailside Museum**, which has changing exhibits on the natural history of the Blue Hills, follow Summit Road to its end at Canton Avenue (Route 138) and turn left. Outside the museum are free animal exhibits; however, unless you are a member of the Massachusetts Audubon Society, you must pay an entrance fee to check out the displays of plants, trees, minerals, birds, etc.

8. From the intersection of Wolcott Path and Summit Road, turn right and retrace your route down Wolcott Path until it merges with Border Path (#1100). Bear left onto Border Path (a granite signpost marks the path).

9. Continue to bear left, following the round green blazes, until the green-blazed trail turns right at intersection #1135; however you are to *continue straight* on Border Path, which circles the northern edge of the reservation.

10. Remain on Border Path for 0.7 mile (4.2 miles total, not including museum visit). A good downhill run will precede an intersection where two paths are separated by an island with a tree in its center (#1175). Turn right and then take an immediate left onto Chestnut Run Path.

Chestnut seedlings grow next to the trail. Unfortunately, the once magnificent trees suffer from chestnut blight, which prevents them from maturing. The fungus arrived here on chestnut trees transported from China more than 50 years ago. Once the trees grow to about 20 feet, the fungus overpowers the trees and they die back. Because the roots survive, the trees can regenerate.

Chestnut

11. Proceed straight on the trail until Unquity Road (5 miles total). Turn right.

12. Continue on Unquity as it soon merges with Hillside Street. Remain on Hillside until you reach the Houghtons Pond Parking Lot. Enter the lot and head to the right side.

13. Find the path that begins on the right side of the pond between the fence and water (next to the public telephones).

14. At the next fork bear left, following the path toward the water. The trail bends around, passing a playground on the right and the pond on the left. Small yellow circles are blazed on trees.

15. Easy cruising now on a wide carriage road through pine groves as you circle the pond, following the yellow blazes. After passing another playground, the path forks. Bear right, leaving the yellow-blazed trail.

16. Turn right at the next intersection onto a wide carriage path blazed with green circles (#2053).

17. Continue to follow the green circles as the path becomes a narrow paved road. At the junction with two dirt roads (#2070), make a hard right onto Bugbee Path (also blazed with green circles), the unpaved road that is a little higher than the paved road. At this point you will have traveled 1.1 miles from the parking area.

18. Proceed for 0.3 mile (1.4 miles) until you reach intersection #2096. Turn right, leaving the green-blazed trail.

19. Continue straight on the wide carriage road through the next fork. Remain on the road until you reach #2140, where you bear right.

20. Continue straight through intersection #2190 until the path appears to be heading out to the road (2.4 miles). Bear left on Forest Path before you reach the barrier that separates the road from the trail.

21. Proceed on Forest Path for 0.7 mile (3.1 miles), pass two huge glacial erratics (boulders dragged off the hills by glacial movement), and turn left at #2175.

22. The trail leads to Chickatawbut Road, where you have the option of turning left onto the paved road for 0.5 mile and reentering the reservation, or attempting to ride over a steep, rocky single-track where you may have to dismount frequently. The third choice is to attempt the trail and if you tire, bail out, which is easy to do as the path parallels the road.

23. If you choose to ride on the road, you can reenter the reservation at the next parking area, across from Hillside Pond about 0.5 mile ahead. After reentering, the trail forks. Bear left and follow the green blazes.

24. After 0.2 mile (3.9 miles total), bear right onto a carriage path. Continue straight through intersection #2081, following the green blazes.

25. At 4.3 miles, turn right onto a gravel driveway leading to a paved storage area.

26. Turn left at #2054, remaining on the paved road for a great downhill run.

27. The path heads toward the bathhouse and up to a No Bicycles Beyond This Point sign. Turn right at the sign, pedal behind the picnic benches, and follow the path until you return to the parking lot.

22

BOSTON HARBOR ISLANDS

GEORGES/LOVELLS/PEDDOCKS

Distance and Difficulty: The trip from Boston to Georges Island takes 45 minutes. Allow 30 minutes to travel between islands on a water taxi. A leisurely walk around 28-acre Georges Island takes about 45 minutes. Touring Fort Warren on Georges Island takes one to two hours. Allow one hour to explore Lovells Island and two for Peddocks.

Much cheaper than a cruise and a lot closer than the Caribbean, this boat tour of the islands in Boston Harbor offers many of the advantages of an expensive voyage. There's the same sense of excitement when the boat leaves land and embarks toward unknown territory. Salt air and cooling breezes both calm and invigorate. After a day near the ocean, one is enveloped by a feeling of total relaxation.

Seagulls hover as passengers dip into their picnic baskets while listening to the captain narrate the history of the harbor and its islands. After cruising for 45 minutes, the ship arrives at its first destination, Georges Island. Visitors can remain on Georges or jump on a free water taxi for further island hopping.

Seven of the 30 Boston Harbor islands compose the Boston Harbor Islands State Park. The water taxi stops at six of them. Since three islands are the most one can explore comfortably in a day, I will guide you through the three largest: Georges, Lovells, and Peddocks. Gallops, Bumpkin, and Grape Islands, although not toured in this book, are certainly worth visiting. You will find no fortresses on these small pristine islands, but rather picnic areas overlooking pebbly beaches, campsites along wooded hills, and hiking trails through woods dotted with wildflowers and berries.

The Metropolitan District Commission (MDC), a state agency that has administered these islands for more than 50 years, staffs friendly, knowledgeable rangers at each one.

Transportation: By automobile: Boston Harbor Cruises boats depart from Lynn Heritage State Park, Hewitts Cove in Hingham, and Boston's Long Wharf. To reach Long Wharf from Route 93, if driving from the north, take Exit 24 (Callahan Tunnel). At the stop sign at the end of the exit ramp, continue straight through a busy intersection to the parking lot near the wharf. From the south, take Exit 22 (Atlantic Avenue/Northern Avenue). Go straight on Atlantic Avenue for 0.3 mile until you reach the parking lot in front of the New England Aquarium. Long Wharf is just north of the aquarium and east of State Street.

By public transportation: Hop on the MBTA Blue Line to the Aquarium station. Long Wharf is just north of the station.

The walks around the island, although generally pretty easy, require some agility to scramble over rocks and balance on sea walls.

Food and Drink: Snacks and drinks can be purchased on the boat to Georges Island, and a small snack bar is located on Georges Island. Drinking water and serviceable barbecue grills are available only on Georges Island.

Restrooms: Located on the boats and all islands.

Fees: At time of publication, the round-trip adult fare to Georges Island was $8.00; seniors, and children, $6.00. The boat to Georges runs on a regular schedule daily from May 1 through Columbus Day. There is no charge for the water taxi that runs daily during the summer. The taxi operates on weekends only between Memorial Day and July 1, and between Labor Day and Columbus Day. For up-to-date information on departure times and rates, call the Metropolitan District Commission at 617-727-5290 or Boston Harbor Cruises at 617-227-4321.

Recreational Options: Swimming only on Lovells Island. Fishing and camping on all islands except Georges (for free permit, call 617-727-5290). Wheelbarrows, lined up at the dock, are available to carry equipment to the campsites.

Background: Most of the islands are drumlins formed during the Pleistocene Ice Age by the glacier as it inched its way southward about 16,000 years ago. As the ice sheet moved, it gathered up clay, sand, and stones, and then compressed this debris into smooth-sloped hills called drumlins.

Native Americans were the first to inhabit and farm the islands. When the English arrived, they continued this farming tradition. By the 19th century, the islands were used mainly to hold fortifications.

Thompson Island is closest to Boston. The water taxi does not stop at this 157-acre island owned by the Thompson Island Outward Bound Education Center, but guided tours are available. Here Outward Bound runs a camp, a school, and educational programs.

Spectacle Island, the second on the right progressing from Boston toward Georges Island, was inhabited initially by Native Americans. During the Revolutionary War it housed a hospital and in the 1800s held a casino and factory. Spectacle Island was literally a dump in the 20th century. Now it is a receptacle for the debris excavated from underneath Boston Harbor to form the third harbor tunnel. When reconstructed, Spectacle will be the highest harbor island and is designated as a recreation area.

Next in the chain is Long Island, which is connected by a bridge to the mainland. Over the years, a fort, hospital, and homeless shelter have occupied the land.

A water treatment plant is located on Deer Island, the large land mass off to the left that connects to the mainland.

GEORGES ISLAND

The first stop, Georges Island, is the most popular. Families head for famous Fort Warren, an imposing granite fortress with inaccessible underground passages and dungeons that housed captured Confederate soldiers during the Civil War. Groups use the island's wide grassy expanses to play volleyball, softball, and soccer or to laze in the sun.

Native Americans were probably the island's first occupants. When the Puritans arrived in Boston, settler James Pemberton was already ensconced on what he called Pemberton's Island, where he remained until his death in 1682.

Water, restrooms, and a snack bar are located between the dock and fort. Pets, swimming, and alcoholic beverages are prohibited.

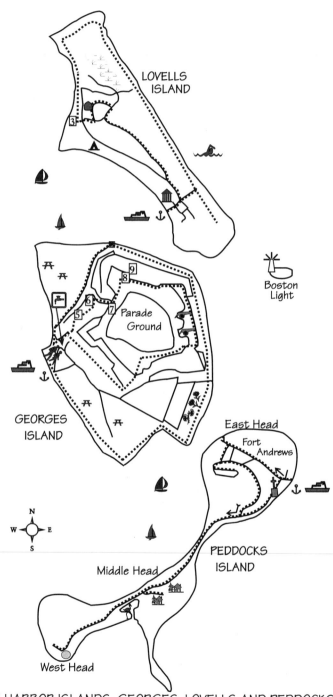

LOVELLS
ISLAND

3

Boston
Light

9
8
6
7
5
Parade
Ground

GEORGES
ISLAND

East Head

Fort
Andrews

PEDDOCKS
ISLAND

N
W   E
S

Middle Head

West Head

BOSTON HARBOR ISLANDS: GEORGES, LOVELLS AND PEDDOCKS

The Walk

1. From the dock, facing the fort, turn right and walk through the wide grassy picnic/play area toward the water for a 45-minute tour around the island's perimeter.

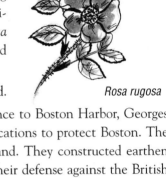

   If you are visiting during late spring or summer, you will be surrounded by the bright pink blossoms of the sand-loving shrub ***Rosa rugosa.*** Often planted to stabilize the sand on beaches and dunes, *Rosa regosa's* showy blooms turn to round bright red rose hips in the fall.

   Rosa rugosa

2. Follow the sea wall as it circles the island.

   Because of its location at the entrance to Boston Harbor, Georges Island was the logical choice for fortifications to protect Boston. The French were the first to fortify the island. They constructed earthen embankments to aid the colonists in their defense against the British during the American Revolution. At the beginning of the 19th century, the United States government set aside money for a major fortification. The sea wall, constructed in 1829, was the first step in the process. The wall slowed the island's erosion, as did forbidding passing ships to remove sand and gravel for use as ballast during storms.

   The sandy beach is covered with black mussel shells. A popular dish in Europe, this mollusk is rapidly replacing the higher-priced clam on menus in Boston restaurants. Better not take any home; mussels harvested from polluted water are not safe to eat.

   After rounding the corner, a view to the south exposes two peninsulas extending into the water. The longer one is the town of Hull; the shorter is World's End Reservation, located in Hingham (explored in chapter 40).

   Near the sea wall on the east side, wildflowers flourish amidst tall sea grass. The harmless-looking tiny purple flowers with protruding yellow centers belong to a vine with a frightening name—**deadly nightshade**, sometimes referred to as **bittersweet nightshade**. The names refer to the poisonous bright red berries that appear in autumn, which first taste bitter, then sweet.

Another lovely plant with an unlovely name, **cow vetch**, decorates the fields with pea-like lavender flowers. Its narrow pairs of leaflets resemble those found on spruce trees. In summer, **oxeye daisies**, with their familiar "he loves me, he loves me not" small white petals, grow all over the island.

Cow vetch

The eastern side of the sea wall has deteriorated, necessitating rock hopping. Interspersed with the large slabs of granite, flat-topped clusters emerge from another common white flower, **yarrow**. Early settlers crushed its fernlike leaves and used them to stop the flow of blood from wounds and to ease itchy rashes. From the boiled leaves they brewed a medicinal tea, believed to break a fever by increasing perspiration.

The view across the ocean to the east reveals Boston Light on Little Brewster Island. Boston Light, our nation's oldest active lighthouse, was first constructed in 1716. It was rebuilt in 1782 after being destroyed by the British during the Revolution in 1776.

(Three other Brewster Islands, Great, Middle, and Outer, are perched behind Boston Light. Great Brewster, to the left of Boston Light and in front of the other Brewsters, is shaped like a whale. Calf and Little Calf lie east of the Brewsters.)

Beyond the battered sea wall on the island's north side sits Gallops Island on the left, Deer Island straight ahead, and Lovells Island, our next stop, to the right.

3. Upon reaching an iron gate, the sea wall suddenly stops. Inch around the gate and head inland toward the fort. Pass the picnic tables. Don't miss the fine view of the Boston skyline from this northwest side of the island.

4. Turn left to enter Fort Warren through its main entrance.

Imagine what manpower was required to construct this imposing fort! Construction began in 1833. Stonemasons, carpenters, laborers, blacksmiths, horses, and oxen spent more than 10 years on Georges Island moving hills, cutting and facing each block of granite, hauling huge stones, and constructing the mammoth fortress.

Because of Fort Warren's remote location, the fortress had to be large enough to fend off enemy attack without help from the mainland.

It was built to accommodate 1,500 troops and artillery. So much granite was needed to form its 12-foot-thick foundation walls that new quarries had to be developed in Quincy and Cape Ann.

Its design, based on 17th-century military theories, is reminiscent of well-fortified French castles. Troops were positioned behind the outer wall (covered with earth to absorb cannon fire), set to attack any landing party. A further deterrent was the moat (now dry), which impeded the attackers and gave the gunners time to aim and fire. Stone ramparts, also covered with earth, absorbed fire and supported cannons. Bastions, or arrowhead-shaped corners on the ramparts, allowed soldiers to shoot the approaching enemy from three different points.

Fort Warren's first prisoners arrived in 1861 during the Civil War. Although the fort often contained more than 1,000 Confederates, only 13 prisoners died, earning it a reputation as one of the most humane prisons on either side of the conflict.

Fort Warren was used for defensive purposes through World War II, after which the Defense Department decommissioned the fort. When the General Services Administration sold the islands in 1957, the MDC purchased Georges and Lovells Islands.

5. Go up the walkway and stop at the guardhouse on the left.

6. After you have finished investigating the guardhouse, continue up the ramp. Before turning right to enter the fort, turn left to visit the *demi-lune,* a French term to describe the half-moon shape of this granite building. Its rounded design allowed soldiers to guard both the north and west sides of the fort and protect the front entrance from attack.

7. Retrace your steps and walk past the immense oak door through the fort's main entrance, called the sallyport.

8. Upon entering the parade ground, where the troops assembled, turn left, head into a small cul-de-sac, and keep your eyes open for the Ramparts Walk sign.

9. Ascend the spiral staircase that leads to the ramparts and signal tower.

10. Head toward the tower, built during the Spanish-American War. Climb to the top for an overview of the fort and surrounding islands.

11. From the base of the tower, walk along the rampart where the cannons had been mounted.

12. Follow the rampart around until you reach the stairway at the southern corner.

13. Unless you wish to investigate Fort Warren further, descend the stairs, leave the fort, and return to the dock to visit Lovells and Peddocks Islands.

Lovells Island

The only island with a lifeguard-supervised beach, Lovells also boasts Lovers Rock, a mysterious underground tunnel, campsites, and remnants of Fort Standish within its 62 acres.

The island was occupied by fishermen and farmers until threats of attack during the Spanish-American War increased Boston's awareness of its own vulnerability. In 1900 the Defense Department built Fort Standish.

Allow an hour to circle the island and visit its sites.

The Walk

1. To reach the beach from the dock, walk past the gazebo straight across to the east side of the island.

   The beach here is rocky, although it becomes sandier as you walk farther into the unsupervised section. Plan on a refreshing dip; the water temperature rises no higher than 60° to 65°.

   If you turn right at the intersection on the path that leads to the beach, you'll walk through the former parade ground where military drills were held. At the southern tip, you'll see remnants of the gun emplacements.

2. After returning to the beach and turning left, you'll soon reach the sea wall.

   From the beach, the eastern view encompasses Boston Light and the four Brewster Islands. The sea wall soon deteriorates, requiring rock hopping. If you are considering heading into the wooded area adjacent to the beach, don't bother. No discernible path runs through this marshy section.

   As you walk around the end of the island, you'll spot more gun emplacements, positioned to protect the island's northwestern tip.

   Be careful of rubbing up against the leaves or flowers of **jimson weed**, which flourishes on the islands. Contact with its pretty white, trumpet-shaped flowers or long, irregularly lobed leaves can cause the skin to swell and turn red. Actually, all parts of this plant are poisonous. It often grows in fields where cattle and sheep have grazed on it and then died. Children have been poisoned when they have eaten its prickly egg-shaped fruit.

The footing is surer on the island's west side, where the beach is covered with ground seashells and small pebbles.

3. Keep your eyes open for a path from the beach that has stairs to the rounded hill rising over much of the island.

An old studded door to the left of the stairs (now boarded up and filled in) led to a tunnel (now partially caved in) that extended as far as Georges Island. Although many tales are connected with this mysterious passageway, the door actually led to a torpedo shoot, and the passageway was nothing more than wide pipelines that connected the mines between Lovells and Georges Islands.

4. After climbing the stairs, turn left at the fork and then bear left to reach Lovers Rock, sitting in a clearing on your left.

The rock marks the site of a tragedy that occurred in 1786 after a winter storm destroyed a vessel carrying 13 passengers. All survived the wreck. They scrambled ashore on Lovells Island and took refuge near a huge granite boulder. Unfortunately, the night was brutally cold and all the passengers froze to death. When rescue crews discovered the bodies, they found two young lovers huddled next to the rock, frozen in a final embrace.

5. Pass Lovers Rock and bear right.

6. At the fork, bear right.

The path winds through a forest of **staghorn sumac**, which has grown from its usual shrub size to tree stature. Staghorn sumac is the dominant vegetation on the harbor islands because it thrives in sandy soil and grows rapidly. In autumn, its leaves turn bright red and its fuzzy red berries draw many varieties of birds. Its name refers to the soft hairy covering on its branches, similar to the downy coating on a stag's antlers when "in velvet." This covering differentiates staghorn sumac from poison sumac, which has smooth, black-speckled branches.

7. The trail leads to a paved walkway that runs down the center of the island. The path to the left leads to the beach on the east side. Turn right to investigate what is left of Fort Standish.

Most of the campsites are located to the right of the roadway. Outhouses sit just beyond the campsites.

If you visit in August, be on the lookout for succulent blackberries. Unfortunately, their thorny branches guarantee challenging picking.

8. The road returns to the first intersection. Turn right to reach the dock.

PEDDOCKS ISLAND

The largest and most topographically diverse island in this tour, Peddocks is divided into three distinct sections. East Head is defined by the remnants of Fort Andrews. Middle Head is filled with summer cottages, and remote West Head contains a freshwater pond and wildlife sanctuary. Allow two hours for wandering around the island.

Located only a quarter-mile from the town of Hull, Peddocks's accessibility allowed Native Americans and English settlers to graze their animals on its 185 acres with no need for fences nor fear of predators. Farming ceased around the turn of the century, when the United States government convinced Eliza Andrews, widow of John Andrews, the governor of Massachusetts during the Civil War, to donate 88 acres of land to be used for defensive purposes.

During the early 1900s, summer resorts shared the island with the military installation. A proprietor of one of the inns, John Irwin, was arrested for conducting gambling houses. Because Irwin was also Peddocks's police chief, he was released with a small fine.

The Walk

1. From the dock, walk straight to East Head, the location of what was once Fort Andrews.

The fort was heavily used during World War I. Troops were trained here during World War II, until the military decided that Peddocks was the perfect spot to hold 1,800 Italian prisoners of war. After the war ended, the fort was decommissioned and the state took over management of the island.

Large, soaring broad-winged and red-tailed hawks as well as a variety of owls nest among the maples, oaks, and fruit trees around the fort. Planted by the army, the largest trees are about 60 years old.

2. After exploring the fort, follow the path that leads to 47 cottages, belonging to hardy individuals who spend the summer without water or electricity.

3. Bear right at the fork to walk on the sandbar to the beach on the north side of the island.

    On this spit of sand between two drumlins you'll discover a vastly different ecosystem. Barraged by blasts of salt air and water, only the hardy plants survive. *Rosa rugosa* and bright yellow **butter-and-eggs**, a member of the snapdragon family, bloom here throughout the summer.

    If visiting in midsummer, keep your eyes open for **highbush blueberries** growing near the cottages. This tall multistemmed shrub has small elliptical leaves that turn bright red in autumn.

    A small salt marsh lies between Middle Head and West Head. Here you may spot such birds as common and snowy egrets, belted kingfishers, oystercatchers, least and common terns, and great blue herons.

4. Continue on to the uninhabited West Head. Dense underbrush in this section prevents exploration anywhere but along the trail and by the water.

5. As the path skirts the southern edge of the island, you'll come upon a small brackish pond (except after a very dry summer) formed by the runoff from West Head. You may see black ducks and mallards paddling around. Two white bars bordering a blue wing patch distinguish the mallard from the black duck.

6. On the return, bear right at the fork to ascend Central Hill on the island's south side, the site of most of the private cottages.

7. Descend the hill and follow the path back to the dock, passing the small white chapel built to serve the soldiers at Fort Andrew. Several couples have exchanged wedding vows here.

23

BACK BAY

BEACON HILL

 Distance and Difficulty: Allow one hour at the John Hancock Observatory. The actual Back Bay–Beacon Hill walk is 2 miles and takes about an hour. Plan on spending at least another hour going in and out of buildings (several of the stops offer tours) and generally poking around.

Where do I bring visitors when I want to show them the quintessential Boston, when I want to impress them with the city's charm and history? To the Back Bay and Beacon Hill. Both adults and children love this walk, which includes all my favorite "must-sees," from Trinity Church to the Ducklings and Swan Boats.

This historical and architectural tour begins on the top floor of the tallest building in New England, at the John Hancock Observatory, which truly offers an overview of Boston. The walk proceeds through the stately Back Bay, meanders around the colorful Public Garden, climbs quaint Beacon Hill to the gold-domed State House, crosses Boston Common, and ends at the Park Street Ⓣ Station.

Transportation: Nearby MBTA stations—Back Bay Station (Orange Line), Copley Station (Green Line). Tour ends at the Park Street Ⓣ Station— Green and Red Lines, about a mile from the starting point. See Ⓣ on map.

Parking: Parking lots are located on Clarendon Street between Saint James Avenue and Boylston Street, on Tremont Street across from Boston Common, and in the Boston Common Underground Garage.

Food and Drink: A few of the many food purveyors are: Spasso, Italian restaurant on the corner of Dartmouth and Commonwealth Avenue; DeLuca's Market, 11 Charles Street; Rebecca's Bakery, takeout on the west corner of Charles and Mount Vernon Streets; Figs, pizza, pasta, and sandwiches, 42 Charles Street.

Restrooms: John Hancock Observatory, Boston Public Library, State House.

Fees: John Hancock Observatory, Swan Boats, Nichols House Museum (617-227-6993).

Recreational Options: Cross-country skiing on Boston Common and the Public Garden, in-line and ice-skating on Boston Common and Commonwealth Mall, tennis courts on the Common.

Background: Until 1857 the Back Bay really was a bay; specifically, a tidal estuary. At high tide, water covered the area from the John Hancock Tower down to the Charles River. At low tide, this section became smelly tidal flats. No one objected when the city's legislature voted to create more land to accommodate the growing population by filling 450 acres of odorous marsh. On each day of the next 30 years, trains with 35 cars ran every 45 minutes carting sand and gravel from a western suburb and dumping it in the Back Bay.

THE WALK

1. Begin at the corner of Trinity Place and Saint James Avenue, at the **John Hancock Observatory** (1). On a clear day, the panorama from the top of the 790-foot tower is well worth the price of admission. However, the observatory offers more than a chance to have a bird's-eye view of Boston; it also provides a visual history through photos and maps, an entertaining diorama of major historical events, and a taped narration of Boston's development by Walter Muir Whitehill, a noted architectural historian.

    This walk travels back in time, starting with the tallest and most controversial addition to Boston's skyline, the **John Hancock Building**. Its construction began in 1968, but it fell victim to major problems and was not ready for occupancy until 1976.

    From a distance the tower, designed by Henry Cobb, an architect in I. M. Pei's firm, was intended as a symbolic marker shimmering in the Boston skyline. Up close, its unusual mirrored facade became a reflective

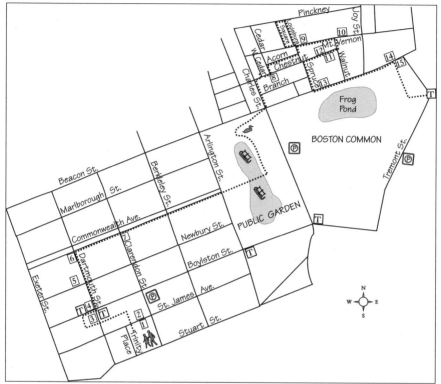

BACK BAY–BEACON HILL

backdrop for the massive stone buildings around it, particularly the celebrated Trinity Church in Copley Square. But the construction of the soaring Hancock tower did more than mirror the church. By disrupting the delicate balance in the water table of the sandy Back Bay, it caused the weighty church to sink. The church's tower alone weighs 11 million pounds and rests on 2,000 wooden pilings which have to remain submerged in water. Engineers monitoring the water level below the church discovered that during and after the tower's construction, the pilings holding up the church were no longer submerged. The John Hancock Insurance Company then had to install pumps to regulate the water level below the church.

Another crisis arose when swirling winds caused many of the windows on the 60-story tower to pop out, fall to the ground, and shatter, threatening the safety of all who passed by. Construction crews quickly walled off the building and then replaced every one of the 10,334 thermopaned glass wall panels with single sheets of tempered safety glass.

At the same time, engineers installed on the 58th floor a tuned mass damper, two rolling weights on a film of oil, to counter wind stress and prevent the building from swaying.

After solving all these problems, a consultant was hired to guarantee the building's safety. Unfortunately, he discovered that the Hancock, under certain conditions, could topple over. To eliminate that possibility, the tower was stiffened from its base to its top with 1,500 tons of diagonal steel braces.

2. Cross Saint James Avenue to **Trinity Church** (2), voted the ninth-greatest building in American history by members of the American Institute of Architects. The members also chose Henry Hobson Richardson, the designer of Trinity Church, as the third-greatest American architect. (Frank Lloyd Wright was number one.)

The Hancock tower may be an eye-catcher, but Trinity Church, constructed in 1877 in the Romanesque style, continues to be a focal point of the Back Bay, with its massive square tower rising above a stolid, craggy granite exterior. Richardson softened the church's large scale by embellishing it with an intricate red-sandstone design and adding a red-tile roof.

The inside of this Episcopalian church is as rich in detail as the outside. Richardson persuaded John La Farge (now often described as "the father of mural painting in the United States") to paint the plastered walls. Note La Farge's paintings on the walls of the tower, in the nave, over the windows, and above the arches. While a few of the colorful stained-glass windows denoting religious events were designed by La Farge, most were created by English and French artists.

Guided tours are available each Sunday, following the noon service. During the summer, a guide is usually available throughout the day to answer questions.

3. Cross Copley Plaza (which hosts an open-air market on summer Sundays and Bostix, where you can purchase tickets to local shows at half-price on the day of the performance) to the Dartmouth Street entrance to the **Boston Public Library** (3). The handicapped-accessible entrance is on Boylston Street.

This perfectly proportioned building, designed by the architects McKim, Mead, and White in the Neoclassical style, was completed in 1895. The library's detailed exterior and interior not only please the eye but also educate. Below the window arches you'll see names of the great masters of art, science, religion, and statesmanship inscribed on the tablets. Nearby hangs the central keystone, where the sculptors Domingo Mora and Augustus Saint-Gaudens carved the head of Minerva, the Greek goddess of wisdom.

From Dartmouth Street, enter the library via the main entrance hall and pass through three pairs of bronze doors sculpted by Daniel Chester French, representing music and poetry (left), knowledge and wisdom (center), and truth and romance (right). Look up at the vaulted ceiling to see the names of 30 famous Bostonians inlaid in the marble mosaic. The huge marble lions protecting the marbled main staircase were sculpted by Louis Saint-Gaudens.

As you climb the stairs, look for the murals lining the main stairwell that were painted by France's greatest muralist, Pierre Puvis de Chavannes, who stated that he "sought to represent under a symbolic form and in a single view the intellectual treasures collected in this beautiful building." On the right staircase wall you'll find three panels depicting pastoral, dramatic, and epic poetry. History, astronomy, and philosophy are depicted on the left. Chemistry and physics are painted on either side of the window. Another major composition of nine Greek muses by Puvis de Chavannes covers the upper corridor wall.

A welcome architectural surprise awaits you after your descent from the main staircase: a spacious courtyard that appears to have been transported from a Roman palace. The benches provide a convenient spot to rest, picnic, or reflect on all you've seen.

Exit from the library on the Boylston Street side through a modern addition designed by the noted architect Philip Johnson. This section serves as the general library, while the original building is used for research.

Guided tours of the building are conducted several times a week. Check at the information desk for the schedule. The library is closed on Sundays.

4. Cross Boylston Street and stop at the **New Old South Church** (4) on the corner of Dartmouth Street.

Its catchy name was created after the Old South Church moved from its original site on Washington Street in 1875. Feast your eyes on its ornate facade of Italian Gothic design decorated with zebra-striped arches, multicolored stone inlays, and intricate ironwork.

5. Continue on Dartmouth Street and cross Newbury Street, home to many upscale shops, restaurants, and art galleries. Don't miss the *trompe l'oeil* on the building owned by the DuBarry French restaurant that faces the parking lot on the corner of Dartmouth and Newbury Streets.

    The mural of the **Café DuBarry** (5) was painted as a tribute to the arts and requires close inspection. Seven of the mural's windows contain details of famous paintings, including the self-portraits of both Picasso and Rembrandt. Peering out from the balcony are such famous entertainers and theatrical characters as Sammy Davis Jr. and the Phantom of the Opera. Crammed on the steps and patio are 62 well-known people who have ties to the Boston area. See if you can spot Ben Franklin, Leonard Bernstein, or Babe Ruth.

6. Walk down Dartmouth to its intersection with Commonwealth Avenue, one of the most elegant streets in Boston. Its 100-foot-wide promenade, filled with trees, benches, and statues, was designed to resemble the Champs-Elysées in Paris.

    Bostonians prospered at the turn of the century, and the new rich displayed their wealth by replicating European grandeur. They rejected the spare Federal-style brick dwellings on Beacon Hill in favor of ornate, massive granite structures. These homes were designed by prominent architects who spared no expense in providing their patrons with luxurious accommodations.

    An excellent example of 19th-century Victorian architecture borrowed from the French Renaissance style sits on the southwest corner of Dartmouth and Commonwealth Avenue. The **Hotel Vendome** (6) was constructed in 1871 for the then incredible sum of one-million dollars. Although known as Boston's most fashionable hotel, with such luxuries as private bathrooms and steam heat, it went the way of many large public buildings and was transformed into condominiums. One of the few restaurants on Commonwealth Avenue, Spasso, occupies its ground floor.

7. Turn right on Commonwealth Avenue. You can either walk on the sidewalk or cross the street and walk along Commonwealth Mall.

If you glance at both sides of the street you'll notice that the dwellings appear to flow together. This harmonious, aesthetically pleasing architecture was not by chance. Strict controls regulated height, setback from the street, and materials used in each building.

Unlike most of Boston's former cart-paths-turned-roads, the streets in the Back Bay were laid out in an orderly fashion. The alleys, built for servant and delivery access, run beside the homes' rear entrances. The first letter of each street name follows the alphabet, beginning at the Public Garden with **A**rlington Street and progressing westward to **H**ereford.

On the corner of Clarendon and Commonwealth Avenue rests the **First Baptist Church** (7). Constructed in 1872, it was one of H. H. Richardson's first designs. He created the rough, mottled facade of this Romanesque-style building by using a local conglomerate stone called Roxbury puddingstone. The square tower is decorated by a frieze modeled by Bartholdi, the sculptor of the Statue of Liberty. The trumpeting angels perched on the tower's corners are responsible for its nickname, "Church of the Holy Bean Blowers."

As you walk the next two blocks toward the Public Garden, look around at the many interesting architectural details. You'll see bay windows and bow-fronts that created more space for light to enter the narrow, flat facades. The top floors, which housed the servants, have the smallest windows, whereas the entry-level floors, where residents entertained guests, often had the largest windows. Note the different roof treatments, the variation in front entrances, and the number and types of chimneys. The multiple chimneys on each roof reflected the inefficiency of the heating methods used at the turn of the century. Most homes relied on gravity hot-water systems that barely heated the bottom two floors.

The Boston Center for Adult Education at 5 Commonwealth Avenue boasts one of the Back Bay's most elegant ballrooms. If the building is open, you may be able to explore the interior.

8. Cross Arlington Street and walk through the iron gates into the **Public Garden**, the first public botanical garden in the United States.

Local citizens conceived the idea for the garden when, disgusted by the foul odor emanating from the marshy area, they voted to fill it. In 1838, 17 Bostonians became "Proprietors of the Botanic Garden," a designation that gave them the authority to plant flowers. Although the land later reverted back to the city, the Massachusetts legislature ordained that the garden be preserved for public use. Now the Boston Parks and Recreation Department is responsible for the upkeep and seasonal transplanting of thousands of plants from the department's greenhouses to the garden.

The formidable bronze statue that overlooks this entrance to the garden is of George Washington. Vandals frequently destroyed his bronze sword, so it is made now of unbreakable fiberglass.

9. Cross the water on one of the world's smallest suspension bridges. The famous **Swan Boats** sit in the pond on your right.

The boats were designed in 1877 by Robert Paget, whose family continues to operate them. You can hop on one of the Swan Boats, perhaps pedaled by a fifth-generation Paget, and go for a 12-minute ride any time between April and November.

Boston's famous Swan Boats are a prime attraction of the Public Garden. (Photo by Marny Ashburne)

10. Turn left onto the path with the large American elm tree on the corner.

11. Bear left at the fork.

The tree on your right with the abundant drooping branches is a weeping European beech.

12. Follow this path and continue bearing to the right.

On the right side you'll spot Mrs. Mallard and her ducklings marching alongside the path. The duck family was sculpted in 1987 by Nancy Schön, who modeled them after the ducks who take up residence in the Public Garden in the children's book *Make Way for Ducklings* by Robert McCloskey. By the way, the names of Mrs. Mallard's eight ducklings are Jack, Kack, Lack, Mack, Nack, Ouack, Pack, and Quack.

13. Continue on the path until you reach the corner of Beacon and Charles Streets. Cross Beacon.

To your left at 84 Beacon Street is the Hampshire House, whose bar, the Bull & Finch, was the inspiration for the award-winning television series *Cheers*.

14. Head up the right side of Charles Street, an area occupied mainly by antique shops and food suppliers.

15. Take your second right onto Chestnut Street. Cross to the left side of Chestnut to begin the climb up the south slope of Beacon Hill, a name derived from a pot of pitch that sat on top of a tall wooden mast. This beacon was placed on the hill's summit and was lit to warn residents of impending danger.

Until 1795, the south slope belonged to John Singleton Copley, an English portrait painter, who told his American agent to sell his land. Five prominent Bostonians formed a syndicate, the Mount Vernon Proprietors, to buy Copley's 18.5 acres for the grand sum of $18,000. As in the Back Bay, the developers carefully laid out the streets. They named most of the main roads after trees and the smaller side streets after parts of trees (such as Branch and Acorn).

The first settlers on Beacon Hill were English people who built simple brick homes that resembled English dwellings. A close inspection of the unbroken facades reveals three distinct styles of house design, each representing the decades in which the homes were built. Facades with arched entrances indicate the Federal style and were built between 1800 and 1820. A doorway flanked by posts that support a horizontal beam called a lintel represents the Greek Revival style popular from 1830 to 1850. Scattered around the hill are a few large-proportioned Victorian entrances constructed between 1850 to 1890. The exteriors often were embellished by wrought-iron balconies, gates, hitching posts, and boot scrapers.

16. Take a quick peek down Cedar Lane Way, lined with tiny homes that formerly housed servants and with backyards of houses facing onto West Cedar Street. Some of the fenced-in gardens open every spring for the annual Beacon Hill Garden Tour.

17. Return to Chestnut Street.

Number 57A, on the corner of Chestnut and West Cedar Streets, belongs to the **Harvard Musical Association** (8). Turn the corner onto West Cedar to find the iron lyre set into the brick facade. The association began in 1837 when several Harvard graduates gathered to perform music together. A major focus of the group was to promote musical taste and science at Harvard, where there was no music department. In 1892, the association purchased this building. A concert hall was added in 1913, courtesy of Julia Marsh, the widow of Jordan Marsh, founder of one of Boston's largest department stores. Her legacy stipulated that the hall be open to the community for pleasure playing and that her paintings hang permanently on the walls.

18. From West Cedar, take your first right onto Acorn Street. Climb up this narrow cobblestone street flanked by simple small homes, once occupied by coachmen who worked for families living in the grander homes nearby.

19. When you reach the end of Acorn, turn left on Willow Street, cross Mount Vernon Street, and make a loop around the park in the center of **Louisburg Square**.

The square's earliest residents solved the problem of park maintenance by creating the first homeowners' association in the country. In 1844, 22 neighbors agreed to "pay an equal proportion of expenses of keeping in repair and embellishing the ground enclosed within said Square." When the Proprietors of Louisburg Square had their trees trimmed, the wood was divided into 22 stacks, one delivered to each house. The wrought iron fence that surrounds the park appeared after boys vandalized the statues of Aristides and Columbus. The Proprietors then voted to forever protect the park from outsiders. Louisa May Alcott moved from her home in Concord to #10 Louisburg Square after she received substantial royalties from her popular books.

Louisburg Square is an excellent example of the Greek Revival style of architecture. The lower row of homes, on the west side, although not quite as elaborate as the homes on the higher level, are beautifully constructed in their understated way. Notice how the entrance floor is elevated so that windows and a service door on the basement level are above ground. This design allowed servants and deliverymen easy access to the kitchen, which was located in the lower level. Because of the great demand for living space on the Hill, many of these basements have become separate apartments.

20. After your exploration of the square, turn left and ascend Mount Vernon Street.

Here you'll find some of the grandest homes on Beacon Hill, many designed by Charles Bulfinch, a member of the Mount Vernon Proprietors. Bulfinch, a highly regarded architect, designed three homes for Harrison Gray Otis, a lawyer and politician, who was one of the wealthiest proprietors. Otis's first house, built in 1796, is located at 141 Cambridge Street. Owned and operated by the Society for the Preservation of New England Antiquities, it is the only Bulfinch-designed house open to the public.

Bulfinch built the twin houses at numbers 87 and 89 Mount Vernon Street. He intended to live at number 87, but as he also was involved in designing and investing in the construction of 18 other buildings, he could not afford to keep it. The energetic Bulfinch also found time to serve as head of the board of selectmen and as Boston's chief of police. Unfortunately, his energy could not compensate for his poor investments and he spent much of his life trying to get out of debt.

The mansion at number 85, completed in 1802, is the **Second Harrison Gray Otis House** (9). The entrance lies adjacent to the cobblestone driveway that leads also to what were stables but now are separate residences. By designing a large free-standing home, Bulfinch tried to set a precedent for future houses in his development. However, most settlers could not afford mansions. Smaller homes joined at a common wall replaced Bulfinch's dream, although his designs did set the standard for homes built in the following decades. Large elegant windows outlined by recessed arches enhanced the floor where hosts welcomed their guests.

Continue up the hill to the low row houses on the right side at numbers 60–50. These dwellings are considerably lower than others on the street because they were originally stables. The owner, who lived behind the stables on Chestnut Street, placed a height restriction on any structure on the property so that the view from her house never would be obscured.

Farther up the street at numbers 57–51 are the four Mason Houses, built by Jonathan Mason, another major force behind the Mount Vernon Proprietors. Hoping to attract further development, Mason commissioned Bulfinch to design homes for his four daughters. Three of the residences have undergone substantial changes. However, the **Nichols House Museum** (10) at number 55 has been preserved. Because Rose Nichols, the former occupant, stipulated in her will that her house and furnishings be left intact and open to the public, curious visitors have the opportunity to explore the interior of this Beacon Hill home filled with its original furnishings. A guide leads 40-minute tours on Monday, Wednesday, and Saturday afternoons from June through September, and occasional afternoons during the other months.

21. Return down the south side of Mount Vernon until you reach Walnut Street. Turn left.

22. Take your first right onto Chestnut Street.

On your left at numbers 6–8 are two houses with a shared entrance that belong to the **Society of Friends** (11). When the dwellings were constructed in 1804, each had a side garden. Twenty years later the new owner built homes in the side lots, a common practice on desirable Beacon Hill.

Between 1910 and 1920, Mr. and Mrs. Edwin Greene purchased both houses and constructed passageways on each floor to link the two buildings. The entire first floor became a music room and the second floor contained a large library. The Greenes were generous and often invited college students to live with them. Upon Mrs. Greene's death in 1955, her son continued the Greenes' beneficent tradition by offering the building to the New England Friends (Quakers) to use as a meeting-house and residence for students of all faiths. The house now has rooms for 20 college students, staff, and a few guests.

Across Chestnut Street at numbers 13, 15, and 17 are the **Swan Houses** (12), which were built as wedding gifts for the three Swan daughters. The matriarch, Hepzibah Swan, was clearly a forerunner of the feminist movement. She wrote in the deed for the home at number 13 that she was "desirous of limiting and appointing part of premises for advancement of her daughter, Christina Swan, free and exempt from control of husband." In 1807, the following year, she did the same for her daughter Sarah. The next year her namesake, Hepzibah, and her new husband moved into number 17.

The homes, again designed by busy Charles Bulfinch, have his distinctive recessed-arch window treatments. Look on the left side for the narrow steep alley used for carriages and cattle to go back and forth from the stables on Mount Vernon Street.

23. Take your next left onto Spruce Street. Branch Street, intersecting on your right, was called "Kitchen Street" because the servants who lived in these small houses entered the fancier dwellings on Beacon and Chestnut Streets through their rear kitchen entrances.

24. Turn left onto Beacon. Proceed up the hill until you reach number 45, the **Third Harrison Gray Otis House** (13), again designed by Bulfinch for Otis.

Apparently Otis was finally satisfied by Bulfinch's third design, as he remained in this residence for 42 years. When the dwelling was built in 1808, it was surrounded by English gardens on each side and a court-yard in the back. The waters of the Back Bay almost reached the front door. Although larger and more elegant than Otis's previous two residences, this mansion had no plumbing. Servants had to haul all the water up from the well in the backyard. Otis trudged to the nearby Tremont House for his weekly bath.

The American Meteorological Society now occupies the house.

Continue up the hill to the **State House** (14), Bulfinch's crowning architectural achievement.

Completed in 1798 for five times the sum originally budgeted, the Massachusetts State House was considered the most outstanding public building of its time. Its success enhanced Bulfinch's reputation and convinced President James Monroe to choose Bulfinch to design the first Capitol building.

The gold dome originally was covered with whitewashed wood shingles. The cupola above the dome displays a pine cone, which symbolized the importance of the lumber industry to the young New England economy. In 1802, Paul Revere's company replaced the leaky shingles with copper, which was painted gray. Seventy years later the dome was gilded with 23-carat gold leaf. The dome's glowing presence now serves as a beacon for visitors and residents. During World War II, however, fearful patriots voted to paint it black to protect the city from possible air attacks.

The building has undergone many alterations and has sextupled its size. If you wish to explore the interior, you can join one of the free guided tours given weekdays from 10:00 A.M. to 4:00 P.M. If you prefer to wander about on your own, ask the guide for the informative free pamphlet "The Massachusetts State House."

25. Cross Beacon Street at the crosswalk. Turn right and head toward Boston Common. Before you descend the stairs, don't miss the large bronze sculpture of **Robert Gould Shaw and the 54th Massachusetts Regiment** (15), situated directly across from the State House. Modeled by Augustus Saint-Gaudens, this war memorial is considered one of the finest works in Boston. This intricate bas-relief portrayed Shaw as commander of the first African-American regiment with some of his troops marching down Beacon Hill. Shaw led an unsuccessful attack in 1863 on Fort Wagner, where his regiment was outnumbered two to one. Shaw and 32 of his men were killed.

Saint-Gaudens spent 14 years working on this unusual sculpture, which reflects the courage of everyone associated with it. The freed African-American Massachusetts residents were courageous in volunteering to fight in a war where capture meant death or a return to slavery. Shaw displayed courage by commanding a troop that had no fighting experience. And Saint-Gaudens, the first white American artist to depict African Americans sympathetically, showed that he certainly was not afraid of public opinion.

26. Proceed down the stairs on the right side of the monument and walk straight across **Boston Common**, the oldest public park in the United States.

    William Blackstone, in 1625, accompanied by his 200 books, first occupied this land. In 1640 his pasture became common land used for grazing cattle.

    The Common consistently has played a significant role in Boston history. During the Revolution, British troops camped here before they marched to Lexington. Public hangings took place on the Common until the gallows were removed in 1817. One of the city's oldest cemeteries, the Central Burying Ground, lies near the intersection of Tremont and Boylston Streets. The Frog Pond, now used for skating in the winter and cooling off in the summer, originally was the site of the first water piped into the city.

27. To reach the **Park Street** Ⓣ **Station**, where the first subway line in the United States was installed in 1895, follow the red brick line in the sidewalk until the first intersection. (If you continue to follow the red brick line, you'll visit historic sites along the 3-mile-long Freedom Trail, which winds through Boston and Charlestown.) Turn left. If you go straight, you'll land at the tourist information center and Tremont Street.

    To return to Copley Square, where the walk began, you can enter the Park Street Station, head for the Green Line, and get off at Copley Station. Or you can extend your walk by one mile by turning right on Tremont Street until you reach Boylston (the next major intersection).

    Cross Boylston, turn right, and follow Boylston Street into Copley Square.

24

ARNOLD

ARBORETUM

 Distance and Difficulty: 3 miles of moderate walking; several hills.

What a way to exercise—strolling along curved walkways and soft dirt footpaths, your eyes dazzled by colorful blooms and your nostrils full of fragrant scents. This tour of the 265-acre Arnold Arboretum travels over rolling hills, through woodlands and manicured gardens as it visits many of the special botanical displays in one of the gems of Boston's Emerald Necklace.

Don't let the idyllic setting fool you. Arnold Arboretum is maintained by Harvard University as an international center for scientific research and education. Its premier collection of more than 5,000 kinds of woody plants are labeled and grouped along the main drive according to genus. Starting at the Hunnewell Visitor Center, the plants are, for the most part, in botanical sequence, from the more primitive plants, such as magnolia trees, to the more complex.

For program information and special events, call 617-524-1718.

Transportation: By automobile: From Boston and Cambridge, take Storrow Drive to the Fenway/Park Drive exit. Follow the signs first toward the Fenway and then to the Riverway, which becomes the Jamaicaway and then the Arborway. Watch for signs directing you to Arnold Arboretum.

From Routes 95/128, exit onto Route 9 east. Follow Route 9 for 7 miles to the Riverway (Route 1 south). Exit to your right toward Dedham and Providence. Proceed along the Riverway to the Jamaicaway and Arborway, following signs to the Arboretum.

From the Southeast Expressway (Route 93), take Exit 11 (Granite Avenue/Ashmont) onto Route 203 west. Follow Route 203 through Dorchester to the Arboretum.

There is limited free parking by the main gate on the Arborway (Route 203) at the junction with Centre Street (Route 1) in Jamaica Plain.

By Ⓣ: Take the MBTA Orange Line and exit at the Forest Hills station. Walk two blocks northwest along the Arborway and enter the Arboretum via the Forest Hills Gate. Take your first right onto a dirt trail named Willow Path which ends at the main gate and the Hunnewell Visitor Center, where this walk begins.

Food and Drink: A number of food shops are on Centre Street in Jamaica Plain. Pick up Centre at the rotary next to the main gate and go north a half-mile.

Restrooms: In the Hunnewell Visitor Center near the Arborway Gate. The center is open weekdays from 9:00 A.M. to 4:00 P.M. and from noon. to 4:00 P.M. on weekends. Portable restrooms are located near the bonsai house.

Recreational Options: Cross-country skiing.

Background: Two forward-thinking men, Frederick Law Olmsted and Charles Sargent, are responsible for the design of and plantings within the Arboretum. In 1872, when the Arboretum was just an idea, Sargent, professor of horticulture at Harvard University, was appointed director. Sargent did not have to choose a location since Benjamin Bussey had donated his farmland to Harvard and specified it be used as a school of agriculture and horticulture. A bequest of James Arnold, the institution's namesake, was to be used for operations. In order to reduce the cost of physically developing and then maintaining the land, Sargent worked out an arrangement whereby the Arboretum would be part of the Boston park system, with the city responsible for the cost of the Arboretum's maintenance.

City planners had hired Olmsted to create a series of parks in and around Boston. He included the Arboretum in his master plan for the park system, now referred to as Boston's Emerald Necklace (see chapter 1). Using his signature style of preserving a natural-looking landscape while creating a scenic surprise at each turn, Olmsted carved roads through the farmland's hilly terrain.

At the same time, Sargent sponsored trips around the world to gather every tree and shrub he considered hardy enough to survive the New England climate. Those from China, Korea, and Japan proved most adaptable. He then organized the huge task of assembling, growing from seed, and planting the collections throughout the Arboretum. Because of Sargent's success, specimens that are now 80 to 100 years old compose the finest collection of mature woody plants in the country.

THE WALK

1. Begin at the Hunnewell Visitor Center, to the right of the walkway, just past the main entrance (Arborway Gate). The center contains a small bookstore, restrooms, and exhibits on botany, horticulture, and the history of the Arboretum.

2. Walk up the road from the visitor center. On the right, **magnolia** and **tulip trees**, which have the most primitive structure, begin the botanical sequence. Although these species do not appear "primitive," they are described as such because of their flowers. In tracing how trees (which reproduce by the sex organs in their flowers) evolved, scientists discovered that the flowers on the magnolia and tulip trees had the simplest reproductive mechanisms.

    Sargent insisted on placing many species of the same plant side by side so visitors could study their differences. Upon examining the labels, you will discover that the collections contain Asian and European as well as American species.

    The tallest specimen in the Arboretum stands on the left, a hundred yards from the visitor center. This **silver maple** tree, distinguished by its peeling gray bark, is more than 105 feet high.

    The collection of **horse chestnut** trees, growing on the right near the cork trees, are best viewed in mid- to late May when their white bell-shaped blossoms are in full bloom. Across the road are more than 130

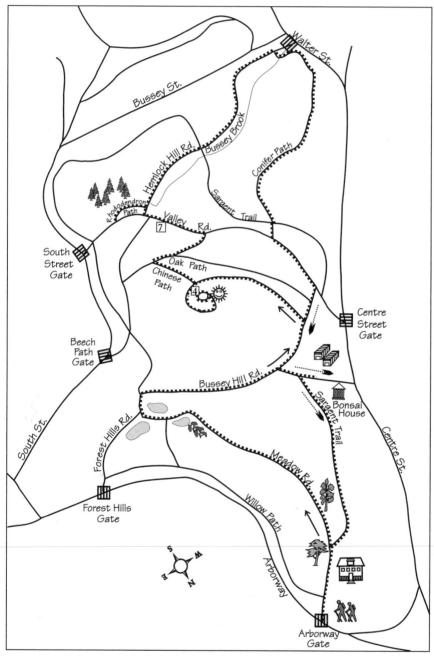

ARNOLD ARBORETUM

varieties of maple trees, at their most colorful in early to mid-October when their leaves turn vibrant orange and crimson.

Down the path from the maples, a wide assortment of **azalea** bushes with their striking multicolored flowers decorate the roadside in May.

The three man-made ponds nestled in the curve of the road are an example of Olmsted's scenic surprises. A pedestrian has no idea the ponds exist until suddenly confronting them. The high ridge, or esker, to your right was created not by Olmsted, but by a glacier 10,000 to 15,000 years ago. A stream of melting glacial water, running under the ice sheet, deposited layer upon layer of gravel and eventually formed this narrow ridge.

Between the two ponds on your left lies the Bradley Collection of Rosaceous Plants, dedicated to species of the rose family, such as potentillas, spireas, pears, cherries, crabapples, and quinces, along with many varieties of wild and cultivated roses. Don't miss this spot in June when the garden is in bloom.

3. Continue around the curve and pass the junction with Forest Hills Road, which leads to the Forest Hills Gate.

    The Arboretum is known worldwide for its collection of 450 varieties of **lilacs**, located ahead on the left. If you are visiting in mid-May, their sweet scent previews the coming visual attraction. One of the largest collections in North America, the lilacs draw thousands of visitors, particularly on Lilac Sunday, the third Sunday in May.

4. Turn left to ascend Bussey Hill. Several of the Arboretum's showcase trees are displayed near the crest of the hill: A dainty **Callery pear** purchased in China in 1908 and a **silk tree** transported from Korea in 1918 stand across from Chinese Path. In late summer and early autumn, the silk tree produces long, pink silky strands that cluster among feathery leaves with numerous small leaflets. A grove of **cedars of Lebanon**, shipped from Asia Minor in 1903, stand on the left side of your descent just before Chinese Path.

5. On the descent, turn left onto the Chinese Path, where you'll see many of the specimens naturalist Ernest Wilson brought back from China in the early 1900s. To the right stands the **dove** tree. Its name refers to its large white leaflike bracts, which resemble doves and appear in May.

To the left and behind the dove tree stands another rare, outstanding specimen, the **paper-bark maple**, distinguished by its cinnamon-colored peeling bark.

The trees with mottled bark are **stewartias**. Their flowers, which resemble camellias, bloom in the summer.

6. Continue down Chinese Path and turn right onto Oak Path.

7. Bear left across the grass until you reach Valley Road.

8. Turn left on Valley Road.

On the right side of the road you'll see a stand of **American and European hornbeam** trees whose gray, gnarled, muscular-looking branches extend toward the walkway.

Ahead on the right, look for the **dawn redwood** tree, a species reputed to have been growing for almost 200 million years and then assumed to be extinct. In the 1940s, a Chinese botanist discovered a stand and sent some seeds to the Arboretum. Because horticulturists were uncertain how well the tree would grow in this climate, its seeds were planted in various locations in the hope that at least one

Hornbeam

area would provide hospitable growing conditions. The dawn redwood proved most adaptable and flourished wherever it was planted.

If you are visiting in summer, look (or walk) down on your right at the Bussey Brook Valley, covered with wildflowers.

9. Turn right onto Hemlock Hill Road.

On your left, watch for the Linda J. Davison Rhododendron Path, that runs along the foot of Hemlock Hill. The **rhododendron** collection, begun in 1886 in this sheltered location, is protected further by the largest stand of native **hemlock** trees in Boston. A gurgling brook and two small waterfalls enhance this cool contemplative spot. It is at its best in June when the "rhodies" are in bloom.

10. Return to Hemlock Hill Road and turn left. In June, showy clusters of pinkish white flowers transform the **mountain laurel** shrubs growing on the left.

   The conifer collection occupies the land surrounding Bussey Brook on the right. Wander among hundreds of kinds of exotic conifers such as the Korean fir, Serbian spruce, and lace-bark and umbrella pines.

11. Remain on Hemlock Hill Road heading toward the Walter Street Gate. Just before the gate, turn right on the Conifer Path, marked by a stand of **gingko** trees. Unusual fan-shaped leaves distinguish this species, which has survived since prehistoric times.

Ginkgo

12. Remain on Conifer Path through the native woodland until it meets Valley Road. Turn left on the road. Bear right, passing the road to the Centre Street Gate, and then bear left passing the road that goes up Bussey Hill.

13. Turn left to the Dana Greenhouses and the Larz Anderson Bonsai Collection.

   On the left are the fields and greenhouses where plants are reproduced and research is conducted. The bonsai collection, displayed from mid-April to mid-October in the small structure on the right, was assembled by Larz Anderson, the former U.S. ambassador to Japan. Many of these tiny trees were planted in Japan in the 18th century. One of the highlights of the collection is the **hinoki cypresses**. Imported from Japan in 1913, the cypresses are reputed to be the oldest bonsai specimens in the U.S. The bonsai house is surrounded by terraces containing 150 varieties of dwarf conifers.

14. Upon leaving the bonsai house, return down the road until you spot Sargent Trail on the left. If you wish to take a shortcut through the woods, turn left. If you prefer to return via the main entrance road, continue to the **T** intersection and turn left.

15. The shortcut via a stone-dust path ascends a ridge, passes North Woods on the right, and continues past the honeysuckles. It ends at Meadow Road, with the **tulip** trees on the left and the **katsura** trees on the right.

Transported here from mountain forests in Asia, the katsura tree sports small heart-shaped leaves that turn yellow, pink, or purple in autumn. The Hunnewell Visitor Center and main gate are ahead.

25

HARVARD UNIVERSITY

HARVARD SQUARE

 Distance and Time: The 2-mile walk in and around Harvard University takes about 90 minutes. For those who enjoy going inside and poking around buildings, add another hour. The art museums deserve several hours. If you're traveling with school-age children, be sure to visit the Harvard Museums of Natural History, which merit several hours as well.

"Colorful, fascinating, historic, awesome" are a few of the adjectives visitors use to describe the eclectic Harvard Square section of Cambridge. Teenagers love to visit Harvard Square because "there is always something going on!" Adults marvel at the diversity of museums, people, stores, and restaurants. What makes this area so alive and exciting is Harvard University, which in 1986 celebrated its 350th anniversary.

This walk around Harvard and its environs explores the area's historic past and also visits many significant additions to its landscape. Allow at least a half-day to see the area, visit a few of Harvard's eight museums, eat lunch, and hang out in the square, an entertaining area teeming with people shopping, eating, and listening to street musicians.

Transportation: By automobile: Harvard University borders the western section of Memorial Drive (Route 2) in Cambridge. Parking in and around the square is either expensive or non-existent. Two adjacent lots are located across from and under the Charles Hotel on University Road off Mount Auburn Street.

By Ⓣ or bus: The best way to get to Harvard Square is via the MBTA Red Line. Eleven MBTA bus routes service Harvard Square.

Fees: Harvard Museums of Natural History (617-495-3045), Harvard University Art Museums (617-495-9400), Longfellow National Historic Site (617-876-4491).

Restrooms: Holyoke Center—Look for a security guard stationed in the street-level arcade. He dispenses free tokens for the usually spotless restrooms. The following Harvard buildings have public restrooms: Widener Library, Science Center, Memorial Hall, Museums of Natural History, and the art museums.

Food and Drink: In and around Holyoke Center: Au Bon Pain, Campo de Fiori, Ma Soba, and Lee's Busy Beehive all offer relatively inexpensive and fast food. University buildings: the first floor atrium in the modern Science Center houses a cafeteria, appropriately named the Greenhouse. The basement level of Memorial Hall contains a coffee shop, a yogurt stand, and a pizza/pasta shop. Within the square, you'll find an array of eating establishments.

Background: When the first settlers arrived from England, they immediately set about choosing a site for the capital of their new colony. In 1630, Puritan leader John Winthrop had selected Newtowne, which remained the seat of government for eight years. In 1636, the Massachusetts General Court agreed to set aside 400 pounds for the founding of a college in Newtowne to educate prospective political leaders and clergy. For decisions regarding building design or method of instruction, the colonists looked to Cambridge University in England, where many of them had been educated. They had such a high regard for their alma mater that they changed the name Newtowne to Cambridge.

THE WALK

1. The tour begins at **Holyoke Center** (1), on the south side of Massachusetts Avenue, just east of the square. From the Ⓣ station, leave by the Harvard Square exit.

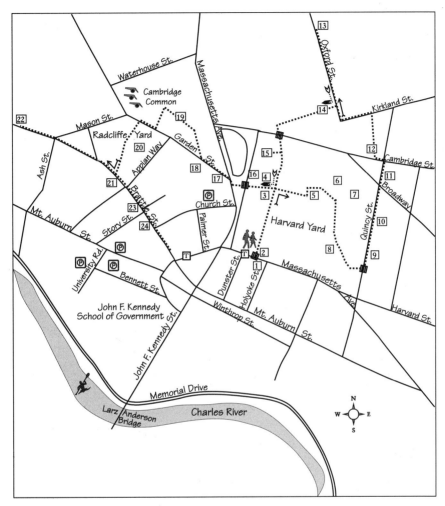

HARVARD UNIVERSITY–HARVARD SQUARE

In good weather tables and chairs surround the entrance to Holyoke Center, courtesy of Au Bon Pain. Inside the arcade you'll find the Harvard Information Office, restrooms, and a number of stalls and shops.

From Holyoke Center, cross Massachusetts Avenue to enter Harvard Yard. Before you pass through the gate, look to your right at the **Benjamin Wadsworth House** (2), which sits on the site of Harvard's first structure. This yellow clapboard house, a replacement for the original structure, was built in 1726 by the colonial legislature for Benjamin

Wadsworth, the ninth president of Harvard. This dwelling subsequently housed nine other presidents.

2. Proceed through the gate and enter Harvard Yard, a name derived from the cow yards that surrounded Wadsworth House.

From the 17th century, when Harvard began with only 12 students, to the present day, with an enrollment of more than 18,000 degree candidates, the yard has been the energetic center of the university. Inspired by the Cambridge University plan of buildings surrounding a grassy center, Harvard Yard has been the prototype for many American college campuses.

Continue straight down the walkway past Harvard's oldest buildings. On your left and right are Matthews and Grays Halls, freshman dormitories. Harvard's oldest existing building, **Massachusetts Hall** (3), sits on the corner facing **Harvard Hall** (4), which served as the center for the old college. Both buildings were built as dormitories on the Cantabrigian model. The rooms were organized into suites, each with a bedroom and study. The ground floor contained a huge hall that was used as a chapel, lecture hall, and dining room. The top floor held the library and adjacent rooms.

3. Turn right and head across the center of "old" Harvard Yard toward a bronze **statue of John Harvard** sitting in front of **University Hall** (5).

This sculpture is known by many as the "statue of three lies." The first lie is that the figure resembles John Harvard: actually, Daniel Chester French, who sculpted the bronze doors of the Boston Public Library, used one of his friends as a model for Harvard's deceased benefactor. Only the statue's skinny legs bear a resemblance to John Harvard, who died of consumption at age 30. The other two inaccuracies relate to the inscription, which reads "John Harvard, Founder, 1638." John Harvard did not found Harvard; it was named after him. Also, the General Court of the Massachusetts Bay Colony founded Harvard in 1636, not 1638.

University Hall, which separates the "old" yard from the "new," was designed by Charles Bulfinch, the most respected architect of that era, who also designed the State House in Boston. Constructed of granite in 1814, University Hall functioned as the students' dining hall. In order to separate the classes, the first floor was divided into four dining

Massachusetts Hall, Harvard's oldest remaining building, was built in 1720. (Photo courtesy of Harvard University)

rooms. The walls did not prevent the classes from interacting; the students often pitched discarded food through the high round openings.

4.   Walk behind University Hall to enter the "new" yard. On your left is **Memorial Church** (6), whose soaring white spire is a landmark on the Cambridge skyline. The church's Georgian style creates the impression that it was constructed far earlier than 1931.

Sever Hall (7), at a right angle to Memorial Church, was designed in 1880 by Henry Hobson Richardson, one of the foremost architects of the day. The hall's massive Romanesque style and detailed brickwork is reminiscent of the highly acclaimed Trinity Church in Boston, which Richardson recently had completed. The varied size and spacing of the numerous windows play a key part in the design of Sever Hall.

Across the "new" yard, where the university conducts its commencement exercises, sits **Widener Library** (8). Widener, Harvard's main research library, contains more than 3 million volumes and is just one component of Harvard's library system—the largest university system in the world. Although signs state that only Harvard affiliates can use the building, you may enter to see the impressive vestibule with murals by famous portrait painter John Singer Sargent on each side of the stairs. Don't miss the three dioramas just beyond the stairway. One depicts the Harvard campus as it looked in 1677. Another is a panorama of pre-landfill Boston in 1775, and the third shows Harvard in 1936.

At the top of the staircase, you'll discover the Widener Memorial Room, a tribute to Harry Elkins Widener, who drowned in the sinking of the *Titanic*. Widener bequeathed his library to Harvard, and his mother added a donation to construct a building to house his book collection.

5. Upon exiting the library, turn right and cross the diagonal path that takes you on top of the underground Pusey Library.

6. Turn left and walk in front of Lamont Library where students in the humanities and social sciences conduct their research. The modern bronze sculpture on your left entitled "Four Piece Reclining Figure" was modeled by Henry Moore.

7. Proceed out of the yard, through the wrought-iron gate, and head left on Quincy Street.

The modern concrete building on your right is the **Carpenter Center for the Visual Arts** (9), the only building in North America designed by the French architect Le Corbusier. The Carpenter Center, described by critics as a piece of sculpture designed for human use, expresses the architect's purpose of exposing students to the arts. If you climb the diagonal ramp to the second level, you can peer into a glass-enclosed exhibition hall. A descent to Prescott Street reveals windowed studios, usually inhabited by artists busily at work.

Continue up Quincy Street to the next building on the right, which contains the **Fogg Art Museum** (10) and the **Busch-Reisinger Museum**. These two museums, along with the Arthur M. Sackler Museum, compose the Harvard University Art Museums, and one fee guarantees admission to all three. The museums are open Monday through Saturday from 10:00 A.M. to 5:00 P.M. and on Sunday from 1:00 P.M.to 5:00 P.M.

The entrance into the Fogg leads to an Italian-style courtyard. Farther inside you'll find European and North American art from the Middle Ages to the present, including major works by Giotto, Rembrandt, Monet, Van Gogh, and Picasso.

The Busch-Reisinger, housed in Werner Otto Hall, contains one of North America's leading collections of German expressionist art, with paintings by Beckmann, Klee, Nolde, and Kandinsky.

8. From the museums, proceed on Quincy Street and cross Broadway. The **Arthur M. Sackler Museum** (11), on your right, focuses on ancient, Asian, and Islamic art. Among its holdings are ancient Chinese jades, rare Persian and Indian miniatures, and Japanese prints and ceramics. Its first-floor gallery often displays special exhibitions.

Continue on Quincy through the next intersection, with Cambridge Street. **Memorial Hall** (12), on your left, occupies the wedge of land bounded by Kirkland, Quincy, and the underpass.

The large brick hall, constructed in 1874, was designed by two Harvard graduates who won an architectural competition to create a memorial to the students and graduates who had fought in the Civil War. They designed a Gothic cathedral whose transept serves as the entrance, while its apse has become Sanders Theatre, an acoustical delight for concerts and lectures. The cathedral's nave holds a large hall decorated with 21 stained-glass windows donated by Harvard classes. The hall recently reverted to its original use as a dining center.

The renovated basement level of Memorial Hall hosts Harvard's first student commons. Among other features, it offers a coffeehouse, a pizza/pasta shop, and student activity rooms.

9. Turn left on Cambridge to enter Memorial Hall. Walk straight through the hall to a second entrance on Kirkland Street.

10. Turn left on Kirkland and take your next right onto Oxford Street.

Follow Oxford until you reach the large brick building on the right that houses the **Harvard University Museums of Natural History** (13). The museums are open Monday to Saturday from 9:00 A.M. to 5:00 P.M. and on Sundays from 1:00 P.M. to 5:00 P.M. One fee allows entrance to the Museum of Comparative Zoology, the Peabody Museum of Archaeology and Ethnology, the Botanical Museum, and the Mineralogical and Geological Museum. The museum shop is on the first floor, while all four museums and the restrooms are on the third floor.

Inside the **Botanical Museum**, you'll find the famous glass flowers, one of the museum's most popular and unusual attractions. The idea for the flowers materialized in 1886 when Professor George Lincoln Goodale, the museum's first director, began his search for a visual means of teaching botany. Color photography had not yet arrived, and dried pressed flowers no longer satisfied Goodale. He happened to see glass models of marine animals created by a German artist, Leopold Blaschka. Goodale traveled to Dresden, Germany, to convince Blaschka to produce all the various parts of plants as well as examples of 850 species. During the years 1887 to 1936, Blaschka and his son blew and shaped 3,000 glass models.

The Blaschkas were so skillful that the flowers look like they have just been picked from the garden. In order to show the tiny plant sections, the Blaschkas sometimes magnified them up to 2,000 times, which meant they had to melt and blow the glass while looking through a microscope. As you walk through the exhibit, don't miss the cases containing lifelike insects collecting and distributing pollen among the plants, and the amazing iris, cactus, and rhododendron models. If you are accompanied by school-age children, consider renting the informative half-hour-long tape that describes the glass flowers exhibit.

If you exit to the left of the Botanical Museum, you'll immediately enter the **Museum of Comparative Zoology**, a terrific place for children. Imagine visiting a zoo filled with stuffed, lifelike replicas of every type of mammal. Then add dinosaurs, sea serpent skeletons, and insect and reptile specimens, along with instructional exhibits on evolution and the development and preservation of fossils. Special changing exhibits geared to school-age children further heighten this museum's appeal. Bird-watchers should not miss the rooms stuffed with birds and birds' nests.

The rooms to the right of the Botanical Museum house the **Mineralogical and Geological Museum**, which features one of world's finest collections of gems, minerals, ores, and meteorites.

Continue on through these galleries in order to reach the treasures from prehistoric and historic cultures found in the **Peabody Museum of Archaeology and Ethnology**. You'll see artifacts from Aztec, Amazon, and Mayan cultures. Don't miss the fascinating Hall of the North American Indian. Exhibits reveal how the North American Indian tribes and Eskimos reinterpreted and molded new concepts into their cultural system in response to contact with European civilization. On the third floor are exhibits pertaining to Latin America. Ethnographic and archaeologic relics from Oceania occupy the fourth floor.

11. Return to the museum's Oxford Street entrance and retrace your steps down Oxford Street. Turn right into the **Science Center** (14), the modern concrete and glass structure on the corner of Kirkland and Oxford.

This sprawling building is the largest and busiest on campus. Walk down the corridor and turn left into the large sunny atrium, usually filled with students who are in and around the cafeteria-style restaurant named the Greenhouse. If you wish to visit the Collection of Historical Scientific Instruments, descend the stairs and head for room B-6. The museum is open Tuesday through Friday from 10:00 A.M. to 4:00 P.M., when Harvard is in session.

To leave the Science Center from the museum, climb the stairs and continue down the corridor toward the building's main entrance. In front of the center rests a cluster of boulders called the Tanner Fountain. This environmental work, reminiscent of New England's rocky landscape, contains dozens of nozzles that emit a fine mist and automatically shut off when there are high winds. During frigid New England winters, the fountain sends out blasts of steam.

12. From the fountain, head back into Harvard Yard through the Holworthy Gate. Tiny **Holden Chapel** (15) is hiding in a small quadrangle between the two buildings on your right.

Although one of the main reasons for the founding of Harvard was to educate ministers, the college did not have a church until 1742, when Holden Chapel was built.

13. Return to the main walkway and continue toward the center of the yard.

14. Take the first right, passing by Massachusetts and Harvard Halls, and walk through the **Johnston Gate** (16).

Nine major gates, all donations to the university, control entrance to Harvard Yard. Although Johnston Gate was constructed in 1890, its brick appears identical to that on Massachusetts Hall, built a century earlier. The designers were able to achieve this weathered effect by placing handmade bricks in a fire. Subsequent builders used this weathering technique, and the brick was dubbed "Harvard brick."

15. Cross the busy thoroughfare (note the brick crosswalks) and turn right, passing the First Unitarian Church on your left.

16. Take your next left onto Garden Street.

Cambridge's founders and Harvard's earliest presidents are buried in the cemetery on your left, referred to as either the **Old Burying Ground** or **God's Acre** (17).

Next to the cemetery rises **Christ Church** (18). Designed in 1761 by Peter Harrison, the country's first trained architect, it is the oldest house of worship in Cambridge. This simple church has no steeple because its congregants requested that Harrison substitute a tower with a belfry. During the Revolutionary War, the church was used as barracks and the organ pipes were melted down for bullets. However, George Washington, ever the dutiful husband, had the church refurbished in order to fulfill Martha's request to attend services there on New Year's Eve, 1775. Feel free to wander around its spartan colonial interior.

The large park on the opposite side of Garden Street, **Cambridge Common** (19), was used initially for grazing cattle, training militia, and holding assemblies. Later, the site was used for public elections and served also as the headquarters for George Washington's army. Now Cambridge Common is a haven for soccer and frisbee players and often hosts arts-and-crafts fairs.

The Civil War Memorial, perched in the center of the common, is just one of several markers scattered about. Three cannons captured from the British in 1775 stand on the west side of the common. Nearby, a sculpted bronze relief commemorates the site where George Washington took command of the Continental army. The text of his orders on July 4, 1775, is inscribed on the reverse side of the plaque.

17. Recross Garden Street to enter **Radcliffe Yard** (20).

Although the Federal-style brick building on the right, Fay House, was the first in the yard, Radcliffe College was not founded until 75 years later, in 1879. The women who attended the Collegiate Institution for Women received instruction from Harvard professors, who often would teach a course at Harvard, rush across campus, and repeat the lecture to the Radcliffe women. The dearth of men at

Harvard during World War II jolted the administration into the realization that it made good economic sense to allow the "'Cliffies" to attend classes with the men, but it was not until the 1970s that the two campuses became coeducational.

The **Schlesinger Library**, the leftmost member of the three linked buildings in Radcliffe Yard, contains papers, books, manuscripts, and photographs denoting the role of women in our nation's history. This collection began in 1898 when Maud Wood Park, a Radcliffe graduate, donated her woman's-rights collection to the college. Within the archives are papers that belonged to such notable women as Harriet Beecher Stowe, Susan B. Anthony, and Amelia Earhart.

18. Continue walking straight through the yard until you reach Brattle Street. Turn right.

The modern building across the street is the **Loeb Drama Center** (21). Although built originally for Harvard and Radcliffe undergraduates, it is shared now by the American Repertory Theatre, a nationally acclaimed regional theater company.

Walk a few minutes more up Brattle Street, also called "Tory Row" because King George's loyal subjects originally occupied the pre–Revolutionary War mansions lining the road.

After you pass the Episcopal Divinity School on the right, you'll reach the **Longfellow National Historic Site** (22), the large yellow frame house at 105 Brattle Street. The internationally renowned 19th-century poet Henry Wadsworth Longfellow lived and wrote here for 45 years. This 28-room, Georgian-style mansion, filled with Longfellow's books, furniture, and art, is open Wednesday through Sunday from 10:00 A.M. to 4:30 P.M. Informative tours on Longfellow's life are offered throughout the day.

The house was built in 1759 by John Vassal, a wealthy Tory. Before the Revolutionary War began, the Vassal family fled Cambridge. Their unoccupied mansion then served as headquarters for General George Washington during the siege of Boston. The estate was purchased in 1791 by Dr. Andrew Craigie, a developer who subsequently died, leaving his widow deeply in debt. She was forced to rent out rooms, and Longfellow, who arrived at Harvard in 1837 to head the Romance language department, became one of her tenants. After Longfellow's marriage to Frances Appleton in 1843, his wealthy father-in-law purchased the mansion and presented it to the couple as a wedding gift. Longfellow and then his heirs occupied the house until the National Park Service took over its management in 1972.

19. Retrace your steps down the right side of Brattle Street and head for Harvard Square.

Number 54, the **Dexter Pratt House** (23), built in 1808, is set back from the street. The name of the bakery that now occupies the site, the Blacksmith Shop, refers to its first owner, a blacksmith in Cambridge named Dexter Pratt, who was the inspiration for Longfellow's poem "The Village Blacksmith." The poem refers to "a spreading chestnut tree" that was memorialized by the sculptor Dimitri Gerakaris. He created a chestnut tree of forged steel and included the anvil, hammer, and tongs that he fabricated and then used to form the sculpture. See if you can spot the bronze pastries that replicate those sold by the bakery.

The last historic home on the tour, at 42 Brattle, is the **William Brattle House** (24), built in 1727 for and named after one of the wealthiest men in Cambridge. Brattle acquired much of his wealth by practicing most of the professions available at that time. He managed to be a doctor, lawyer, and minister along with commanding all the militia.

The walk ends here in the commercial section of Harvard Square. At last count, 18 bookstores were scattered around the square. If you follow Brattle Street to its end, you'll spot the Harvard Coop on the left. Here you'll find a wide variety of items, from Harvard memorabilia to posters, books, and sundries. Opposite the Coop is an entrance to the Red Line MBTA station.

26

MOUNT AUBURN

CEMETERY

 Distance and Difficulty: 2 miles of relaxed walking on paved walkways and unpaved footpaths.

Forget that Mount Auburn is a cemetery; think of it as a top-notch 174-acre arboretum with so many historical monuments that it's listed in the National Register of Historic Places. Within this wooded Westminster Abbey are 10 miles of paved roads and grassy paths that wind around ponds, fountains, and sculptures. A granite medieval-style tower rises above the treetops to offer terrific views of Boston, Cambridge, and the Charles River.

Hosting more than 4,000 native and foreign trees (many of which are labeled), 130 species of shrubs and ground cover, and more than 30,000 annuals, Mount Auburn's holdings rival major arboretums. Conceived as the first rural cemetery in the country, it contains more than 86,000 graves, including those of Oliver Wendell Holmes, Henry Wadsworth Longfellow, Winslow Homer, Mary Baker Eddy, and Julia Ward Howe.

An annual stop for migrating birds, the cemetery draws binocular-draped birders to view more than 80 species every spring.

This 2-mile tour, while highlighting many famous graves, memorials, and plantings, just touches on Mount Auburn's numerous treasures. For more information, contact the Friends of Mount Auburn Cemetery (617-547-7105), which sponsors walks, tours, and lectures. The cemetery is open daily from 8:00 A.M. to 7:00 P.M.

Transportation: By automobile: Follow Route 2 or Route 3 to Route 16 at the Mount Auburn/Brattle Street intersection on Fresh Pond Parkway in Cambridge. From this intersection (multiple traffic lights), follow Mount Auburn Street (Route 16) west for two blocks to 580 Mount Auburn Street. Drive through the iron gate and park around the traffic circle on the right.

By public transportation: Take the MBTA Red Line to Harvard Square. From the square, catch either the #71 or #73 bus or walk 1.5 miles down Brattle Street through the Fresh Pond Parkway intersection. Continue on Brattle until it joins Mount Auburn Street. Then cross Mount Auburn to the cemetery on the left.

Food and Drink: Many restaurants are in Harvard Square, 1.5 miles east of the cemetery.

Restrooms: Located in the administration building to the left of the entrance.

Recreational Options: None. No dogs allowed.

Background: By the beginning of the 19th century, Boston had become increasingly crowded. Even the deceased were jammed together in small burial grounds. After unsanitary cemeteries were blamed for a yellow fever epidemic that killed 16,000 people in New York City, Dr. Jacob Bigelow, a professor of medicine at Harvard, advocated acquiring Stone's Woods in rural Cambridge, where the dead could be buried in natural surroundings. He convinced the Massachusetts Horticultural Society, which desperately wanted a garden for botanical research, to purchase the land and repay the loan by selling burial plots. Bigelow, an avid botanist, named the cemetery's main roads after trees and the side paths after varieties of shrubs and flowers.

Mount Auburn Cemetery immediately became the place to be buried, and many prominent Bostonians were interred there. Visitors from all over the country were so impressed with its design that Mount Auburn quickly became the model for rural cemeteries. Each weekend thousands of local residents arrived in their carriages and drove around admiring the grounds and vegetation. Its popularity convinced legislators of the need for public recreation land, sparking the development of the metropolitan park system. Now, 170 years later, Mount Auburn Cemetery continues to be a popular spot for a Sunday outing, a means of escaping the congested city and reaping the benefits of Dr. Bigelow's foresight.

THE WALK

1. Begin at the granite Egyptian Revival–style entrance gate, designed by Dr. Bigelow. Proceed straight, passing on the left offices, restrooms decorated with stained-glass windows, and Story Chapel, where memorial services are conducted.

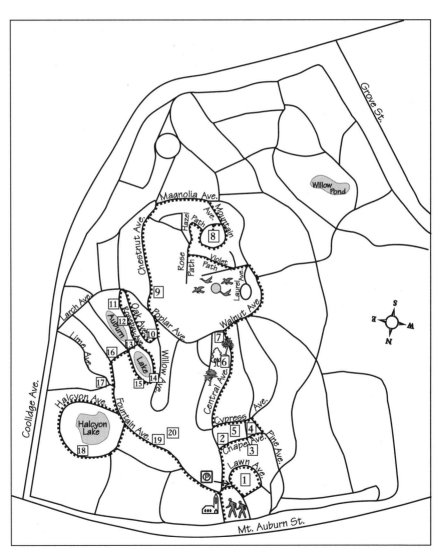

MOUNT AUBURN CEMETERY

Before the invention of cars, visitors entered by carriage or foot. If they rode their horses, they had to leave them at the gate. Now bicycles, as well, must remain in the bike rack by the front gate.

2. Take the first right and circle around **Asa Gray Garden** (1), named for the distinguished botanist. Standing around the fountain are the unusual **handkerchief and Japanese snowbell trees** and the more common **flowering and kousa dogwoods**. In late May, the handkerchief and dogwood trees produce large decorative white bracts, or leaves that surround tiny flowers, and clusters of small bell-shaped white blooms droop from the branches on the snowbell tree.

3. Return to Central Avenue, turn right, and proceed to Chapel Avenue.

On the left corner of Chapel, surrounded by a cast-iron fence, a common embellishment of 19th-century graves, sits a statue of **Nathaniel Bowditch** (2). Robert Hughes created this first life-size bronze sculpture in the United States more than 150 years ago. Bowditch, an accomplished navigator who at age 29 commanded his own ship, is known for his sailing guide, *American Practical Navigator*. Hughes alludes to Bowditch's profession by carving a globe and sextant next to him.

Farther along Chapel, on the right, lies the Gothic Revival–style **Bigelow Chapel** (3), designed by Dr. Bigelow, who imported the stained-glass windows from Scotland in the 1840s. The crematory stands to the left of the chapel.

Across from the chapel, sculptor Martin Milmore has carved the **Sphinx** (4), a rather unusual Civil War memorial, commissioned by Bigelow to commemorate the preservation of the Union and the destruction of African slavery.

4. Go to the rear of the Sphinx, turn left on Cypress, and follow it back to Central.

On the left side of Cypress, next to Hyacinth Path, sits the **Harrison Gray Otis Memorial** (5). Otis, a prosperous 18th-century merchant, was one of the developers of Beacon Hill.

5. Turn right on Central.

If you look closely at the gravestones, you may detect recurring imagery. One of the most common symbols is a draped urn, which signifies death. Another recurring image is a winged figure carrying a child, which often refers to women or children who died at an early

*"American Union Preserved"—the unusual Sphinx monument
to Civil War heroes in Mount Auburn Cemetery.*

age. Sheaves of wheat pertain to the wheat harvest and indicate that the deceased lived to a ripe old age. The metamorphosis of a butterfly symbolizes the passage of time. The poppy image, signifying sleep and eternal rest, is a popular motif, perpetuating the continual association between death and sleep. In fact, the word "cemetery" is derived from a Greek word meaning "places of sleep."

After walking for a few minutes on Central Avenue, you will pass on the left the life-size statue of Reverend Hosea Ballou, an influential Universalist minister.

Three impressive trees enhance the left side of the road. The handsome **American elm** hopefully will not fall victim to the pervasive Dutch elm disease that has been killing these popular trees for more than 60 years. The huge 100-year-old **sugar maple** will be at its most magnificent in autumn, when its leaves turn dazzling shades of orange and red, whereas the **flowering dogwood** is best viewed in spring when its fragrant pink flowers perfume the air.

Also on the left, a boulder surrounded by ivy covers the grave of **Fannie Farmer** (6), who wrote the first cookbook to contain recipes with precise measurements for the ingredients.

Farther ahead sits the detailed memorial to William Harnden, inset with symbols of the express-package business he founded.

6. Follow Central until it meets Walnut Avenue. Turn right.

On the left corner of Central and Walnut stands a **ginkgo** tree (7), distinguished by its fan-shaped leaves. A native of China, this species has survived from prehistoric times. Most arboretums prefer to display the male ginkgo trees because the decaying fruit issued from the female not only has a foul smell but becomes mushy and difficult for the grounds crew to remove. The female ginkgo is more popular in China, where the kernel of the fleshy, plumlike fruit is considered a delicacy.

7. Follow Walnut until Laurel Avenue joins on the left. Cross Laurel Avenue and turn left onto Violet Path, a dirt trail that borders Consecration Dell.

8. Take the right fork onto a path that overlooks the dell.

A number of trails run through the dell and around the vernal pool. During spring, the pool hosts spotted salamanders, while the dell is a favorite spot of migrating birds. Imagine hundreds of birds resting in the dell; then visualize hundreds of birders peering down at the birds. This secluded little valley has remained virtually unchanged since the consecration ceremony was held here in 1831.

9. Bear right on Rose Path, which merges immediately with Hazel Path on the right (there may not be a marker for Rose Path).

10. Proceed on Hazel Path to **Washington Tower** (8), which rises 62 feet above the summit of Mount Auburn. Dr. Bigelow designed this round stone structure to be reminiscent of guard towers used for protection during the medieval age. It contains a gallery, battlements, Gothic-style windows, and a spiral stone staircase. Bigelow urged Mount Auburn's trustees to build this structure to gain a panoramic view from the top and to serve as a landmark for the cemetery itself. The view from the top of the tower reveals such Boston landmarks as the gold-domed State House, Prudential and Hancock skyscrapers, buildings of Harvard University, Bunker Hill Monument in Charlestown, and the Charles River flowing through the suburbs.

11. After your descent from the tower, turn right to walk down the hill.

12. Turn left on Magnolia Avenue.

13. Take the next left onto Chestnut.

At the junction with Hawthorn Path on the left side stands an eye-catching tree whose branches cascade to the ground. This unusual **weeping European beech** tree (9) is one of several that decorate the cemetery. A popular tree around the turn of the century, it was planted in public parks and around stately mansions. This variety of beech began as a mutation of an ordinary beech tree, which was then propagated by grafts or cuttings. (If propagated from seed, there would be no guarantee that the seedling would have the characteristic drooping branches.) The arching branches are not as apparent on saplings; the tree must reach a certain size before its branches become long enough to droop. This particular weeping European beech is approximately 100 years old.

14. Continue straight on Chestnut as it intersects with Poplar. Cross Poplar, turn left, and head on to Willow Avenue.

15. Take your first right onto Oak Avenue, which overlooks Auburn Lake.

In the right corner stands the **sawleaf zelkova** tree (10), distinguished by small pointed leaves. A species of elm, this Japanese native was touted as a replacement for the American elm, which has fallen prey to a fungus. A hardy, fast-growing tree with broadly spreading branches, the sawleaf, or Japanese zelkova, often is planted along city streets.

16. Turn left onto Rosebay Avenue for a closer view of Auburn Lake and the magnificent specimens that thrive in this moist environment.

A multistemmed **fern-leaf beech** (11) displays leaves that resemble lacy ferns. Growing near the water is a rare **weeping katsura** (12) tree. During hot weather its heart-shaped leaves curl to retain moisture. In autumn they turn bright yellow and orange.

After passing a clump of rhododendron bushes, you'll spot a tree with reddish bark with its branches drooping over the water. The **bald cypress** (13) requires moist soil and often is found growing in swamps. In order to provide oxygen for its submerged trunk, its roots issue bulbous growths, often called knees, which rise straight up out of the water. Native to mild climates, the bald cypress is rarely seen this far north. The name results from the annual autumn shedding of its green, feathery, hemlock-like leaves. Because

Bald cypress

its wood is so durable and resists rotting, cypress is often used for outdoor construction.

17. Pass the bridge and continue straight around the second pond.

After rounding the northern tip of Auburn Lake, you'll pass a **sweet bay magnolia** tree (14) whose white flowers, resembling lily pads, appear in June.

Near the magnolia towers a **dawn redwood** (15), one of the largest and oldest species in the world. Introduced to the United States and Mount Auburn Cemetery in the 1940s, this fast-growing redwood is as tall as trees twice its age.

18. Turn left at the bridge onto Auburn Court.

The Bourne Crypt is flanked by two unusual **Japanese cryptomeria** trees (16). Their soft, thick, peeling dark-orange bark and lacy leaves, which resemble fern leaflets, are similar to the giant sequoia, a member of the same family.

19. Cut through the crypt courtyard and turn left on Fountain Avenue.

*The memorial to Christian Science founder Mary Baker Eddy
stands in the beautiful landscape of Mount Auburn Cemetery.*

20.	After passing another katsura tree and the grave of the physician and writer **Oliver Wendell Holmes** (17), located at the intersection with Lime Avenue, turn right onto Halcyon Avenue to circle Halcyon Lake.

Halfway around the lake stands the imposing memorial for **Mary Baker Eddy** (18), the founder of the Christian Science movement.

21.	After circling the lake, turn right on Fountain Avenue.

On the left side of Fountain is the grave of **James Russell Lowell** (19), who in the 19th century was editor of the *Atlantic Monthly* and later minister to Spain and then Great Britain. Above, on the ridge, lies the well-known poet **Henry Wadsworth Longfellow** (20), a former Harvard professor and Brattle Street resident.

22.	Continue down Fountain Avenue to return to the entrance gate.

27

Fresh Pond

Reservation

 Distance and Difficulty: 2.5 miles of easy walking.

A hidden treasure, favored by local residents and Harvard students, Fresh Pond Reservation offers a 2.5-mile loop around pristine Fresh Pond Reservoir. Located 1 mile from Harvard Square and 6 miles from downtown Boston, this tranquil 150-acre reservation is separated from the hubbub that surrounds it by a border of dense foliage. Once inside the reservation, the scenery across the path from the reservoir continually changes, from woodland to meadow, playing fields to marsh, and even includes several manicured holes on a public golf course.

Two parks and several playing fields allow all family members to enjoy some form of recreation. In fact, the loop is short enough for parents to alternate jogging with manning the swings. Fresh Pond is so popular with dogwalkers that the reservation provides machines that dispense pooper-scoopers.

Transportation: By automobile: Fresh Pond Reservation is west of Boston and just south of the Alewife MBTA station and the Fresh Pond rotary. It can be reached by following Route 2 east or west to Fresh Pond Parkway. The reservation lies on the corner of Huron Avenue and Freshpond Parkway. Only

Cambridge residents, identified by automobile stickers, are allowed to park in the reservation lot. Paid parking is available in the Alewife MBTA Garage. If you purchase food at the Ground Round restaurant or Bread & Circus food market on Alewife Brook Parkway across from the reservation, you certainly can park in their lots.

By rapid transit Ⓣ: Take the Red Line to the last stop, Alewife. The station is a half-mile from the reservation. From the station, turn right at the traffic lights on Route 2/Alewife Brook Parkway and walk over the bridge. Remain on the right side of the busy road and head toward the Ground Round restaurant on the corner next to the rotary.

Food and Drink: A water fountain is on the side of the new Water Works Building. Cheddar's Pizzeria, 201 Alewife Brook Parkway, tucked away in a minimall on the right side en route from Alewife station to Fresh Pond Reservation, offers takeout homemade soups, sandwiches, salads, and pizza. Closed Sundays. Next door, if you prefer sitting, the Ground Round is known for its hamburgers. Across the street (there is a push-button traffic light control) is Bread & Circus, a terrific food market that offers a wide variety of takeout items perfect for picnics.

Restrooms: Located inside the Alewife MBTA Station, and on the outside of the new Cambridge Water Works Building.

Recreational Options: Cycling, cross-country skiing, in-line skating.

Background: Now a watershed for the city of Cambridge, Fresh Pond formerly was known worldwide for its ice. In 1805, Frederick Tudor cast a cold eye on New England winters and saw ice. He wisely concluded that what Boston had in abundance, tropical climates desperately needed. Tudor spent many winters overseeing workers who sawed tons of ice from the north and east shores of the pond. Ox teams transported the ice to the Boston waterfront, where it was shipped all the way to the West Indies. With the development of the railroad, Tudor, then referred to as the "Ice King," installed tracks and replaced oxen with railroad cars.

Along with contributing to Frederick Tudor's wealth, Fresh Pond and the land that surrounded it functioned as a popular recreation spot for Harvard students, local residents, and visitors. Beginning in 1796, the Fresh Pond Inn, on the eastern promontory now occupied by Kingsley Park, was a fancy hotel, serving food and drink for 30 years. It also boasted bathing and

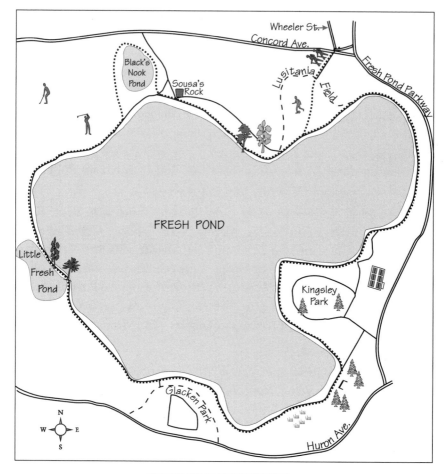

FRESH POND RESERVATION

athletic facilities, boats, horses, and sleighs. Oliver Wendell Holmes, Harvard class of 1829, reported that he and his friends celebrated their commencement at Fresh Pond Inn, where they enjoyed a "most superb supper," undoubtedly enhanced by vast amounts of claret, champagne, and madeira.

By 1880, Cambridge installed a pumping station and removed all private buildings so as to protect their 155-acre water supply. Five-foot-wide pipes carry the water 6 miles east from Cambridge Reservoir to the new treatment plant at the main entrance on Fresh Pond Parkway, where the water is filtered, cleaned, and held for several days.

THE WALK

NOTE: CONSTRUCTION IN AND AROUND THE NEW TREATMENT PLANT MAY EFFECT THE ROUTE.

1. From the Ground Round restaurant parking lot, next to the rotary at the junction of Concord Avenue and Fresh Pond Parkway, carefully cross Concord Avenue. An entrance to the reservation is directly across from Wheeler Street.

2. Head down a paved path and cross Lusitania Field, where soccer, softball, and baseball games often take place.

3. Upon reaching Fresh Pond, turn right onto either the unpaved path close to the water or the paved bikeway.

    Both paths pass through a grove of **white pine** trees, characterized by five long thin needles in each cluster. Several varieties of moisture-loving trees grow along the banks of the reservoir. The **red maple** can be distinguished by the distinctive red color on its flower clusters in early spring, reddish fruit and leafstalks in late spring and summer, and crimson leaves in the autumn. **River birch** has reddish brown bark that curls into thin sheets on young trees and thickens as the tree matures. Its small double-toothed leaves turn yellow in autumn.

    White pine

    A half-mile into the loop you'll reach Sousa's Rock, named for Joe Sousa, a former track coach crippled with arthritis who rested on the rock during his walk around the pond. His friends named the rock after him and posted the sign.

4. Turn right to circle Black's Nook Pond, a junglelike environment with overgrown honeysuckle and greenbrier encroaching on the path that circles the tiny pond and leads to the golf course. To return to the Fresh Pond Loop, head south across the grass (and watch for errant balls).

5. Turn right to continue on the trail that runs between Little Fresh Pond and Fresh Pond.

    Trees and shrubs grow near the water on both sides of the trail. **Black willow** trees are readily recognized by their dark trunks and irregular spreading branches. Their thin narrow leaves often have tiny heart-shaped knobs at their stems. **Black ash** have seven to 11 small, dark green leaflets that grow from one stem. Another plant commonly found near water is the **marsh elder**. A large nondescript shrub, the elder is recognized more easily in autumn, when clusters of dark berries droop from its branches.

Glacken Park, which contains a large playground, tennis courts, playing field, and a fountain where a cooling shower provides relief on a hot day, is located on Huron Avenue just past the golf course. To gain access to it from the main trail, look for the path up the woodland ridge.

The trail passes an open, grassy "rest area" before passing through a section referred to as the Pines. Here, an anonymous benefactor hauled a four-foot, 500-pound marble bench down a narrow footpath and placed it in a hilly glen amidst a grove of tall pines. What makes the bench so notable is the lengthy inscription from Virginia Woolf's novel *Orlando* chiseled on top. To see the bench, bear right, cross the railroad tracks, and climb the hill into the forest. The bench is on the left, precisely planted to overlook the pond.

6. After walking a total of 1.8 miles, you'll reach scenic Kingsley Park, site of the former Fresh Pond Inn. An upper path winds through a dense hemlock grove as it loops around and returns to the main trail. A lower unpaved loop skirts the shore before it rejoins the main trail.

7. After the loop, turn left onto the main trail, with the pond on your left. The Cambridge Water Treatment Plant sits on the right. Visitors are welcome to enter the building to see how the Cambridge filtration system works.

8. Continue to follow the trail around the pond for another half-mile until you return to Lusitania Field. Turn right and cut through the field to the path that leads to the Fresh Pond rotary.

28

MIDDLESEX FELLS RESERVATION

EASTERN SECTION

 Distance and Difficulty: Approximately five miles. Fairly strenuous—involves climbing and descending rocky slopes.

Feel like going on a four-hour challenging hike in the mountains of Vermont? Save time and gas and head for the 2,000-acre Middlesex Fells, located just seven miles north of Boston. It boasts jagged peaks overlooking panoramic views, extensive woodlands, and well-kept trails to test your agility and stamina.

Middlesex Fells Reservation owes its existence to the foresight of Charles Eliot, the founder of Boston's metropolitan park system, who in 1893 was so taken with this area's natural beauty that he fought to have it protected from future development.

The eastern half of the Fells, so named by English settlers to describe its barren rocky hills, affords more opportunity for invigorating hiking than the flatter western section, situated west of Route 93. This tour begins on a trail through historic Virginia Wood and leads to the Rock Circuit Trail, a loop around the eastern Fells interrupted by nine rocky outcroppings.

Transportation: By automobile: Traveling north on Route 93, take Exit 34 toward Melrose and Stoneham, following signs to the Stone Zoo. Turn right at the traffic light, proceed 0.9 mile, passing the zoo on your right. Turn left on Pond Street, the first left after the zoo parking lot. Park in the cleared parking areas on either side of Pond Street.

Traveling south on Route 93, take Exit 35 (Winchester Highlands) toward Melrose and Stoneham. At the end of the exit ramp, turn left and then turn right at the stop sign, following signs to the Stone Zoo. Go through the set of lights and take your first left after the zoo parking lot onto Pond Street.

By commuter rail: From North Station take the Haverhill/Reading Line to the Wyoming Hill stop in Melrose. Go west on West Wyoming Avenue for 1 mile until you reach the trailhead on the left side of Pond Street, a quarter-mile past the intersection with the Fellsway. (Wyoming becomes Pond Street at the traffic lights when it enters the Fells.)

Via the Ⓣ and bus: Take the Orange Line to Malden Center. Hop on the #130 bus to Stoneham. Exit at the intersection of Wyoming/Pond and Fellsway or as close to the trailhead on Pond as possible. Continue on Pond for a quarter-mile until you reach the trailhead for Virginia Wood on the left.

Food and Drink: Friendly's, on the corner of Main and South Streets (on the automobile route from Route 93 to the Fells); J J Grimsby, on the corner of the Fellsway and West Wyoming Avenue; Chicken Express, convenience store, market, and bakery on Wyoming Street, near the train station.

Restrooms: Friendly's.

Recreational Options: Cross-country skiing, mountain biking, rock climbing.

Background: Beginning in the 17th century, Spot Pond and environs drew millers, woodsmen, and farmers. The millers dammed the Spot Pond Brook to provide water power for their mills. By the 19th century the steam engine had replaced the water wheel, and instead of grinding grain or sawing wood, the mills manufactured rubber, medicines, and textiles. Manufacturing here ceased by the 20th century and the Commonwealth of Massachusetts began to accumulate available land and set it aside for recreational purposes. In 1894 the state acquired its first parcel in the Middlesex Fells when the Tudor family donated the Virginia Wood property in memory of their daughter. This donation, the first gift of land for public purposes in the country, became the prototype for similar bequests throughout the world.

THE HIKE

Although these directions refer to some of the carriage roads and hills by name, don't expect to find these names posted on the trails. The carriage roads and hills are labeled on the map and hopefully will help orient you.

1. The trailhead, located on the south side of Pond Street, begins behind a Virginia Wood sign near gate #42. Several trails originate along the road and they all eventually merge. Begin at the middle trail, bounded by three boulders that bar vehicle entrance.

2. You soon will cross a bridge over Spot Pond Brook to access the Virginia Wood Trail, marked by pink blazes on trees. The bridge spans a dam constructed by the Civilian Conservation Corps (CCC) and the Works Progress Administration (WPA) in the 1930s. It replaced one built by Ebenezer Bucknam in 1790 to create a millpond that would help power his sawmill. The #4 attached to a wooden stake on your left corresponds to the Spot Pond Brook Self-Guided Tour. Written by rangers employed by the Metropolitan District Commission (MDC) the agency that has administered the Fells since 1896, the Spot Pond Tour, marked by yellow blazes, visits the sites within the Spot Pond Brook Archaeological District.

3. To continue the quarter-mile historic tour, turn left soon after crossing the bridge and follow the yellow blazes on the trees. Look to your left for marker #5, where Bucknam's sawmill once stood. The stones near the water formerly housed the tub wheel used to generate power for the mill.

4. Ahead on the left, a short path leads to marker #6 at Middle Mill Pond, created in 1812 by John Rand, who took advantage of the surrounding rocky ledge and dammed the water to create power for his water wheel. A small mill village grew up around the pond.

5. Return to the path and continue until you reach #7 to see remnants from a mill that once sat on the rim of the gorge. The bridge and spillway were relatively recent additions, built more than 60 years ago by the CCC.

   Nearby, #8, located in a grove of huge 250-year-old hemlock trees, indicates where Spot Pond Brook flows over the ledge to the ravine below.

6. Continue on, following the stream until you reach the large earthen dam at the end of the pond, marked by #9. Look closely to find the

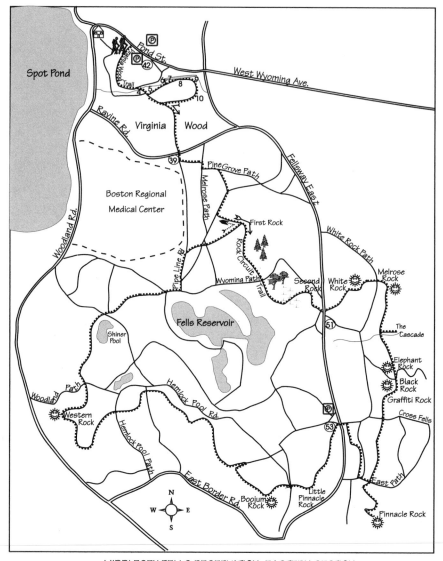

MIDDLESEX FELLS RESERVATION—EASTERN SECTION

stone chamber, constructed in 1862, at the bottom of the dam. This chamber housed eight steam engines that supplied power for Nathaniel Hayward's rubber factory.

Marker #10 stands in the spot formerly occupied by Hayward's home and rubber mill, where workers produced boots, buckets, and chamber pots.

7. Follow the yellow blazes until you meet the Virginia Wood Trail. Turn left and resume following the pink blazes.

If you visit this section in autumn, you'll notice clusters of dainty **white wood asters** decorating the sides of the trails. These flowers are just one of the many varieties of white and blue asters that thrive in New England woodlands. The showy orange pea-like blossoms on the **bird's-foot trefoil** also brighten the sides of the carriage paths. Its name is derived from the footlike shape of its pods.

White wood aster

8. Cross Ravine Road. Reenter the woods at gate #39, take the first left, and continue on the pink-blazed Virginia Wood Trail.

9. Cross Melrose Path. At the fork, bear right and begin to climb while watching for the pink blazes.

10. At the next fork at the top of the hill, turn right onto the carriage road.

11. Look carefully on your left for a narrow trail. The pink blazes may be hard to find since a fire destroyed many of the large trees. Follow this narrow path as it climbs to the top of "First Rock" (author's creative designation, later referred to as "a.d.").

12. On First Rock, the Virginia Wood Trail ends and the more strenuous Rock Circuit Trail begins. From now on, white blazes will determine your route. The trail is generally well marked, but if you become confused, return to the last white blaze and try again. Follow the white blazes up a bluff and then down to the right.

13. After descending, the path enters another densely grown **hemlock** grove with no undergrowth.

The hemlock tree has short, shiny flat needles that are dark on top and have two white lines on the underside. These hemlocks are older and larger than the reservation's oaks and pines; in the 19th century the latter were cut down to supply wood for sailing vessels, while the coarse-wooded hemlocks were spared.

The Rock Circuit Trail crosses Wyoming Path and enters an area of **white** and **black oak** trees and a stand of white birches. Although commonly referred to as white birch because of their smooth white bark, these small trees are a species called **gray birch**. Because they are among the first trees to sprout in burnt-out areas or clearings, they are referred to as a pioneer species. After the birches have become established, other varieties of trees, such as oak, can use the birch's canopy for pro-

Gray birch

tection. Eventually the tiny oak seedlings grow tall enough to tower over the small birches and block the sun. Without sufficient sunlight, the gray birches weaken and die.

If climbing over the granite slabs during summer, you will be engulfed by the fragrant smell of the **sweet pepperbush** growing in wetlands near the trail. In fall, its pointed clusters of white flowers are replaced by spikes of dry gray fruiting capsules.

14. The path heads away from the Fells Reservoir and ascends Second Rock (a.d.). Looking down reveals a paved road below (Fellsway East). Unfortunately, a huge pine tree blocks the view of the coastline in the town of Revere. As you descend into the woods, you will be paralleling the road. Follow the white blazes to a carriage road.

15. Turn left onto the carriage road that leads to the busy Fellsway.

16. Exercise caution crossing the Fellsway and watch for a trail, guarded by large rocks, blazed white. *Do not* follow the carriage road behind gate #51 on your right.

17. The Rock Circuit Trail veers to the left for the climb to White Rock. At the next fork, bear left.

18. After about one hour of hiking, and well into the climbing-up-and-over-and-down-rock routine, note that the white blazes on the boulders form a right angle indicating that the trail turns left. This left turn leads to White Rock, where you will have a clear eastern view of Tobin Bridge stretching over the Mystic River.

19. Bear left, descending eastward, and then turn right onto White Rock Path.

20. On White Rock Path (a carriage trail), walk about 40 feet and watch for white blazes on a trail to your left that leads to the next outcropping, Melrose Rock.

Multicolored Melrose Rock resembles a brick wall. Its jagged southern slope resulted from glacial action that tore away sections of stone as it inched its way southward. From the peak, you'll spot the Boston skyline.

21. The trail continues to climb before it descends to the right (southwest side). Here you may spot pretty pink mushrooms, *Russula emetica*, which may be good-looking but aren't good eating. This species actually protects the potential nibbler, as it has such a disgusting taste that it never makes it to the intestines.

    Maple-leaf viburnum grow beside the path. This shrub produces clusters of small white flowers in the spring. During autumn the flowers turn into dark purple berries and the leaves, which resemble those found on maple trees, turn a dazzling pink-purple color.

22. After descending from the rocks, at the next fork by a stream, either make an optional left turn to visit the Cascade, which features a waterfall in the spring, and return via the same route, or bear right and continue on the Rock Circuit Trail.

23. Huge **Elephant Rock** (a.d.), the next peak although not the highest, yields the best view so far. Here no trees interfere with a vista of Boston. The trail proceeds over a ridge and descends. Follow the white blazes as the trail skirts the southern section of the ridge and then veers right.

24. Turn left onto the fire road for about 30 feet before bearing right toward Black Rock, probably so named because of the intertwining dikes of black diorite in its crevasses.

    By now, you may have detected a pattern in the shapes of these peaks. Approximately 16,000 years ago, the southerly movement of the Laurentide Ice Sheet ground down the northern sides of hills, which made them more gradual and sloping. The glacier, as it continued its movement south, dragged away huge chunks of frozen ice and granite from the southern sides of these hills, creating steep craggy cliffs. The isolated granite boulders scattered around the hills, called glacial erratics, are the remnants of the frozen chunks the glacier severed from the slopes.

    Black Rock offers an even better view than Elephant Rock: the Boston skyline, Atlantic Ocean off the coast of Revere and Winthrop, and planes departing from Logan Airport.

Elephant Rock in Middlesex Fells offers a southward panorama of metropolitan Boston.

Prepare for a steep descent from Black Rock and then another climb to Graffiti Rock (a.d.).

25. At Graffiti Rock make a sharp left turn. The white blaze pointing left may be obscured by the graffiti. Cross the Cross Fells Trail (blue blazes) as you continue to ascend and descend through this overgrown section. The trail passes through wetland decorated with tiny streams, moss, ferns, and a gigantic glacial erratic sporting white blazes pointing to the right. A radar tower sits off to the right.

26. After about two hours of hiking, you reach East Path (carriage road) and the spur for Pinnacle Rock. To reach Pinnacle Rock, cross East Path and follow the white blazes. Return to East Path by the same route.

   If you don't wish to visit Pinnacle Rock, turn right onto East Path, bear left onto another carriage road, and then keep your eyes open for the Rock Circuit Trail heading off to the right.

27. The trail veers off to the left and climbs White Rock. Look for the white blazes on the rocks. You will enter a grove of baby **pitch pine trees** growing through the rock formation. This hardy species, whose distinguishing characteristic is its long stiff needles that grow in groups of three, prefers rocky, sandy soils.

28. Recross the Fellsway, pass through gate #53, and take an immediate left onto the narrow trail blazed with white paint.

29. You next ascend Little Pinnacle Rock (a.d.), after which you cross two carriage roads on your way to Boojum Rock, which boasts a 180° panorama. If you look south you'll spot the Blue Hills, the highest point in the Boston area, explored in chapter 21. Descend to your right.

30. When you reach a large boulder, you'll notice a big white cross, a geodesic survey marker for surveying planes.

31. At the fork, go left following the white blazes (a right turn leads to Hemlock Pool).

32. Cross a carriage road and bear to the left.

33. Cross Hemlock Pool Path and walk by a grove of birch trees. Pull off a leaf and chew on its stem for a burst of wintergreen flavor.

34. The last ascent is to Western Rock (a.d.), with a view to the west that radiates color during peak foliage. To descend, turn right and cross another carriage road.

35. Cross the blue-blazed Woodland Path. When the trail forks, bear right and continue to follow the white blazes.

36. Pass Shiner Pool on the right and cross the intersection of two carriage roads to access a narrow path.

37. At the top of the hill, turn right. The trail passes near the fence for the Fells Reservoir, which holds the water for the towns of Malden, Melrose, Medford, Stoneham, and Somerville.

38. Continue on the road next to the reservoir for about 200 feet. Turn left onto Pipe Line Road.

39. Take the second right (New England Memorial Hospital is off to the left).

40. Cross two carriage roads on the return to First Rock and the junction with the Virginia Wood Trail. Turn left, following the pink blazes.

41. Turn right onto the carriage road.

42. Take the first left and head downhill.

43. At the bottom, turn left, make a quick right, and then left again.

44. Cross Ravine Road and continue to follow the pink blazes on your return through Virginia Wood to Pond Street.

29

BREAKHEART

RESERVATION

 Distance and Difficulty: 2.5 miles of fairly level hiking and 0.5 mile of rocky hilly terrain.

Tucked away amid strip malls and fast-food joints on Route 1 in Saugus lies a gorgeous 675-acre reservation which is truly one of the hidden gems close to Boston. Visitors are amazed at what they discover in Breakheart Reservation: miles and miles of scenic, varied, and sometimes strenuous hiking trails, picturesque ponds for swimming, and hemlock groves for picnicking, as well as paved walkways perfect for cycling, in-line skating, and cross-country skiing.

This 3-mile hike, while circling the reservation, meanders along the banks of the Saugus River, where such wildlife as ospreys, herons, cormorants, ducks, and otters feed and breed, and scrambles over rocky Fox Run Trail. The last leg of the tour cruises around man-made lakes where archaeologists have uncovered Native American artifacts more than 10,000 years old. Because this route encompasses five ecosystems—river flood plain, barren ridges, hemlock forests, oak woodlands, and moist wetlands—its changing landscape and vegetation make for terrific hiking.

Call 781-233-0834 for specific information about the reservation.

Transportation: By automobile: From Boston take Route 1 north, or from Routes 128/95 take Exit 44 onto Route 1 south toward Boston. From Route 1, exit onto the Lynn Fells Parkway toward Melrose and Stoneham. Turn right onto Forest Street, following the sign to Breakheart Reservation. Pass the Kasabuski Ice-Skating Rink on your way to the small parking lot on the left. If the parking lot is full, you can park at the rink.

By Ⓣ and bus: Unfortunately, Breakheart is not reached easily via public transportation. The closest connection is through Lynn. From Boston, you can either take a train from North Station via the Rockport/Ipswich Line to Lynn Central Square, or take the #426 bus from the Haymarket Station in Boston (on the Orange and Green Ⓣ Lines) to Lynn Central Square. Then pick up the #429 bus to North Saugus. Exit at the Saugus Plaza Shopping Center. Breakheart is less than a mile southwest of the plaza. Walk through the parking lot to Lynn Fells Parkway. Turn right on Lynn Fells Parkway and walk for half a mile to the entrance on Forest Street.

Food and Drink: Route 1 is loaded with every conceivable type of snack shop and restaurant.

Restrooms: Located in the bathhouse at the north end of the reservation, near the Pearce Lake beach and parking lot, the restrooms are open from Memorial Day to Labor Day.

Recreational Options: On- and off-road biking, in-line skating, cross-country skiing, swimming, fishing.

Background: The reservation's unusual name, Breakheart, probably originated during the Civil War when soldiers used the land as a training site. According to local legend, the young homesick recruits found the location, which at that time was "lonely and remote from civilization," to be heartbreaking.

Native American tools, arrowheads, and cooking implements were discovered near the Saugus River and can be found now at the R. S. Peabody Foundation for Archaeology at Phillips Academy in Andover (see chapter 30). Native Americans, seeking a source for food as well as a means of transportation, camped near the river during the winter. The stone-studded land supplied material for their tools and weapons. When the weather turned warm, they paddled to the ocean.

Throughout colonial times, the river continued to serve as the center of activity and farmers settled along its banks. During the 1800s, mills replaced farms. The dam site off the Saugus River Trail serves as a reminder of that era.

Before the Metropolitan District Commission (MDC) purchased Breakheart in 1934 and the Civilian Conservation Corps transformed it into this reservation, it served as a private hunting and fishing preserve.

The Hike

1. From the parking lot adjacent to the headquarters building, enter the reservation via paved Pine Tops Road.

2. Turn right at the barrier onto the Saugus River Trail.

3. Turn left at the next junction onto the Lodge Trail, where the hunting lodge constructed by the land's previous owner, Benjamin Johnson, once stood. Immediately turn right just after the bench and descend the stairs to visit the Rhododendron Grove, also a Johnson contribution.

   The **Rhododendron Grove** grows in a vernal pool—one that fills with water during the spring and dries up during the summer. Don't miss this spot in late May when the "rhodies" flaunt their large pink blossoms and the **mountain laurel** display showy white clusters. Birders should visit the pool in spring when such birds as the scarlet tanager and the Baltimore oriole enliven the grove with their songs.

4. The path loops back to the Saugus River Trail, where you turn left. To follow the trail, keep your eyes open for yellow paint blazed on trees. If confused, return to your last yellow blaze and try again.

   Continue straight for 0.3 mile, passing stone walls and **gray** and **yellow birch** trees, both indications that the land had been farmed. During the 17th and 18th centuries, farmers cut down trees and cleared the stone-dotted fields. They stacked rocks to form walls that contained their cows and goats and marked boundaries of their land. When the farmland reverted to woodland, birch trees, a pioneer species, were among the first to appear. While growing, the birches provide protection for the pine, oak, and maple seedlings that eventually replace the birches.

Yellow birch

5. If you wish to visit the dam that was built in 1814 on the Saugus River to supply energy for a linen mill, bear right, following the yellow blazes on the trees. The rock formations that resemble stone walls are remnants from the foundation of the dam, which was destroyed when the river overflowed its banks. The pond to the left of the dam was created when gravel was removed to construct Route 1.

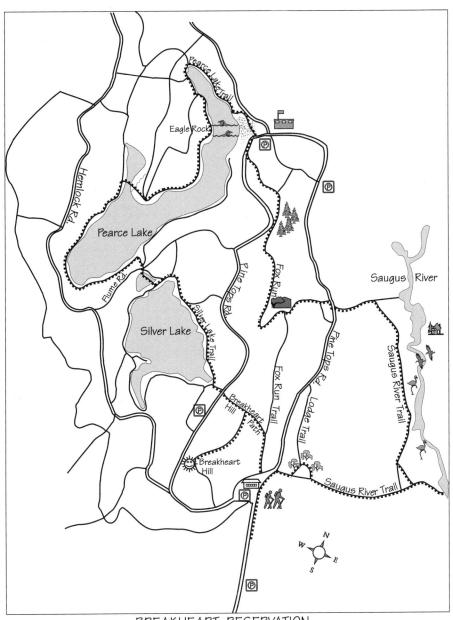

BREAKHEART RESERVATION

6. Upon returning from the short dam side-trip onto the Saugus River Trail, turn right.

The path soon will parallel the river. You may hear and see such birds as the red-winged blackbird, yellow warbler, great blue heron, and black double-crested cormorant.

Growing near the river are moisture-loving plants, including the **highbush blueberry, sweet pepperbush**, and many variety of ferns, such as the large **cinnamon fern**. Look for grand arching fronds growing from a central, thickly matted hairy rootstock. Its name refers to the golden cinnamon-colored fertile leaves that are interspersed with the fronds. Another moisture-loving fern that grows near the river is the **sensitive fern**, whose broad, almost triangular leaves and thick center membrane differ from the delicate lacy leaflets found on most ferns. The sensitive fern derives its name from its sensitivity to the cold, which causes it to die after the first frost.

On the opposite bank of the river sits Camp Nihan. One of its four cabins is visible across the water. The MDC rents its cabins and camp-sites to nonprofit groups.

7. The trail crosses a road and then forks as it heads away from the river. Although both trails lead to Pine Tops Road, stay to the left on the continuation of the yellow-blazed Saugus River Trail.

8. Upon reaching Pine Tops Road, turn right for about 200 feet and then at the speed bump turn left onto Fox Run Trail. The huge boulder, named Painted Rock, previews the rocky terrain that you will soon experience.

9. Follow the trail as it bends left. At the next fork, bear right and continue to follow the yellow blazes.

10. At the wooden stake at the trail intersection, turn right to climb the steps toward a massive wall of granite embedded with scrapings caused by glacial movement.

Continue to climb up and over the ridge, formed from dirt and stones deposited by the melting glacier more than 12,000 years ago. After hiking a quarter-mile, you'll see a grove of huge 200-year-old **hemlock** trees growing in the chasm below.

The trail descends, traverses a plank bridge over a tiny stream, and then climbs another ridge. In spring, look for delicate pink **lady's-slipper**, a variety of orchid, to provide a pleasing contrast to the severe gray granite.

Proceed farther along the ridge, a harsh growing environment for most plants but one for which the sturdy **hair-cap moss** is well adapted. In spring the moss provides a soft, rich green blanket along the slope. When the weather becomes hot and dry, it stops growing. To reduce evaporation, the exterior of its tiny star-shaped leaves turns brown and the leaves fold up to protect the chlorophyll. After a heavy rain, the leaves uncurl and return to their original green color.

Lowbush blueberry and **huckleberry** bushes prefer this rocky acidic soil and supply hungry summer hikers with small tasty berries.

When you finally reach the top of the ridge, look west to spot other peaks in the reservation, such as Eagle Rock, perched beyond Pearce Lake; Crow Hill; and the highest point, Castle Hill, which rises above the challenging Ridge Trail.

11. While on the ridge facing the lake, turn right, still following the yellow blazes on rocks and trees. This path leads to the beach parking lot and bathhouse.

12. Head toward the beach, walk across the sand with the water on your left, and look for the boardwalk and then the trailhead for Pearce Lake Trail. The narrow path around Pearce Lake and Silver Lake hugs the shore and is marked by blue blazes. Lifeguards supervise swimming from July 1 to Labor Day in this mile-long lake.

Benjamin Johnson, the previous owner of the property, created the lakes by damming two spring-fed marshes. He had hoped to attract waterfowl and improve the fishing for his hunting and fishing preserve.

13. After walking for a few minutes, you will reach a clearing, covered with wood chips, that opens onto the lake and provides a peaceful rest stop. Continue to circle the lake, following the blue blazes as you cross a bridge that extends over the dam and waterfall. Fork left and remain on the trail next to the lake.

14. At the next fork, both trails are blazed blue. For those who seek another peak, turn right toward Eagle Rock. If you prefer level ground, bear left and continue circling Pearce Lake.

15. Cross the plank bridge and then turn left with the lake on your left. Don't take the paths on the right that lead to Hemlock Road.

    Hanging over the western end of the lake are very old **blueberry bushes** whose stems are as large as small tree trunks. If you're hiking in the summer and your timing is good, you may beat the birds to the berries.

16. The next fork appears at the spot where the path curves around the southern tip of the lake; continue to hug the water's edge as you cross over a cluster of rocks that bridge a tiny stream. Watch your footing on this rocky section.

17. Before the second stream crossing, turn right. Walk over a tiny bridge and head to the right.

18. Pass under Flume Road and then over the water-filled flume.

19. After climbing 11 steps, you reach an intersection at Silver Lake. Take the path to the right that leads to the dam linking the two lakes.

20. Turn right or left to circle the lake. If you prefer a shorter route, turn left. Follow the blue blazes and continue to follow the shore until the trails merge just before Pine Tops Road.

21. Cut through another parking area, turn left, cross the road, and go through the barrier to get on Breakheart Hill Path.

    A right turn off this path leads to Breakheart Hill, the last peak for climbing enthusiasts. Remnants from an old truck engine remain on top of the hill. Sixty years ago, the engine powered a rope tow to pull skiers up the slope.

    The panorama from the summit encompasses surrounding suburbs, the Boston skyline, and Logan Airport with the ocean beyond. After descending Breakheart Hill, continue on the trail that leads to Hemlock Road. Turn left to reach the entrance.

    For those who do not wish to climb Breakheart Hill, continue down to the bottom of the hill.

22. Bear right onto Fox Run Trail and return to the reservation entrance.

30

PHILLIPS
ACADEMY

Art, Archaeology, and Ambling

 Distance and Difficulty: Allow three hours to visit the museums and walk two easy miles around the sanctuary.

Rarely can a secondary school match the facilities of a top-notch college. Phillips Academy in Andover is an exception. Its picturesque campus contains two terrific museums with extensive holdings in art and archaeology, a major library, and the Moncrieff Cochran Sanctuary—all in a setting that reflects its English heritage. Founded during the Revolutionary War, Phillips Academy is the oldest boarding school in the nation. Its many privileged alumni have provided funds for these high-quality offerings.

This tour passes several noteworthy buildings on the way to the Robert S. Peabody Museum of Archaeology and the Addison Gallery of American Art. These interior explorations are balanced by a two-mile loop around the Moncrieff Cochran Sanctuary. The best time to visit the sanctuary is the end of May, when hundreds of azaleas, rhododendrons, and mountain laurels are in bloom.

Transportation: By automobile: Take Route 93 north (19 miles from Boston, 12 miles from the Routes 128/95 interchange) to Exit 41, Route 125 east toward

Andover. Turn right on Route 125 for 2 miles. Turn right on Route 28 for 4 miles to the campus. Turn right on Salem Street and park on the side of the road.

By commuter rail: From North Station take the Haverhill Line to the Andover Station. The station is located 1 mile from Phillips Academy. From the station, turn right on Ridge Street and then left on School Street. Follow School to Route 28 (Main Street). Take the first left onto Salem Street, where the tour begins.

By bus: Trombley Commuter Line runs buses from the Transportation Building in Park Square, Boston (978-937-3626).

Strolling through the Moncrieff Cochran Sanctuary.

Food and Drink: The Andover Inn is located on the campus on Main Street. One mile away on Main Street in Andover Center are Bruegger's Bagels and Bertucci Pizzeria.

Restrooms: Located in the Robert S. Peabody Museum of Archaeology and Addison Gallery of American Art.

Recreational Options: Cross-country skiing through the sanctuary.

Background: In 1642, John Woodbridge purchased land from the resident Native Americans in Cochichowick, an Indian name meaning "place of the great cascade," for six pounds and a coat. Woodbridge changed the name Cochichowick, which may have referred to the Shawsheen River which flows in the south end of town, to Andover, the English homeland of its settlers.

More than 100 years later, following the United States's split from England, Americans began to redirect their energies from simply surviving to educating their young. Samuel Phillips moved from Cambridge to Andover in 1778 to establish a "public free school or Academy" committed to teaching "youth from every quarter." The constitution assumed that "youth" meant males only: Abbot Female Academy did not open until 1828. One hundred and fifty years later, the country's oldest male and female schools merged to become Phillips Academy, referred to by its students and graduates as Andover. Recognized as one of the country's finest preparatory schools, Andover today educates 1,180 students from all over the world.

THE WALK

1. From Salem Street, return to Main Street (Route 28).

    On the right facing the green sits the **Oliver Wendell Holmes Library**, named after the famous poet and physician who graduated in 1825. As the second-largest secondary-school library in the country, it contains more than 102,000 volumes and subscribes to 260 periodicals.

    To the left, the 159-foot granite and brick **Memorial Bell Tower** dominates the corner. Beneath the tower, constructed in honor of the Phillips Academy graduates who died during World War I, rests a copper box containing such souvenirs of the period as newspapers, books, magazines, photographs, a baseball, and a pack of cigarettes.

2. Turn right on Main Street. Walk one block to the corner of Phillips and Main Streets to the **Robert S. Peabody Museum of Archaeology** on the left side of Main. It is open Tuesday through Friday noon to 5:00 P.M. and Saturday from 10:00 A.M. to 1:00 P.M. The museum is closed in August. For information on current exhibits and programs, call 978-749-4490.

    In 1901, Robert S. Peabody, class of 1857, donated his collection of 40,000 archaeological specimens to Phillips Academy. He also included funds to maintain and enlarge the collection and to build a structure to hold and display his specimens. The collection, which now includes more than 500,000 artifacts, reflects Peabody's passion and respect for the Native Americans who first inhabited the land. One of the top Native American museums in the country, the Peabody Museum contains holdings that range from Paleo-Indian to contemporary, and represent nearly every indigenous culture area in North America.

    The first floor of the museum displays changing exhibits, often relating to archaeological sites in New England. A diorama to the left of the stairway depicts activities in an Algonquin village situated on the banks of the Merrimack River about 500 years ago. Hanging on the

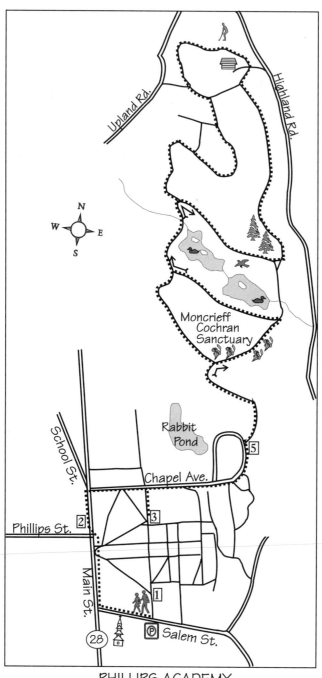

PHILLIPS ACADEMY

right is a terrific mural by the artist Stuart Travis. It portrays members of various Indian tribes and locates them on a map of the United States. Watercolors on the stairway illustrate a variety of artifacts from the museum's collection. Upstairs a diorama, also by Travis, represents a cutaway of the Pecos Pueblos of New Mexico showing native life in their clay-terraced dwellings in 1600. A library and more permanent exhibits are located on the second floor.

The philanthropic Peabody family has its name attached to two other museums in the Boston area: the Peabody Museum of Archaeology and Ethnology at Harvard University and the Peabody Museum in Salem, known for its Chinese, Japanese, and Pacific Islands ethnological collections. Both are the result of bequests from George Peabody, Robert's uncle.

3. To reach the Addison Gallery, turn left onto Main Street and make the first right on Chapel Avenue.

The **Addison Gallery of American Art**, the first building on the right, was named after Mrs. Addison Cobb, a friend of Thomas Cochran, the museum's benefactor. Cochran, who also donated funds for the chapel and sanctuary, limited the collection to works by American artists. The gallery opened in 1931 with 400 pictures from Cochran's collection. Now the museum houses more than 11,000 pieces by such well-known artists as Stuart Davis, Edward Hopper, Hans Hofmann, Jackson Pollock, John Singleton Copley, Winslow Homer, George Bellows, Benjamin West, Alexander Calder, and Phillips Academy alumnus Frank Stella. In addition to its permanent collection of paintings, prints, sculptures, and photographs, the Addison Gallery also organizes special exhibitions by American artists.

The museum is open Tuesday through Saturday 10:00 A.M. to 5:00 P.M. and Sunday from 1:00 to 5:00 P.M. It often hosts free concerts, lectures, seminars, and recitals. For information on current exhibits and events, call 978-749-4015.

4. Return to Chapel Avenue and turn right to visit the **Moncrieff Cochran Sanctuary**.

5. Bear right at the cul-de-sac.

6. To enter the sanctuary, turn right and walk through the stone arches.

The Moncrieff Cochran Sanctuary, built with funds contributed by Thomas Cochran, is now less than half its original size. In 1928, Cochran donated 150 acres of land around Rabbit Pond for a sanctuary to be built in memory of his brother, Moncrieff. He constructed two islands in the middle of the pond and brought in flocks of swans, ducks, and geese. A seven-foot-high fence circled the entire property. Cochran ordered the fence to be installed two feet deep in the ground to prevent animals from burrowing under it. He also supplied the funds for and supervised the planting of hundreds of flowering shrubs that lined three miles of gravel road.

By damming a brook and carving out two ponds, Cochran created a sanctuary for birds. When Cochran died in 1937, the birds were sold or set loose, and the bird sanctuary became a nature preserve.

7. Follow the path into the sanctuary. When the path forks, bear right.

The path is lined with large **rhododendron, azalea,** and **mountain laurel** bushes. Although all belong to the heath family, each has its own distinguishing characteristics. Both the laurel and rhododendron keep their dark green leathery leaves throughout the year, whereas the azalea drops its smaller leaves in winter. The rhododendron leaves tend to be larger and more rounded at their base than the mountain laurel. All produce clusters of showy flowers from mid-May to early June. The white or pink blooms on the mountain laurel are smaller than the pink, lavender, or white bell-shaped rhododendron blossoms. The tubular, vase-shaped azalea blossoms may be pink, red, orange, or yellow.

8. Turn left onto a path that loops around two man-made ponds.

As you circle, you'll see birdhouses and benches where you can sit and watch the wildlife that feed and nest in and around the ponds. In 1942, students began to use the second pond as a natural swimming pool. Thirteen years later, contamination due to an unusually hot, dry summer forced its closing.

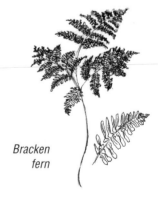

Bracken fern

Hemlock and pine trees shade the paths. The undergrowth includes a variety of ferns, including the large **cinnamon fern**, the three-leaved **bracken fern**, and the

sensitive fern, with its thick center membrane and broad triangular leaves.

9. Turn right onto the main trail. Cross a granite bridge over the brook that feeds the ponds.

10. Turn right at the next fork to complete the loop around the ponds.

11. Turn left at the fork into a more heavily wooded section of the Sanctuary.

    Tamarack

    Soon you will pass through a grove of **tamarack** trees, also known as **eastern larch**. These unique trees can be distinguished by clusters of soft needles extending from both sides of their branches. The tamarack is a conifer and certainly looks like an evergreen, but it has a most unevergreenlike habit—it sheds its needles every autumn.

12. Bear right at the next junction and circle around the log cabin on the left, between two grassy areas that served as golf putting greens.

    The cabin was built in 1931 from rough-hewn logs transported from New Hampshire. Although intended to serve as a center for undergraduate gatherings, it is also used now for alumni and faculty functions.

13. Continue straight past a path that leads to Upland Road and bear right at the next fork to pass by the area where Cochran's birds were contained in coops.

14. Continue straight to complete the sanctuary loop.

    The path passes through a section landscaped with rhododendrons, azaleas, mountain laurel, and viburnum before it enters a heavily wooded area, more reminiscent of a remote forest than a former bird sanctuary.

15. After passing the ponds and returning to the entrance path, bear right to head back to the cul-de-sac and Chapel Street.

31

IPSWICH RIVER

WILDLIFE SANCTUARY

 Distance and Difficulty: Several loops, totaling almost four miles on level terrain.

What a great place for kids! They can play detective as they walk the trails snooping for clues of beaver habitation, such as gnawed trees, mounds of dirt, dammed water, and beaver lodges. They can clamber up and around the Rockery, the former owner's attempt at replicating an Italian grotto. They can watch a tame black-capped chickadee hover, waiting for an extended finger. Once perched, the chickadee will patiently wait for a tidbit of food. Children can climb to the top of the observation tower to search the marsh for a green-backed heron hunting for a snack. Families can choose among ten miles of trails over gentle terrain in this Massachusetts Audubon Society (MAS) facility.

Birders as well as children delight in this spot. Sitting on 2,800 acres of diverse habitats, including woodlands, marshes, ponds, and the Ipswich River, the sanctuary harbors hundreds of bird species whose songs provide a delightful accompaniment to the walk.

Because much of the sanctuary consists of wetland, visitors should bring mosquito repellent.

Transportation: By automobile: From I-95, take Exit 50 onto Route 1 north. Follow Route 1 until you reach the traffic lights at the intersection with Route 97. Turn right onto Route 97 south. Take your second left onto Perkins Row. The sanctuary is 1 mile ahead on the right.

By commuter rail: From North Station take the Ipswich Line to the Hamilton/Wenham Station. The distance from the station to the sanctuary is 4.6 miles. From the station on Main Street turn right, and then turn left on Asbury Street. Remain on Asbury for 1 mile to the blinking light at the intersection with Highland Street. Turn right. At the fork, bear left and continue on Asbury for 2.2 miles to the **T** intersection with Ipswich Road. Turn left on Ipswich Road. Take the next left onto Perkins Row. Remain on Perkins Row for about 1.3 miles until you reach the sanctuary.

Food and Drink: In Hamilton on Railroad Avenue across from the train station are the Black Cow and the Weathervane. In the shopping center adjacent to the station is the Coffee Table. Topsfield Bagel Company and Coffee House, 38 Main Street, Topsfield, is 1.5 miles from the Sanctuary. Take Perkins Row to Route 97 and head north until you reach Main Street.

Restrooms: Located in the red building northeast of the parking lot.

Fees: Adults, $3; children and seniors, $2. No charge for MAS members. Open from dawn to dusk except Mondays (978-887-9264).

Recreational Options: Cross-country skiing.

Background: In 1643, John Winthrop, the first governor of the Massachusetts Bay Colony, gave 500 acres to Simon Bradstreet, another Englishman who eventually succeeded Winthrop as governor. Bradstreet never actually lived on the land but leased it to local farmers. The large white house perched on top of Bradstreet Hill was built in 1763 by one of Bradstreet's heirs, Samuel. Bradstreet's descendants continued to live in the house and own the land until 1898, when Thomas Proctor purchased the property to display his considerable collection of trees and shrubs.

Proctor was interested in growing specimens of all North American tree species, as was Charles Sargent, the first director of Arnold Arboretum, owned by Harvard University and located in Boston (chapter 24). Both Proctor and Sargent grouped their trees according to genus in order to better compare their botanical details. Proctor also followed Sargent's example of

sailing around the world to Japan and China to search for exotic tree specimens in Far Eastern climates that were similar to Massachusetts.

The Massachusetts Audubon Society purchased the property in 1949,
several years after Proctor's death.

THE WALK

Trail conditions change. Before you head out, inquire at the office about any
trail closings.

As in all MAS sanctuaries, the trails are clearly marked. The square
numbered signs mark trail junctions. If you are facing a blue sign, you are
heading away from the parking area. A yellow numbered sign indicates you
are walking toward the parking area. Stay on the trails and away from the
brush to avoid ticks. Tuck your pants into your socks and carefully check your
clothes, shoes, and hair after your walk.

1. From the building where you pay your entrance fee, head north toward
    the #2 intersection. The **pachysandra** ground cover that lines the
    impressive entrance path signals that Ipswich River Wildlife Sanctuary
    will not be a typical woodland sanctuary.

2. Proceed straight on the Rockery Trail (marked R), one of Proctor's
    many carriage roads that wind through the reservation. The spreading
    branches of the **catalpa** tree extend over the path. In June, its clusters of
    spotted white flowers, which resemble orchids, adorn large heart-
    shaped leaves. Nearby grow **winged euonymous** bushes whose branches
    are covered with woody irregular bark that looks like wings.

    Beavers are indirectly responsible for the fancy boardwalk that
    crosses what is now marsh. Before their dams redirected the flow of
    water and submerged the trails, this section was dry land. Many trees
    and shrubs died because their roots were covered by water. The trees
    that remain, especially the beeches whose outer layers of bark have
    been gnawed away by the beavers, are struggling to survive.

    Among the abundant wildlife that live in and around the marsh are
    several varieties of frogs, such as leopard, bull, and spring peepers.
    Numerous species of birds, including wood and black ducks, mallards,
    mergansers, teals, green-backed herons, sandpipers, bitterns, and
    egrets, rest, feed, and nest in the wetlands.

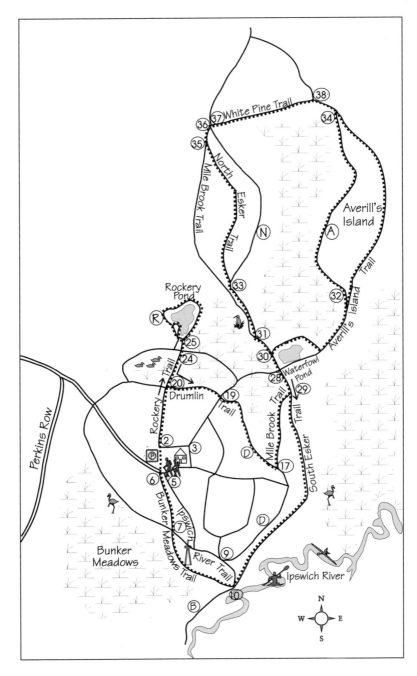

IPSWICH RIVER WILDLIFE SANCTUARY

You may have noticed a green coating on the surface of the water. Although it looks like algae, it is actually a water plant called **duckweed** which has adapted to its aquatic environment by producing a root system that floats on top of the water.

3. Continue straight through intersections #20 and #24. Cross the stone bridge, a preview of the sanctuary's superior masonry.

    The **katsura tree** on the left, distinguished by its unusual mottled bark, was brought here from Japan.

4. To circle Rockery Pond, turn left at #25 and cross another bridge that spans the southern tip of the point. The path forks and later merges. Choose either the one that takes the high ground or the path that runs closer to the pond.

    Welcome to the Rockery, Proctor's replica of an Italian grotto, a landscape that took nine years to create. Fifty laborers excavated the pond and filled it by diverting the flow of water from the surrounding marsh. Mules hauled huge boulders, remnants of the Ice Age, from nearby farms to the Rockery. Under the direction of a Japanese landscape architect, masons labored for five years to create arches, steps, walls, and bridges. Proctor then surrounded the stonework with thousands of rhododendron and mountain laurel bushes.

    Behind a rock formation on your left stands a **cork tree**. Robins flock to the tree in the fall to feed on its abundant black berries.

    A close inspection of the pond may reveal painted and snapping turtles swimming near the water's surface. Although both have dark top shells that blend with the color of the logs and water, the underside of the painted turtle is orange and yellow, while its neck has yellow stripes.

    Cork tree

5. A loop around the pond leads to a **Carolina hemlock** grove filled with huge multistemmed trees with reddish bark and long interlocking branches.

    Just after the grove, a **sawara cypress** tree, transported from Japan, remains rooted to the spot where Proctor planted it 90 years ago.

Proctor returned from his Far East tree-purchasing mission in the dead of winter to discover the ground frozen solid. What to do with his new exotic trees? After frantic research, he purchased all available salt-marsh hay. His workers hauled hundreds of bales of hay to the home-stead, spread it around the Rockery, and set it on fire. The burning hay thawed the ground so the workers could plant the cypress and other new trees. To identify the sawara cypress, look for an evergreen with very small, scalelike leaves; diminutive, pea-sized cones that ripen from green to brown; and red-brown bark peeling in narrow strips.

If you look closely at the ground as you circle the pond, you may spot small mounds of mud that beavers pile near the water to mark their ter-ritory. After beavers heap the mud, they secrete a scent that lingers on the dirt. This scent sends an unmistakable message to other beavers: Do not trespass!

The beaver lodge sits on the eastern side of the pond. Look for sticks, branches, and a huge hump of dirt rising out of the water. You probably won't see any beavers because they are active only after sun-set. According to the sanctuary director, beavers may not always have been nocturnal but adapted to protect their hides, so to speak; hunters, their biggest enemy, shot them during daylight.

Several varieties of maple trees line the path. The trees with shiny, smooth olive green, brown, and white striped bark are **striped maples**. Their common name is **moosewood** because moose eat the bark in win-ter. As the trees age their striped bark turns solid gray. On the water side sit **silver maples**, a variety that thrives near ponds and rivers. Both the striped and silver maples produce leaves that turn bright yellow in autumn.

6. After you circle the pond and return to #25, proceed back through intersection #24 to #20. Turn left onto the D (Drumlin) Trail, so named because of its hilly contour formed by glacial debris.

7. Follow the D Trail past intersection #19 to #17. Turn left onto the M (Mile Brook) Trail.

8. Continue straight past #29 and cross the stone bridge, keeping the Waterfowl Pond to the right. Turn right onto the path that passes behind the pond and leads to the A (Averill's Island) Trail to explore

the northern section of the sanctuary. This 1.5-mile loop covers a very different environment. Surrounded by wetlands, the eastern and western sections wind through peaceful, natural woodland.

9. Turn left onto the A Trail. The trail splits at #32 and merges again at #34. The trail on the left side is a little hillier than the one on the right.

10. After the paths merge at #34, cross the bridge and bear left at #38 onto the White Pine Trail.

11. Follow the wide carriage path to #37. Turn left and cross the wetland to #36.

12. The lower trails in this section are often submerged, so it is better to head for the ridge on the N (North Esker) Trail. To reach this trail, you must first get on the M Trail and then bear left at #35 onto North Esker Trail.

   This long narrow ridge of sand and gravel, called an **esker**, was formed about 12,000 years ago when the glacier started to recede and melt. As it melted, immense cracks formed under the thick ice. The water, carrying sand and gravel dragged along by the glacier, poured through the widening cracks. The sand and gravel accumulated, eventually filled the cracks and formed the ridge you see today.

13. Proceed south through intersections #33, #31, #30, and #28. When you reach intersection #29, bear left onto the E (South Esker) Trail and continue south for a half-mile on another high narrow glacial ridge that rises above the marsh on the left. At the fork in the trail, head toward the gazebo.

14. At #10 the trail merges with two other paths adjacent to the canoe slip, where Massachusetts Audubon members can rent canoes for $5 an hour. The path follows the river for a few hundred feet and then ends.

15. To reach the observation tower from the canoe slip and intersection #10, follow the path that runs alongside the marsh. Climb the observation tower and, if you have binoculars, watch for waterfowl feeding in the wetlands or wildlife on the river.

16. After descending from the observation tower, follow the path north. Proceed straight through intersection #7 and remain on Bunker Meadows Trail to the parking lot.

32

GARDEN IN
THE WOODS

 Distance and Difficulty: three miles of easy walking.

Attention, flower lovers! If you wish to view wildflowers flourishing in their natural habitats, head for Garden in the Woods, New England's biggest and best wildflower showcase. As you meander along well-manicured trails that wind through 45 acres of varied terrain, you can feast your eyes on more than 1,600 varieties of native wildflowers growing in specially designed gardens. Most of the plants have color-coded labels so you can learn their names, country of origin, and whether the species is rare or endangered.

Owned and operated by the New England Wild Flower Society, the garden, located in Framingham, opens April 15 and closes October 31. The garden is open from 9:00 A.M. to 5:00 P.M. every day between April 15 and June 15. Between June 16 and October 31, the garden is closed on Monday.

Transportation: By automobile: From Routes 128/95, take Exit 26, Route 20 west. Drive 8 miles on Route 20 to Raymond Road, the second left after the traffic lights in South Sudbury. Follow Raymond Road 1.3 miles to Hemenway Road.

By commuter rail: From Back Bay or South Station, take the Framingham Line to Framingham Station. The station is approximately 5 miles from Garden in the Woods. From the station, proceed north on Route 126 (Concord Street). Take the second left onto Union Avenue. Follow Union for 1.7 miles as it crosses Route 9 and the name changes to Edgell Road. Remain on Edgell, crossing under the Massachusetts Turnpike. After traveling for 2.1 miles on Edgell, turn right on Water Street. Take your first left onto Hemenway Road. Follow Hemenway 1.2 miles to the garden.

Hop Brook Trail. (Photo by John Lynch)

Food and Drink: The Charcuterie, Sudbury Farms, and Star Market are on Route 20 in Sudbury, a half-mile west of the intersection with Raymond Road.

Restrooms: Toilets and a water fountain are located in the visitor center.

Fees: Adults, $6; children (6–15), $3; seniors, $5. Call 508-877-7630 for more information.

Recreational Options: No dogs allowed.

Background: Credit the creation and design of the garden to Will Curtis, a landscape architect who in 1931 purchased 30 acres of land from a railroad company. In 1932, he and Howard Styles collaborated on the design of a naturalistic landscape to display native perennials. In 1965, he donated the garden to the New England Wild Flower Society.

THE WALK

1. Begin at the visitor center/museum shop, where you pay your entrance fee.

   In the nursery on your right, plants are propagated either for planting in the gardens or for sale to the public. Wildflower enthusiasts flock to the garden the second Saturday in June for the annual sale.

   On your left lies the Introductory Garden, a preview of coming floral attractions, where some of the plants now in bloom are displayed with their color-coded signs. Red indicates a species rare or endangered throughout North America. Orange signifies rare or endangered throughout New England, and yellow means rare or endangered in one or more New England states. Plants not endangered have brown labels. In the upper left corner, you'll see either N, signifying the plant is native to North America, or EX, which means the plant is an exotic that originated in another continent. An NZ on the brown label indicates that you are looking at a naturalized plant, one that originated on another continent but now is well established in North America.

   If you follow the solid line on the map, you'll walk through all the main habitats of the garden. The dotted line indicates the alternate routes, which contain additional plantings.

   The numbered stakes along the Curtis Trail are keyed to descriptions in the self-guiding tour booklet for sale in the visitor center.

   A gorgeous spring blossom rises from the **trillium**, whose many varieties are displayed in the garden. Its name is derived from its three petals, three sepals, and three leaves. Look for the double trillium, which flaunts double soft white petals. Double trillium, a member of the lily family, doesn't reproduce in the usual manner. Because its seeds have become part of the flower itself, horticulturists propagate the plant by cutting and dividing its thick roots. Native Americans found many uses for trillium. The leaves were cooked and

Trillium

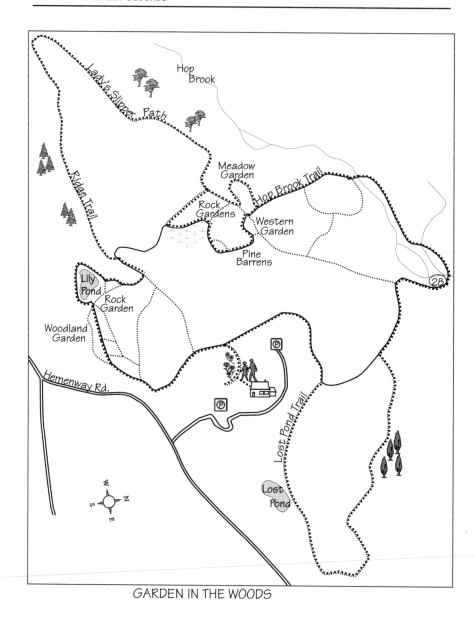

GARDEN IN THE WOODS

eaten as greens, while the underground rootstalks were chewed for the curative powers of their juice.

2. On your left, a woodland canopy allows some sun to peek through and energize the shrubs below. A close look at the lowest level of the garden reveals a layer of herbaceous, ground-hugging plants. If you visit in early spring before leaves appear on the trees, you may discover small

light-blue flowers from the **wild blue phlox** or the **foamflower's** tiny white flowers in a feathery, foamlike cluster.

3. Beyond the woodland garden lie the lily pond on the left and rock garden on the right. Plants growing in the rock garden's alpine conditions bloom for such a short period that they must attract pollinators quickly. Mother Nature has obliged by bestowing them with flamboyant flowers. Plants growing in the lily pond have enough moisture to bloom for a longer period of time and thus don't need such showy blossoms.

    On the southwest side of the lily pond is the moisture-loving **interrupted fern**. Its name refers to the interrupted space left in the center of each fertile leaf after its dark green leaflets have first turned brown, then withered, and finally disappeared by early summer.

4. Circle the pond, where painted turtles may be sunning themselves on the banks.

    The next incline, called Variegated Alley, contains an assortment of plants with white and green leaves.

    A glacial riverbed, called an esker, is off to your right. When the glacier receded 12,000 to 15,000 years ago, ice two miles thick melted and produced immense cracks. The melting water, carrying sand and gravel that originally had been dragged along by the glacier, rushed through the widening cracks. The sand and gravel accumulated and eventually filled up the cracks. Great chunks of ice broke off, melted slowly, and formed deep kettle holes on both sides of the esker. What was originally a riverbed under the ice is now higher than the surrounding terrain.

5. On the left lies the Ridge Trail, an optional 10-minute, slightly hilly loop through a pine forest and oak woodland.

    If you hike in May, look for the delicate **lady's-slipper** scattered among the trees. One of the largest native orchids, it flourishes in forests yet stubbornly resists growing in gardens.

6. The Ridge Trail ends at a group of plantings that display a range of North American habitats: rock garden, bog, pine barren, meadow, and plateau.

    Many of the plants in the limestone rock gardens are not found in New England. The limestone, shipped from New York, creates an alkaline environment for plants, while New England plants are accustomed to acidic conditions caused by soil composition and the presence of such trees as oak, pine, and spruce. Note how the porous limestone allows the plants to grow on top of and in between the rocks.

7. The bog or swampy section contains such plants as the odoriferous **skunk cabbage**, lovely **marsh marigold**, and the huge **cinnamon fern**.

Pitcher plant

If you are visiting during the first couple of weeks in June, watch for the dark-red solitary blossom of the unusual **pitcher plant**. Look down into its pitcherlike leaves for an unsuspecting insect lured there by its beautiful bloom and inviting odor. Unable to crawl up and out, the insect falls into the rainwater collected in its bowl-like base and drowns. The plant then secretes an enzyme that aids in the digestion of the insect. The digestion process produces the nitrogen necessary for the plant to survive in nutrient-poor soils.

8. Next on the right are plants that grow in the pine barren section of New Jersey. **Turkey beard** and **pixie moss** thrive in this acidic, sandy soil. In early spring turkey beard resembles sea grass, but in June it more closely resembles a turkey's beard. It sends out a two-foot-long stalk bearing an elongated cluster with bristlelike leaves at the top and a bunch of small white flowers below. Pixie moss sports white flowers also, but they cover the ground like a carpet.

Proceed next to plants that thrive in arid western plateaus. **Prickly pear cactus** has adapted to dry conditions by using its pads as storage containers. During spring rains, the pads expand to absorb moisture, which makes them stand erect. After hot dry summers, moisture from the pads travels down to the roots, leaving the pads gray and limp like a dirty washcloth. A showy yellow bloom appears on its flat, fleshy green pad in June.

9. Continue to the Meadow Garden on your left. Varieties of grasses grow among big bright wildflowers, such as the blazing yellow **coneflowers** with their drooping petals, clusters of orange blossoms on the **butterfly**

weed, red tubelike petals on the **bee balm**, and the dazzling gold petals on the **black-eyed Susan**.

Coneflower

10. Bear left onto the Hop Brook Trail, which runs through a typical New England wooded landscape. Here, as on the Ridge Trail, pink lady's-slippers decorate the woods in late May. After crossing three tiny bridges, you will be accompanied by Hop Brook meandering beside the trail.

The number 28 posted near the trail refers to the **scouring rush** plant that has been around since prehistoric time. It hardly looks like a plant, as all you see is a variegated stalk with a bloom that resembles a dead bud. New England settlers used the stalks to scour their pots and pans.

12. The Hop Brook Trail leads to a grove of **junipers**. Many of the trees have double or triple trunks, which indicates that the trees had been cut for timber or firewood.

13. Turn left onto the Lost Pond Trail to find the New England Garden of Rare and Endangered Plants. The Lost Pond Trail offers 10 minutes of tranquil hiking. Its name refers to the vernal pool on the left side of the trail on the second half of the loop. Vernal pools fill with water in spring and dry up in summer. Salamanders are well suited for this environment. They mate in spring when the pool offers protection for their eggs. In summer, young and old salamanders protect themselves from predators by burrowing in the muddy remains of the dried-up pool.

14. From the end of Lost Pond Trail, turn left to return to the visitor center and parking lot.

The road leaving the parking lot runs one-way, to the right. Follow the sign to Hemenway Road. Turn left at the bottom of the hill onto Eisenhower Road and left again onto Catherine Road.

33

BROADMOOR
WILDLIFE
SANCTUARY

 Distance and Difficulty: 2.7 miles of easy walking.

Scenic Broadmoor Wildlife Sanctuary boasts several environmental attractions to lure both wildlife and humans. The eastern edge of this 600-acre sanctuary borders the Charles River, home to great blue herons, osprey, kingfishers, and wood ducks. River otters, muskrats, and even a few foxes prowl near the riverbanks searching for food. Wide-open meadows, dense forests, moist wetlands, meandering streams, and picturesque ponds further enable Broadmoor, a Massachusetts Audubon Society (MAS) facility, to succeed in its mission of providing an attractive environment to birds and other wildlife in order to educate visitors in nature and ecology.

While exploring the trails around Indian Brook and the Charles River, this tour stops at historic mill sites and identifies some of Broadmoor's varied vegetation and wildlife.

Transportation: By automobile: From Routes 95/128, take Exit 21 (Route 16) west toward Wellesley. Remain on Route 16 for 7 miles through Wellesley Center and South Natick until you reach the sanctuary at 280 Eliot Street (Route 16).

By commuter rail: From Back Bay or South Station take the Framingham Line and exit at Natick. The station is 2.3 miles from the sanctuary. From the station on Main Street, head south on Main (Route 27) for 0.3 mile until the road forks. Continue straight onto Cottage Street (Route 27/Main Street bears right). Remain on Cottage until you reach a T intersection. Turn left onto Everett Street, which merges into Eliot Street. Turn right onto Eliot. The sanctuary is just ahead on the left.

Food and Drink: The nearest food shops are on Eliot Street in South Natick, 1.8 miles east of the sanctuary. The Dancing Goat is a coffee shop, and Corrado's serves takeout subs and pizza.

Restrooms: Composting toilets are located in the Nature Center.

Fees: Adults $3; children and seniors, $2. Free to members of Massachusetts Audubon Society. Open dawn to dusk except Mondays. Call 781-235-3929 for more information.

Background: Native Americans settled in and around Broadmoor because of its close proximity to the Charles River and one of its tributaries, Indian Brook. When the plague of 1616 decimated Broadmoor's Native American inhabitants, the Massachuset, a tribe of Christian converts led by Reverend John Eliot, replaced them. In 1692, Eliot hired Thomas Sawin, a local carpenter, to build a gristmill by the banks of Indian Brook. The tribe then could grind its own corn instead of carting it to Medfield and Watertown. Huge millstones are remnants of a later gristmill built on Indian Brook.

THE WALK

Here, as on other MAS properties, blue trail markers indicate trails heading away from the visitor center, while yellow markers signal trails leading back to the visitor center. The square numbered signs note trail junctions.

BROADMOOR WILDLIFE SANCTUARY

1. Depart from the solar-heated Nature Center and turn left.

   There may be activity in the swallows' nest boxes, located on the right of the trail. If you are visiting in mid-May when eggs are hatching, you may witness mother and father swallows catching insects in midair and carrying them back to the boxes to feed their young.

2. Bear left at the #2 marker onto the Mill Pond Trail.

   A quarter-mile from the Nature Center lies a 110-foot bridge over Indian Brook and the marsh. Indian Brook provided a trade route for Native Americans by linking the Charles River with the Cochituate Lakes. From the lakes, Native Americans paddled north along the Sudbury, Assabet, and Concord Rivers to the Merrimack River to trade with tribes in northern and western sections of New England.

   Wildlife abounds in this section of the reservation. You may spot painted turtles sunning on old logs, long-dark brown minks running swiftly near the shore, or light-brown muskrats swimming through the wetlands.

   If you are walking in the spring, you may hear the *wichedy, wichedy* sounds of the common yellowthroat, or the whistled *peter, peter* of the tufted titmouse. Gray wings and back, white breast, and the characteristic tuft on top of the head describe the tufted titmouse. It's easier to spot the bright yellow throat on the common yellowthroat. A black masklike band around the eyes distinguishes the male from the female.

3. After crossing two bridges, bear left at the 3M marker while remaining on the M (Mill Pond) Trail.

   The trail hugs the brook as it passes through red maple wetland, oak woodland, and then a white pine forest. **Partridgeberry** creeps along the forest floor. During spring, pairs of its white tube-shaped flowers peek out above round, shiny green leaves. In autumn, these flowers give way to red berries.

   If you are touring in May, keep your eye open for delicate pink blooms, courtesy of the **lady's-slipper**. Its name refers to the slipperlike pouch formed by its lower petal. Even though you may see a number of these orchids growing in the woods, resist the temptation to pick them. Because their anthers lie well within the petals, the lady's-slipper is a difficult flower to pollinate. Bees must enter the bloom via a small slit in the petal. When the bee exits through a hole in the rear wall of the flower, it rubs against an anther that releases pollen. After the bee has managed the intricacies of entering and exiting, it then must go through the whole process again if it is to pollinate another lady's-slipper. During summer, the pollinated plants retain their shriveled blooms, while the unpollinated plants dry up and die.

Another pink orchidlike plant that decorates the woods during spring is the **fringed polygala**. Its other name, **gaywings**, refers to its shape, which resembles a tiny tailless airplane. Whereas the bloom on the lady's-slipper droops from the top of a slender stem, the flower on the low-growing polygala rises from its underground stem.

Fringed polygala

After the trail curves to the right, a stand of tall **witch hazel** shrubs line the path. One of the latest-blooming plants, witch hazel waits until autumn to display clusters of spidery yellow flowers. The blooms adapt to cold weather by curling back into a bud. When the temperature rises, the petals open. Liquid extracted from its bark and branches is the main ingredient in the time-honored lotion used to treat bruises, bites, and sore muscles.

4. Cross the small Mill Pond Bridge above the Mill Pond Dam. Here the water falling to Indian Brook powered a gristmill and sawmill. Continue straight past the #5 marker onto the short H (Hemlock) Trail.

    This loop runs alongside a stream through a dense **hemlock** forest. Many groves of grand old hemlocks remain in New England forests, because loggers preferred fine-grained lumber suitable for building to this coarse-wooded evergreen. Characterized by two flattened rows of short flat needles, hemlocks thrive in moist environments.

5. The H Trail returns to the C (Charles River) Trail just after crossing the stream. Turn left.

6. Turn left at #8 onto the W (Wildlife Pond) Trail to view colorful wood ducks, Canada geese, painted turtles, and river otters that may be in or around the pond.

7. Turn left at #9, crossing the dam and tiny waterfall, to continue on the C Trail.

   The path runs between South Street and a meadow. Listen for the *sweet, sweet, I'm so sweet* call of the yellow warblers that may be searching the meadow for insects.

8. Bear right at #10, cross South Street, and proceed on the C Trail.

9. Proceed straight at the fork at #11 toward the Charles River.

   This section begins in a hemlock forest and then passes through an oak woodland with an undergrowth of witch hazel. Examine the oak branches and leaves to discover galls, little round balls that are green in spring and turn red in fall. The oak tree grows galls when an insect deposits an egg on its tissue. After the egg hatches, the oak protects itself by increasing its production of tissue to surround and isolate the larva. The insect then feeds off the new tissue rather than other parts of the tree.

   The trail parallels the Charles River for a quarter-mile. Watch for great blue herons or kingfishers searching the river for a midday snack. Both have long beaks that enable them to pluck fish out of the water.

Swamp tupelo

   The arching branches of the **swamp tupelo** trees form right angles over the river. In autumn the trees' shiny red elliptical-shaped leaves create a dazzling display as they reflect off the water.

   After leaving the riverbed and completing the loop, you will pass a stand of **white pine** saplings. To determine their age, count the number of whorls, or arrangement of branches growing from the same joint.

The distance between whorls reveals the growing conditions. A large spread reveals a year with plenty of sun and moisture.

10. Bear right at #11, recross South Street, and continue straight at #10 onto the B (Boundary) Trail, with views on the left side of the field and Wildlife Pond.

11. Continue straight past the site of the sawmill that operated here in the 19th century. Cross through the #5 intersection toward the dam, waterfall, and remnants of the gristmill at the #6 intersection.

    All that remains of the gristmill are two large round granite stones that were used to grind grain into flour. Flowing river water turned wooden gears which rotated the top stone. Dried corn kernels, lying on the stationary bottom stone, were mashed by the rotating top stone.

12. Continue straight to the #7 intersection. Turn right onto the S (Blueberry Swamp) Trail.

13. Remain on the S Trail until the #12 intersection. Turn right.

14. At the junction with the M Trail at #3, bear left to return to the visitor center.

34

WELLESLEY COLLEGE

LAKE WABAN

 Distance and Difficulty: Allow an hour to explore the art museum and one to two hours for the greenhouses and arboretum, depending on your interest in horticulture. Walking time between the museum and greenhouses and between the arboretum and lake is about 10 minutes each way. The lake's circumference is 2.5 miles.

The Wellesley College campus, often described as among the most beautiful in the world, boasts a variety of high-quality, no-cost offerings: the new, modern Davis Museum and Cultural Center, Margaret C. Ferguson Greenhouses, Hunnewell Arboretum, and Alexandra Botanic Garden. Exercise aficionados can stroll around the campus or on the path near the shore of Lake Waban. The lake intensifies the beauty of the campus by reflecting both the landscape and buildings as well as the lush, colorful foliage growing beside the water.

Transportation: By automobile: Wellesley College is located at 106 Central Street in the town of Wellesley, 12 miles west of Boston and 3.5 miles west of the Route 16 exit (21B) off Routes 95/128. Proceed on Route 16 for 3 miles. In Wellesley Center Route 16 veers to the left. Continue straight on Route 135. Turn left at the traffic light onto the Wellesley College entrance road, named College Road, which bisects the campus.

Lake Waban reflects the Wellesley College campus.

From College Road take the second right and then another right into the parking lot. The parking lot is bounded by tennis courts and the lake.

By commuter rail: From Back Bay or South Station take the Framingham Line to Wellesley Square. The campus is on Route 135, less than a mile west of the station.

Bus: Wellesley Senate Bus from Harvard Square, MIT, Massachusetts Avenue and Beacon Street, and Woodland Station (Green Line–D) runs Friday night, Saturday, and Sunday. Call 617-235-0320, ext. 2670.

Food and Drink: Wellesley Center has a number of places: Truly Yogurt sits on the corner of Grove and Washington Streets. Farther east on Washington Street are White Mountain Creamery, Bruegger's Bagel Bakery, and Au Bon Pain. Within the college, the Collins Cafe is located next to the Davis Museum and Cultural Center.

Restrooms: Located in the Davis Museum.

Background: Wellesley College is a prestigious women's college whose scenic campus is as widely praised as its high-achieving students. The campus originally belonged to its founder, Henry Fowle Durant, whose expressed wish was to transform his country estate into the most beautiful female college in the world. To accomplish that end, Durant, a brilliant and successful Harvard-educated trial lawyer turned evangelical Christian, chose Hammatt Billings as the architect.

Billings's canvas was Durant's estate—300 acres of hills, woods, and meadows bordering Lake Waban. His first building, College Hall, rose five stories and overlooked the lake. It contained the president's office, library, chapel, and dining room, all decorated in a luxurious manner. The living quarters for the solely female faculty and students also occupied the same building. When this magnificent structure burned down in 1914, it was replaced by a series of brick Gothic Revival–style buildings.

In 1902, Frederick Law Olmsted Jr., whose father conceived Boston's Emerald Necklace (chapter 1), helped design the campus, botanical garden, and arboretum. Olmsted's design differed from what was typical for the time. Instead of scattering buildings around the 500-acre campus, he grouped compatible buildings in one area, contributing to the formation of one of our country's most aesthetically pleasing campuses.

With an enrollment of approximately 2,200 students, Wellesley has withstood the trend of women's colleges toward admitting men and continues to remain in the top tier of academic institutions.

THE WALK

1. From the service parking lot, head for the Davis Museum and Cultural Center, housed in a modern brick building a few hundred yards up the road from the parking lot.

2. Climb the wide stair tunnel, a solution to the design problem of constructing a building on a site that is higher than the buildings around it. After your ascent to the concrete plaza, you'll find the museum on your left.

    The **Davis Museum and Cultural Center**, which is free and open to the public, opened in October 1993. Museum hours are Tuesday, Friday, and Saturday 11:00 A.M. to 5:00 P.M., Wednesday and Thursday 11:00 A.M. to 8:00 P.M., and Sunday 1:00 to 5:00 P.M. To hear a recording of current exhibits and programs, call 781-283-2051.

    The Davis Museum houses nearly 5,000 objects from Wellesley's art collection, which was established in the late 19th century. Its 10 roomy galleries display only one-fifth of its holdings, ranging from classical

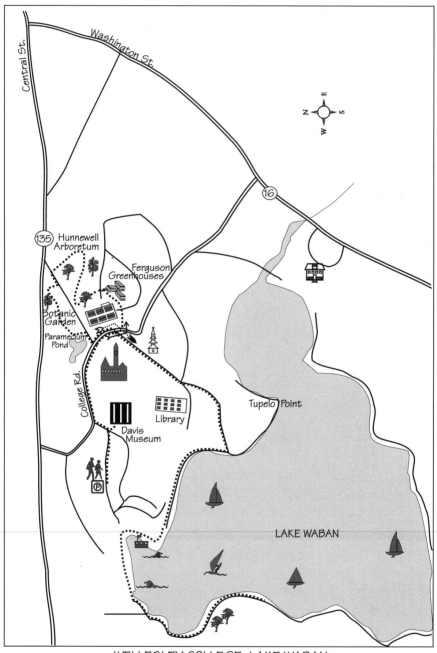

WELLESLEY COLLEGE-LAKE WABAN

through contemporary sculpture, along with 15th- through 20th-century paintings, prints, drawings, and photographs. Among the artists represented are Picasso, Monet, Calder, Degas, Cézanne, Léger, Rodin, Hoffman, and de Kooning. Wellesley alumnae donated the collection, which includes such diverse offerings as Chinese jades, Greek vases, African sculptures, Costa Rican figures, and a Brillo box constructed by Andy Warhol.

Rafael Moneo's design of Davis Museum has received much praise. He stacks the galleries vertically and links them by a central staircase that scissors back and forth between the rooms. You'll find modern and contemporary art in the galleries on the second floor and 19th-century, Renaissance, and Baroque on the third. Schist, a coarse-grained rock composed of flaky parallel layers of minerals, covers the entry-level floor. The light airy galleries draw much of their illumination from the atrium on the top floor, where a series of overhead clerestory windows also highlight a sculpture court. Adjacent to the galleries, tall windows are located conveniently above benches, so you can sit and contemplate framed views of the campus.

The Cultural Center also contains a gallery for special exhibitions, in addition to a cinema and cafe.

3. To reach the greenhouses from the museum, turn right on the Davis Museum and Cultural Center access road.

4. Take the next right onto College Road. Follow College Road, passing on the right the Academic Quad with its tall Gothic-style tower.

5. Turn left, heading toward the modern Science Center, and walk to its right. The **Margaret C. Ferguson Greenhouses and Visitor Center** sit on the northeast side of the Science Center.

The Margaret C. Ferguson Greenhouses, open daily from 8:30 A.M. to 4:30 P.M., house more than 1,000 kinds of plants from all regions of the world. Eleven greenhouses contain the college's permanent collection, which focuses on demonstrating the diversity and adaptations of orchids, ferns, and desert and tropical plants, as well as subtropical, temperate, and aquatic plants. Four greenhouses serve as horticulture classrooms, while two others provide botanical research facilities for faculty and students.

From the entrance, walk by the Friends' Office and Assembly Room. A right turn leads to a greenhouse containing desert plants. The next room displays seasonal plants, followed by a very large greenhouse where the tropical plants grow. Subtropical plants grow in the room next door. If you continue straight you'll find water plants, and if you turn right you'll see the orchid area.

6. To reach the **Hunnewell Arboretum** and **Alexandra Botanic Garden** from the greenhouses, turn right onto the driveway/ access road.

7. Continue to the intersection with a paved road. Turn left. A small Botanic Garden sign is perched on the corner among the shrubs. Take an immediate left onto a grassy slope into the arboretum/botanic garden.

In 1921, trustees of Wellesley College set aside 22 acres for the study of trees, shrubs, plants, and birds. They hired Arthur Shurtlett and Frederick Olmsted Jr. to design the arboretum. Its construction and planting was administered by Professor Helen Davis, the director of the gardens for 17 years.

Although parklike, the garden's primary purpose is to encourage the study of plants. Different species of a genus are planted near each other so as to invite comparison. Some of the attributes that interest professors and students are rate of growth, size, form, susceptibility to disease, and attractiveness to birds. Each plant has two labels: one displays its scientific name and the second notes the date it was acquired. Some sections of the arboretum purposely are not landscaped, so students can study the insect and fungus activity that results from decaying leaves, flowers, and branches.

As you walk through the arboretum, you may notice small saplings encased in white plastic tubing. In order to minimize expenditures, new trees are purchased when very young. The plastic protects the saplings from the elements.

8. Proceed about 50 yards down the slope. The trickle of water you hear on the left flows from a grotto. Ferns and wildflowers thrive in this moist area. Marsh marigold, coral bell, and bleeding heart are a few of the varieties that bloom here in the spring.

Farther ahead on the left are several species of Japanese maple trees. Small plaques on the trees memorialize a child or classmate.

9. As you round the corner, you'll walk through Wedding Point, a popular place for ceremonies in late May and early June when the azaleas and rhododendrons are in full bloom.

   The Jennings Biblical Garden is to the left of Wedding Point. Hawthorn, fir, ash, and spruce trees, along with additional plants also mentioned in biblical texts, grow in this section.

10. Bear right and head for the small concrete pond.

11. Walk past the left side of the pond, with Carolina rhododendrons and a huge **stewartia** tree, distinguished by its mottled bark, on your left.

12. When face to face with a large pitch pine tree (needles in clusters of three), bear right.

    If you visit in late May, the sweet fragrance of the **lilac** bushes on your left perfume the air.

13. Upon reaching a paved path, turn left, heading for the big yellow Fiske House, which houses Wellesley College faculty.

14. At the parking lot, immediately turn left onto an asphalt walkway that leads to the **Alexandra Botanic Garden**.

    The walkway passes over a tiny waterfall from a stream that meanders through the garden to Paramecium Pond.

15. After passing crab apple and cherry trees on the left, look to the right to spot a wrought-iron sculpture named "Wild Spot." At this point, leave the paved walk and head onto the well-worn path that follows the stream to Paramecium Pond. Clusters of tiny light-blue forget-me-nots thrive on the moist banks of the stream.

    A number of unusual trees grow in this section. Among them are **tulip trees** which produce bright green and orange tuliplike flowers in spring; **dawn redwood**, whose hemlocklike leaves drop each fall (it was believed to have become extinct 20 million years ago until rediscovered in China

Tulip tree

in 1944); **Ohio buckeye**, a relative of the horse chestnut; **cork trees**, most commonly found in Spain and Portugal; and a **weeping Japanese cherry tree**.

16. Continue toward Paramecium Pond. Benches are placed conveniently for those who wish to rest before proceeding back to College Road.

17. Turn left on College Road.

18. Take the next right, passing the Academic Quad on the right and Houghton Memorial Chapel on the left. Continue straight. Before you reach Lake Waban, you'll pass on the right tennis courts, the Margaret Clapp Library, and the Continuing Education building.

19. Continue walking to the shore. Turn right onto a path that runs near the water.

   The route crosses two beaches and runs by the Wellesley Boathouse before it enters a woodland on the west side.

   Soon you'll see Do Not Trespass signs indicating the boundary line of Wellesley College.

   Look across Lake Waban for a view of the grandiose Hunnewell estate, with its sculpted bushes and trees. Built in 1852 by H. Hollis Hunnewell, a grandson-in-law of Samuel Welles, for whom the town of Wellesley was named, the mansion has six terraces which contain more than two acres of shrubs.

20. To reach the parking lot from the lake, follow the road behind the boathouse.

35

HAMMOND POND RESERVATION
WEBSTER CONSERVATION AREA

Distance and Difficulty: two miles of easy walking.

Nestled behind the parking lot of a sprawling suburban mall, two combined recreation areas offer well-marked trails through 200 acres of woodlands. The entrance path to Hammond Pond Reservation follows the shore of serene Hammond Pond, where ducks, geese, and snapping turtles edge out their companions as they compete for scraps of food. On the woodland side of the path, rock climbers attempt to scale sheer cliffs that rise to the treetops.

Webster Conservation Area is located farther in the reservation, seemingly removed from the bustle of Route 9. It contains a 22-acre deer park, home to more than 30 bucks, does, and fawns. If you rattle the fence, the normally reticent deer may appear. Beyond the deer park, tucked in back of the MBTA tracks, lies Houghton Garden. Meticulously landscaped flower beds frame ponds and streams that flow through this idyllic spot. The western side of the reservation, across Hammond Pond Parkway, boasts startling glacial rock formations, including Gooch's Cave and Cake Rock.

Transportation: By automobile: From Route 9 (Boylston Street) in the Chestnut Hill section of Newton, exit onto Hammond Street, which leads to the one-level shopping area anchored by Star Market and Bloomingdale's clothing store (not to be confused with the Atrium or the Mall at Chestnut Hill, both west of Hammond Street). Turn left into the parking lot and drive behind Star Market toward Bloomingdale's. Park in the small parking lot behind Bloomingdale's, near the woods to the left of Hammond Pond.

By the Ⓣ: Take the MBTA Green Line–D toward Riverside and get off the train at Chestnut Hill. The reservation is a half-mile from the Chestnut Hill stop. Proceed south on Hammond Street past the Longwood Cricket Club, until you reach the shopping center. Turn right into the parking lot for Star Market and walk along the north side of the lot, past Hammond Pond until you reach the trailhead.

Food and Drink: Star Market, Legal Seafoods, and Friendly's are located in the mall adjacent to the reservation.

Restrooms: Bloomingdale's, Legal Seafoods, Friendly's.

Recreational Options: Cross-country skiing, rock climbing.

Background: Hammond Pond Reservation is named for Thomas Hammond, who farmed the land in the mid-1600s. It is administered by the Metropolitan District Commission (MDC), which manages 16,000 acres of conservation land within metropolitan Boston. The 114-acre northern half, Webster Conservation Area, belongs to the city of Newton, which purchased parcels of land, beginning in 1968 from the Stone and Houghton families.

THE WALK

1. Begin at the entrance to Hammond Pond Reservation, to the left of Hammond Pond, at the north end of the parking lot. Walk through the metal gate and remain on the wide main path as it runs north through the woods.

    On the left, walls of rock beckon climbers who practice here before they head up to New Hampshire's White Mountains. Closer inspection of the seemingly smooth rock surface yields a jumble of different stones, called puddingstone, presumably because its gray-grape color and texture resemble old-fashioned pudding. This conglomerate, the official

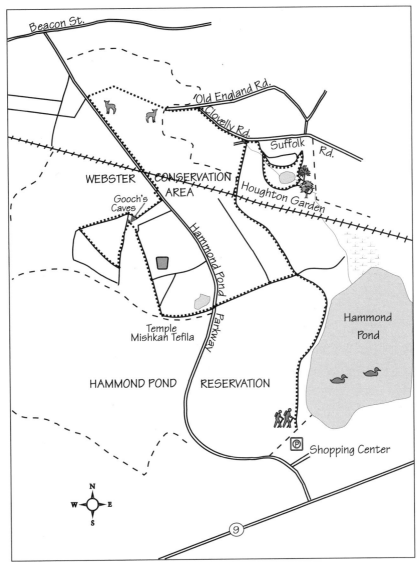

HAMMOND POND RESERVATION-WEBSTER CONSERVATION AREA

rock of Massachusetts, was formed from compressed outwash of ancient rivers and is estimated to be 600 million years old. Tightly packed mud forms its light purple background, which holds a conglomeration of granite, quartzite, and volcanic rock.

The path bends toward the pond, allowing a closer inspection of the waterfowl.

2. Ignore the paths going off to the left and right and continue on the trail in what is now the Webster Conservation Area for a half-mile through woodland filled with beech and oak trees and an understory of huckleberry and blueberry bushes. After the trail heads away from Hammond Pond, look for an old cranberry bog on the right. Pass over the tiny plank bridge that spans Hammond Brook.

3. Proceed through the gate to the MBTA tracks. Frequent commuter trains rumble along the rail bed, so take care when crossing the tracks.

4. Go straight onto Suffolk Road. Turn right and then right again through the main entrance gate to **Houghton Garden**.

    In an ongoing creative effort spanning 40 years, Mr. and Mrs. Clemence Houghton, previous owners of this property, dammed a swamp and artfully diverted the flow of water to form ponds and streams to enhance their natural-looking garden. They constructed stone bridges and walkways and then planted flora native to the region as well as several species of exotic trees.

5. To begin your tour of the garden, take the first left, passing the flower beds maintained by the Chestnut Hill Garden Club. Follow the path as it circles the tiny pond, adorned by honeysuckle, azalea, and rhododendron bushes whose colorful blooms brighten the landscape in late May and early June.

    Sourwood

    Don't miss the Japanese sweet gum and sourwood trees planted by the Houghtons in the Conifer Garden in the southeastern corner. The **Japanese sweet gum** is spotted most easily in autumn, when its star-shaped leaves turn a brilliant red and prickly brown fruit balls droop from its branches. The **sourwood**, an ornamental tree found more commonly in southern states, is best viewed in spring when it flaunts white bell-shaped flowers that resemble lily of the valley. Early settlers named the tree after attempting to quench their thirst by chewing on its twigs.

The green film on the pond's surface is not algae but **duckweed**, the world's smallest flowering plant. Look carefully among the duckweed to spot frogs and painted turtles sunning themselves on rocks.

6. Continue to circle the pond, crossing and recrossing the stream that meanders through the gardens. The Ⓣ tracks will be on your left now. Return to the entry path and exit through the same gate back onto Suffolk Road.

7. Turn left on Suffolk, which becomes Clovelly Road, and follow it until it ends at a gravel driveway at 100 Old England Road (Clovelly is now named Old England Road).

8. Walk 100 feet up the driveway toward the chain-link fence and path that circle the deer park. Rattle the chain on the gate to alert the deer, who may then pay you a visit. Although it's possible to circle the park by following the path next to the fence, for this tour remain on the path only until you reach Hammond Pond Parkway.

You may be wondering why a deer park was plunked down amid shopping malls. The deer, having lived in the park for more than 30 years, were here long before the malls. When the city of Newton bought the land from the family of Edwin Webster, a founder of Stone & Webster engineering company, the deer that Webster kept as pets were included in the purchase. Newton Recreation Department now cares for the 22-acre park and more than 30 deer, twice the original number.

9. At Hammond Pond Parkway, turn left and walk next to the deer park with the parkway to your right. After you walk on the bridge above the Ⓣ tracks, carefully cross the busy parkway and continue heading south, with the western section of Webster Conservation Area on your right.

10. Follow the two-rail wooden fence. Just after the fence stops, turn right onto a narrow path heading into the woods. A Webster Conservation Area sign may be posted as you enter. Look for blue blazes on a tree.

11. From the entry path, turn right, following the orange-and-green-blazed trail as it loops around the huge boulders that form **Gooch's Caves**. This formation of rocks—many revealing evidence of glacial scarring—was used for shelter by Native American hunting parties.

12. After the cave loop, proceed south on the blue-and-orange-blazed trail to the immense **Cake Rock**, favored by youngsters for its climbing potential. Its cupcake-like shape was formed from layers of Cambridge sandstone.

13. Remain on the blue-blazed trail as it continues south toward Temple Mishkan Tefila and then bears left, passing Farm Pond on the left.

14. After reaching Hammond Pond Parkway, carefully cross the thorough-fare and get on the path into Hammond Pond Reservation.

15. Remain on the path until it intersects the main trail through the reservation. Turn right to return to the parking lot.

36

HABITAT

WILDLIFE

SANCTUARY

 Distance and Difficulty: two miles of easy walking.

Habitat's convenient location and friendly atmosphere make it an ideal spot for a family outing, as well as a peaceful place to exercise and commune with nature. Habitat is only 7 miles from Boston, less than 1 mile from Belmont Center, and accessible by public transportation, yet few people are aware of its existence. Now that the Massachusetts Audubon Society (MAS) is managing the property, word is getting out that this 89-acre sanctuary offers many pleasant options.

The sanctuary entrance is impressive. A shady parking lot leads to a wide circular drive in front of a grand neo-Georgian colonial that houses the Visitor Center. A glance out the center's back window reveals formal gardens that have witnessed many a wedding. The friendly staff is eager to share information and give directions.

From its inception, Habitat's primary goal has been to stimulate children's interest in the natural world through outdoor experience, so much of the programming, facilities, and even the trail markers are geared to youngsters.

Among its offerings are a vegetable garden planted and cared for by children, a half-mile-long nature trail, and the Unnature Trail, where kids learn to look closely at the environment by searching for items that do not belong. Habitat exudes an upbeat attitude. Its manageable size, well-tended trails, and emphasis on children make it clear that Habitat has a mission and is proud of it.

Transportation: By automobile: From Route 2, take Exit 59 (Route 60, Pleasant Street) toward Belmont. Go about 0.7 mile and turn right on Clifton (traffic light). Turn left onto Fletcher. Remain on Fletcher for 0.3 mile and then turn left on Juniper Road. The sanctuary sits on the right 0.3 mile down the road.

Tending the children's garden at Habitat Wildlife Sanctuary.

By Ⓣ and bus: Take the Red Line toward Alewife and exit at Harvard Square. From the square, hop on the #74 bus to Belmont Center. Exit at the last stop at the corner of Alexander Avenue and Leonard Street. From the bus stop, go west on Alexander a short block to Pleasant Street (Route 60). Turn right on Pleasant and then make an immediate left on Somerset Street, a great street for walking, as few drivers like to navigate over its many potholes. After hiking up Belmont Hill for a half-mile, turn right onto Juniper Road. Habitat is on your left.

By commuter rail: From North Station, take the Fitchburg Line to the second stop at Belmont Center. Exit the station and head for Leonard Street, which runs through Belmont Center. Either bike or walk through Belmont Center until you reach Alexander Street and then follow the route from the bus stop in the above directions.

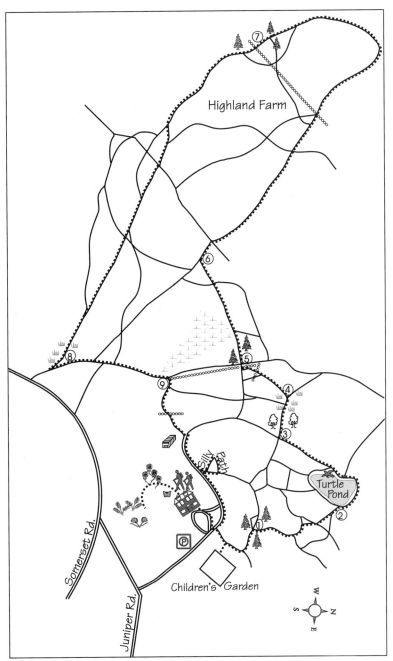

HABITAT WILDLIFE SANCTUARY

Food and Drink: A number of shops are on Leonard Street in Belmont Center, less than a mile from Habitat. Among them are Starbucks, Bruegger's Bagel Bakery, and TCBY yogurt.

Restrooms: Located in the visitor center.

Fees: Adults, $3; senior citizens and children, $2; free to members. Open dawn to dusk except Mondays. Call 617-489-5050 for more information.

Recreational Options: No dogs; no picnicking.

Background: As visitors soon surmise, the imposing visitor center and surrounding property belonged originally to owners of wealth and privilege. Ruth Hornblower Atkins Greenough Churchill, whose family once owned the entire summit of Belmont Hill, built the brick mansion in 1914. An ardent environmentalist, Churchill designed and planted diverse habitat areas to attract wildlife. She then encouraged school groups to use her property for nature study. Insistent that her estate continue to function as an environmental education center, she set aside 26 acres of her land to be used for natural history education. A year after her death, in 1971, the private, nonprofit Habitat was established to educate children. Fourteen years later, Churchill's son, Elisha Atkins, left Yale University after spending 30 years as a professor and then dean of Yale Medical School to direct Habitat.

In July 1994, the Massachusetts Audubon Society consolidated its Highland Farm holdings with Habitat and took over management of both properties. MAS had purchased the 45-acre Highland Farm in the 1960s. Originally part of a 205-acre parcel owned by Winthrop Chenery and called Highland Stock Farm, the property included a racetrack for thoroughbred horses, now the Belmont Hill Club. Chenery was among the first farmers to successfully breed purebred Holstein-Friesian cattle, imported from Holland. Their descendants now produce most of our country's milk.

MAS is continuing the Habitat tradition of running a summer nature-study day camp and offering educational programs for adults and children year-round.

THE WALK

1. From inside the visitor center, exit through the back door to view the formal gardens planted by the property's previous owner, Ruth Churchill.

Fountains and birdbaths enhance the gardens filled with annuals and perennials, a picturesque and popular place for weddings. The rose garden lies directly ahead. To the left, a butterfly garden displays plants that attract butterflies, such as **bee balm**, whose showy red flowers also lure hummingbirds. Butterflies find the orange bugle-shaped **trumpet creeper** vine irresistible.

2. Turn left to reach the wildflower and fern gardens, designed by Will Curtis, who also created Garden in the Woods (chapter 32).

In autumn, the wildflower garden is filled with **white wood asters**, whose small white petals surround lavender centers. You may spot another species of white flower that has a small fuzzy head bunched into flat-topped clusters, with the unlovely name of **white snakeroot**. While fine in a flower garden, white snakeroot can be deadly if allowed to grow in pastures—not for the cows who graze on it but for the humans who drink the cows' milk. A more benign plant that also produces small white flowers is **smooth Solomon's seal**. Its bell-shaped flowers, hanging from dark-green arching stems, turn into dark blue berries in the fall.

Smooth Solomon's seal

During spring, the ground is covered with bright yellow **trout lily**, red bell-shaped **columbine**, dainty white **anemone**, **hepatica** with its six small pink petals, and **trillium**, so named because of its three large white petals surrounded by three pointed leaves.

Mrs. Churchill was fond of ferns, and more than a dozen varieties grow here. At first glance, ferns tend to look similar to one another. Close inspection reveals significant differences. The **ostrich fern's** large size and gracefully arching fronds which resemble ostrich feathers distinguish it from other ferns. **Christmas fern** may look familiar because its fronds, which remain green throughout the year, are used to create Christmas decorations. The fronds on the **maidenhair fern** curve around like a horseshoe and grow in a row from

Christmas fern

slim straight stalks. The distinctive characteristic of the **New York fern** is tiny leaflets
on both the bottom and top of the frond.

New York fern

3. Leave Mrs. Churchill's gardens, head
   back through the Visitor Center, and go
   left around the circular drive.

4. Turn left onto the path next to the
   Wildlife Nesting Area sign.

5. Turn right at the gate to visit the
   Children's Garden, bird blind, and the
   community gardens, where gardeners
   rent plots for $50 per year.

   Naturalists teach children's gardening classes here in the spring.
   Activities include spreading manure, planting vegetables and flowers,
   and harvesting crops. A bird blind, where students can observe birds,
   stands beyond the garden.

6. From the Children's Garden, return to the wide wood-chip-covered
   trail and head into a **white pine** forest.

   Count the pine needles to distinguish red from white pine. The stiff,
   thick red-pine needles are two to a cluster, whereas white-pine clusters
   are composed of five light, thin needles. The largest trees are more than
   100 years old. You can determine the age of a pine tree by counting the
   layers of branches, or whorls, and adding five years, the average time it
   takes a tree to sprout and grow its first whorl.

7. Bear right at the triple fork (1) toward Turtle Pond.

   As you walk among the pines, you may hear stereophonic chirping
   noises. Chipmunks are making these sounds
   to warn neighboring chipmunks to stay out
   of their territory.

8. Upon reaching a stand of **white birches**, the
   path forks. Bear right to circle Turtle Pond
   (2).

   Ruth Churchill dammed and dredged a
   marsh to carve this pond, and planted the
   birches soon after. Lenticels, the short horizontal markings on white birch bark, allow

*White
birch*

air to flow through to its trunk. Once the tree reaches a certain size, the lenticels can expand no more and the bark peels off into its characteristic strips.

Moisture-loving **spicebush** grows near the water. Crushing one of its long smooth leaves and smelling the spicy aroma reveals the reason for its name. In spring, pale yellow flowers appear before the leaves. In autumn, bright orange berries hang from its umbrella-shaped branches.

Jewelweed is another plant that thrives in shaded moist areas. Another name for this golden-orange flower is **touch-me-not**, a reference to its delicate seed capsule which bursts when touched.

Mrs. Churchill created this pond in order to attract wildlife. Here, painted turtles bask on partially submerged logs; bullfrogs bathe near the pond lilies; green, great blue, and black-crowned night herons feed around the pond. Many varieties of birds nest amidst the dense foliage and in the shrubs, including kingfishers, phoebes, catbirds, Baltimore orioles, and vireos.

9.   After walking three-quarters of the way around the pond in a counter-clockwise direction, follow a path away from the pond.

10.   Turn right onto the meadow trail (3), into the meadow and up the hill. The path runs by apple trees.

   One of the trees is dotted with small holes pecked out by a yellow-bellied sapsucker, a member of the woodpecker family. He was both sucking sap and searching for insects trapped in the sap.

11.   Continue straight (4), ignoring all other paths, and then bear left into a forest of hemlock and beech trees.

12.   Bear right, pass through two stone walls, and head onto the Fern Trail (5).

13.   At the T intersection, turn left onto a rocky path.

   A **red maple** swamp and several varieties of ferns are on the left. It's easy to spot the **sensitive fern** because of its broad leaves and thick membrane which runs from top to bottom. This fern is sensitive to cold and dies at the first frost. The lacy **lady fern**, growing in circular clusters, also prefers shady moist conditions.

14.   The path leaves the swamp and enters a woodland of oak trees with an occasional **eastern red cedar**, distinguished by its shaggy bark. Sun-loving

cedars are often the first trees to pop up once farmland reverts to forest. Cedars remain until more dominant trees, such as oaks, begin to grow taller than the cedars and steal their sunlight.

15. Turn right at the next **T** intersection (6) and begin the Highland Farm loop.

16. Proceed straight past the paths that intersect the trail. Cross through a stone wall, loop around, and pass through it again. Just before the second stone wall crossing, the path forks and then rejoins (7).

   This section runs through a grove of white pines containing many saplings. The distance between the whorls of branches indicates the quality of the growing season. A sunny yet moist season produces a wider span than one with less rain and few sunny days.

17. Continue straight as the trail passes through an oak woodland and returns to the meadow. Turn left at the **T** intersection (8).

18. Cross the red maple swamp via the wooden footbridge. When you reach the stone wall, turn right and proceed 100 feet up a slight incline (9).

19. Turn left and cross over the stone wall. As you turn, look for the Habitat sign posted on a tree.

20. Head into the pine forest and proceed toward the brick building. Watch for the roof of the greenhouse, down the incline to the right.

21. From the greenhouse, head up the paved walk, past the brown building on the right.

22. Turn left onto the Turtle Pond Loop.

23. Take an immediate left to walk down the Unnature Trail (formerly named Silly Path), stocked with items that are out of place in a natural environment (10).

   If you are accompanied by children, direct them to count how many unlikely things they can find (like a toothbrush on a branch).

24. Follow the Unnature Trail back to the paved walkway. Turn left to return to the Visitor Center.

37

DeCordova Museum
Sandy Pond

 Distance and Difficulty: The walk around Sandy Pond on level, somewhat bumpy terrain covers three miles. Add another half-mile for the Sculpture Park tour. If you choose to visit the museum, allow about an hour.

The tour around DeCordova Museum and Sculpture Park in Lincoln merges art with nature in one of the most exquisite settings in the Boston area. Perched high on a hill overlooking Sandy Pond, Julian de Cordova's castle overlooks 35 acres of rolling terrain, much of it decorated with contemporary sculpture. The museum itself exhibits contemporary American art, while a complex of studios on the property provide art education to adults and children. After the overview of Sandy Pond, also known as Flint's Pond, we descend to the water to experience one of Henry Thoreau's favorite walks, a 3-mile exploration on wooded trails that circle the water.

Transportation: By automobile: From Routes 95/128, take Exit 28B, Trapelo Road, west toward Lincoln. Remain on Trapelo Road for 3 miles until you see the sign for DeCordova Museum on the right.

DeCordova Museum and Sculpture Park has a large parking area located at the end of the entrance road.

By commuter rail: From North Station, take the Fitchburg Line to Lincoln. The DeCordova Museum is a mile and a half from Lincoln Station. From the station, cross Lincoln Road to enter the bike path. After a half-mile, turn left onto Mackintosh Lane. Follow Mackintosh for a quarter-mile. Turn right onto a hiking trail over a gas line. Bear right at the fork and head toward a school. Upon reaching the school grounds, hug the edge of the yard, near the woods. Follow the schoolyard around until you are almost parallel with the school. Turn left on the path that heads into the fields. At the next fork, bear right. This path leads to the extension of Trapelo Road named Sandy Pond Road. Just before the path reaches the road, it forks again. Bear left to reach the entrance road to the DeCordova Museum.

Food and Drink: The Café at DeCordova, located on the fourth floor of the museum, is open Tuesday through Sunday from 11:00 A.M. to 4:00 P.M. and serves light luncheonfare. The Mall at Lincoln Station has a small coffee shop named the Whistlestop which sells light sandwiches, drinks, and muffins. Donalon's, a food market also located in the mall, sells sandwiches and drinks.

Restrooms: At the Mobil gas station on the south side of the train station (located in the drugstore). Inside the DeCordova Museum store to the right of the lower parking area.

Fees: There is no charge for walking around the Sculpture Park; however, adults pay $6 to enter the museum. The fee for senior citizens, students, and children is $4. Galleries are open Tuesday through Sunday from 11:00 A.M. to 5:00 P.M. Call 781-259-8355 for more information.

Recreational Options: Cross-country skiing around Sandy/Flint's Pond.

Background: A major reason why Julian de Cordova built his summer home in this location in the suburb of Lincoln was the panoramic view of Sandy Pond. Now a reservoir for the town of Lincoln, Sandy Pond was used first as a hunting ground by the Musketaquid tribe, who sought its abundant fish and wildlife.

Thomas Flint, after whom the pond was named, arrived in Lincoln from England in 1640 carrying a royal grant that gave him title to 750 acres, including the pond. During the years of colonization, trees were cut for fuel

DeCordova Museum. (Photo by George Vasquez)

and lumber, and livestock grazed on the land. In 1778, Zachariah Smith purchased property from the Flints on the west and north shores of the pond, where he planted cherry, apple, pear, and quince trees.

According to town legend, Henry Thoreau preferred Flint's Pond to Walden Pond. However, Captain Ephraim Flint, a descendant of Thomas, refused Thoreau permission to build his cabin along the shore. After Thoreau settled at Walden Pond, he continued to spend hours walking the trails around Flint's Pond. Each trip around the pond apparently fueled Thoreau's anger at Flint for denying him permission to live there. The name of the pond may have been changed to Sandy Pond in deference to Thoreau, who wrote in *Walden*, "Flints' Pond! Such is the poverty of our nomenclature. What right had the unclean and stupid farmer whose farm abutted on this sky water, whose shore he had ruthlessly laid bare, to give his name to it."

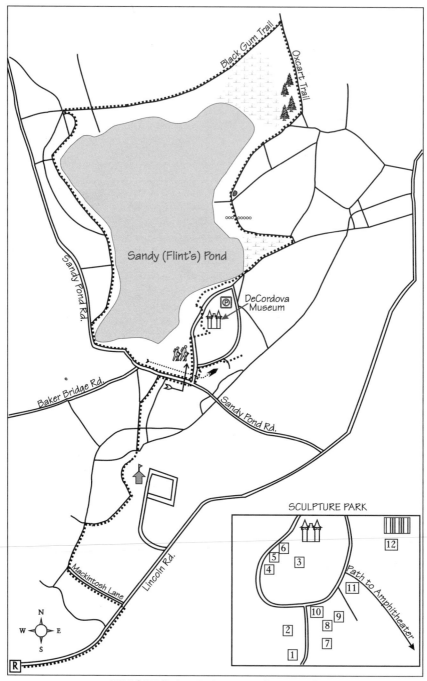

DECORDOVA MUSEUM--SANDY POND

Before the pond supplied the town with water, it was a popular spot for boating. To satisfy the demand for a place to dock and launch boats, the Lincoln Boat Club was constructed in 1893. It proved so popular that a dance hall was added on the second floor.

Around the same time, Julian de Cordova and his wife, Elizabeth, purchased 35 acres of land near the pond. They built a simple shingle-style summer retreat on a knoll overlooking the water. Fifteen years later, Julian's business success as president of the Union Glass Company and decades of traveling around the world inspired the de Cordovas to convert their dwelling to a Moorish castle and landscape it with stone walls, curving walkways, and broad grassy expanses. A collector of everything that took his fancy, de Cordova bequeathed his estate to the town of Lincoln with the stipulation that his home become a museum. Because his collection, which included paintings, tapestries, vases, and sculpture, had little artistic value, the town sold it and used the proceeds to purchase contemporary art crafted by New England artists.

In March 1998, the DeCordova opened a 15,000-square-foot wing which more than doubled its exhibition area. This addition enables the museum to strengthen its mission: to display and interpret the artworks of New England artists.

THE WALK

1. The tour begins at the entrance to the Sculpture Park. From the parking lots, walk to the main entrance at Sandy Pond Road. As you meander around the grounds, you'll find more than 40 modern and contemporary works created with a wide variety of materials, from evergreens cut precisely into topiary to metal sculptures that move with the wind. The Sculpture Park includes permanent works from the museum's collection as well as borrowed pieces in changing outdoor exhibitions.

   This tour will stop at some of the works. Because pieces are moved or returned to the sculptor, some sculptures may not be in their designated places. The comprehensive Sculpture Park Guide which describes all the pieces is on sale for $9.95 at the museum and store.

2. The beginning of the tour visits some of the sculptures on the left side of the entrance road. The last leg stops at the pieces on the right. The

sculpture nearest the entrance on the left side of the road was created by John Buck, who has named his bronze work **Dream World** (1). The title refers to an imaginary world that exists in our subconscious. The thin, elongated human form appears to balance between two discs. The left ball represents the real world while the contrasting flattened disc refers to the world of the subconscious.

3. The tower formed from discarded plastic in 1993 by Konstantin Simun memorializes the sculptor's son. When Simun emigrated from Russia to America, he no longer could afford his usual mediums, stone and bronze, so he worked with trash he found along the street. **Totem America** (2) is constructed of such recycled plastic materials as empty detergent bottles and abandoned orange highway cones.

4. As you climb the hill toward the mansion, cross the road and head onto the wide expanse of grass that lies below the museum. Walk toward the center of the lawn to find shrubs clipped to resemble English gardens. **Three Gardens** (3) by Mags Harries resembles three different enclosures that function as architectural elements when seen from above and enhance the grounds in a naturalistic way when viewed from the lawn.

5. Head back toward the road and continue your ascent until you reach a line of sculptures on the right. The first, a train or armored-tank-like contraption, is named **Mass Art Vehicle** (4). George Greenamyer's intriguing title may refer to art in Massachusetts or to art as a unified body of matter with no specific shape.

6. The soaring bronze **Venusvine** (5) appears to be formed from wooden vines. Richard Rosenblum has "tried to create a piece that flips back and forth between nature and art" in order to demonstrate the unpredictable and beautiful balance between the two.

7. The next piece is one of my personal favorites. The biomorphic forms in Dennis Kowal's steel sculpture titled **Migration–Series No. 7** (6) remind me of work by sculptor Henry Moore.

8. Follow the road to the top of the hill. Pass the museum and watch for the stairs leading to the water.

9. Descend the stairs and turn right onto a path that follows the shore into the woods.

Many **chestnut** seedlings grow near the trail. Look for long oval leaves with serrated edges. You will not find any large chestnut trees. About 50 years ago, a fungus wiped out most of Massachusetts' chestnut trees. Now seedlings sprout from old rootstocks, but when they reach five to 10 feet the fungus invades their stems and weakens the trees, and they soon die.

The path skirts wetland. Here you'll spot **bracken fern**, whose three fronds grow from one stem, and **sensitive fern**, which has a thick center membrane and broad, almost triangular leaves. The name "sensitive" fern aptly describes its reaction to cold weather: its lacy fronds die at the first touch of frost.

Witch hazel

If you're walking in late fall, you may spot the spidery yellow blooms from the **witch hazel** shrub. When the temperature drops, its petals curl into a bud. When it warms up, the petals open. Liquid extracted from the bark and leaves is used as an astringent.

10. Turn left at the No Bikes sign.

11. Bear left at the fork and head back toward the water.

During your walk, you often will be able to see the pond on your left side, a reassuring indication that you are heading in the right direction.

The path becomes quite rocky. A wood plank bridge crosses a stream and the trail cuts through a stone wall.

Hundreds of years ago, settlers used the ubiquitous stones deposited in New England by glaciers to build their homes, fence in their livestock, and serve as boundaries for their farms. These remaining stone walls scattered through the woods serve as reminders of this farming era.

12. Stop at the large glacial erratic that has a tree growing through its center. A poignant story accompanies the memorial plaque attached to this unusual formation. On January 7, 1971, Aureet Bar-Yam was walking her dog around the pond. The dog ran down the narrow path that extends from the rock to the water and scampered out on the ice. The young woman followed him but her weight broke the thin ice. Her screams alerted passersby, who immediately called the police and told them to rush to Sandy Pond. Unfortunately, the police arrived too late.

Take a quick detour down the narrow path that leads to the water. This overlook, flanked by granite outcroppings, offers a panoramic view of Sandy Pond. In autumn, the reflection of red, yellow, and orange leaves on the water creates a spectacular sight.

13. Return to the trail and remain on the path that first hugs the water and then heads into a grove of tall **hemlock** trees.

For an energy boost, the August hiker should be alert for small dark berries hanging from **blueberry** and **huckleberry bushes** that line the path. Huckleberries can be distinguished from blueberries by the little seeds in their center that crunch when chewed. Huckleberries are also darker and shinier.

In spring the hiker is rewarded with fragrance, not fruit. Near the trail, white flowers from tall **viburnum** bushes perfume the air.

14. Turn left onto Oxcart Trail, bordered on both sides by a stone wall.

15. At the fork, turn left onto the Black Gum Trail. The path now has veered away from the water to avoid the marshy terrain. The garden of lacy ferns bordering the path is thriving in the moist soil.

The trail is undoubtedly named for the **tupelo,** or black gum trees that grow on the left side near the marsh. Black gum trees are easy to spot in the fall, when their elliptical leaves turn bright red, and dark blue berries sprout from their stems.

Continue straight through the next intersection.

16. After walking on the Black Gum Trail for approximately 0.7 mile, bear left and cross a bridge constructed of oak logs.

17. Make a succession of left turns, keeping the pond on your left side, as the trail now skirts the pond's south side.

18. Remain on the path adjacent to the pond until you reach an open field that leads to Sandy Pond Road. Turn left and walk on the side of the road for a few minutes, passing the water treatment plant, formerly the site of the Lincoln Boathouse, until you come to the entrance road to the DeCordova Museum on your left.

19. Turn left onto the entrance road.

The return up the entrance road stops at the sculptures on the right side.

20. The compact formation of welded steel pieces with a haphazard, unfinished look is by Alexander Liberman and is named *Cardinal Points* (7). Liberman has used remnants of discarded oil-storage tanks to create this work.

21. Although the components of Mark di Suvero's orange steel spatial sculpture are more refined, they too refer to familiar objects. *Sunflowers for Vincent* (8), which lies straight ahead, spreads out and moves through space, drawing our eyes in many different directions.

The Musical Fence by Paul Matisse. (Photograph by Marc Teatum)

22. To the right of di Suvero's work stands ***Three Lines*** (9), a stainless-steel work by George Rickey. Here, gusts of wind determine the design of the narrow 18-foot metal spikes.

23. Walk ahead to the grove of hemlocks. Hidden beneath the trees lies Gail Rothschild's powerful piece ***Woman in the Nineteenth Century: A Conversation*** (10). *Woman in the Nineteenth Century* is the title of a book by Margaret Fuller, an intelligent woman who was not allowed to attend college because she was female. She believed that higher education was the key to women's advancement. To advance her goal, Fuller wrote books and articles and organized groups. The back of each chair displays quotations written by men about Fuller; on the front are statements by Fuller. The oversized steel rocking chairs, which resemble 19th-century wooden Windsor chairs, function as cages to contain their female occupants in positions of subjugation.

24. While following the road, bear right at the fork, passing the museum school offices on the left of the road.

25. Turn right down the paved walkway that leads to the museum store and gallery, studios, and classrooms. Several interesting sculptures are positioned around the school complex.

    Unlike most museum pieces that forbid touching, ***The Musical Fence*** (11) by Paul Matisse was designed to be played. Matisse suggests that you "strike the bars gently for the best sound."

    The larger-than-life fiberglass head was created by Philip Grausman, one of America's finest contemporary representational sculptors. ***Leucantha*** (12) is an enlargement of a photograph of Grausman's ex-wife, choreographer Martha Clarke.

    From this spot, you can walk beyond the studios to inspect the amphitheater, the site for Sunday afternoon summer concerts; visit the school gallery and store; or climb the hill to the museum.

    Museum guides offer free tours of the Sculpture Park every Saturday and Sunday at 1:00 P.M. from May to October and tours of the museum every Wednesday at 1:00 P.M. and Sunday at 2:00 P.M.

38

Moose Hill

Wildlife Sanctuary

 Distance and Difficulty: three miles of easy hiking, with a moderate climb to the bluff.

You may not spot moose lumbering through the woods in Moose Hill Wildlife Sanctuary, but you will see and hear a variety of birds as you hike through this 1,800-acre reservation. The oldest and second-largest Massachusetts Audubon Society (MAS) sanctuary, Moose Hill offers more than 15 miles of well-marked trails that loop through woodland and wetland, up to bluffs and down to valleys.

This 3-mile tour examines the sanctuary's varied topography and assorted plant life, while climbing Bluff Head on its western side and then crossing into the more tranquil eastern section to meander through pine forest and wetland. The tour includes optional side trips to Moose Hill, Hobbs Hill, and the Kendall Whaling Museum, which houses an extensive collection of whaling artifacts.

Transportation: By automobile: From Routes 128/95, follow Route 95 south toward Providence to Exit 10. At the end of the ramp, turn left toward Sharon. Travel a quarter-mile and turn right onto Route 27 toward Walpole. Proceed a half-mile and turn left onto Moose Hill Street. Follow the Massachusetts Audubon signs to the parking lot on the left.

By commuter rail: From Back Bay or South Station, take the Attleboro Line to Sharon. The sanctuary is one and a half miles from the Sharon railroad station. With your back to the station, turn left on Depot Street. Take your first left onto Moose Hill Parkway. Continue on Moose Hill Parkway (bearing right at the junction with Upland Road) to the visitor center on the right.

Food and Drink: Life's a Deli is located on Depot Street near the railroad station in Sharon Center.

Restrooms: In the visitor center and next to the barn, west of Moose Hill Street.

Fees: Adults, $3; children and seniors, $2. Open dawn to dusk except Mondays. Free admission to members of Massachusetts Audubon Society. No dogs. Call 781-784-5691 for more information.

Kendall Whaling Museum: Adults, $2; children and seniors, $2. Open Tuesdays through Saturdays 10:00 A.M. to 5:00 P.M., (781-784-5642).

Recreational Options: Cross-country skiing.

Background: Moose Hill, one of the first private wildlife sanctuaries in the country, was established in 1916 when Dr. George Field, a noted biologist, donated 225 acres of land to the Massachusetts Audubon Society. This donation allowed MAS to expand its original mission of educating members on the environment to include environmental preservation as well. Since Field had stipulated that his estate be used as a bird sanctuary, MAS hired ornithologist Henry Higbee to oversee the property. Five years later, Moose Hill had accumulated 700 acres. Recently, MAS purchased an additional 410 acres for Moose Hill that include Wolomolopoag Pond and Wolomolopoag Bog.

The sanctuary offers a wide range of activities for adults and children, in addition to school programs and a natural history summer day-camp.

THE HIKE

1. From the Visitor Center, which contains a gift shop, library, and art gallery, cross Moose Hill Street. Walk between the stone pillars across from Moose Hill Parkway and you'll be on the B Trail.

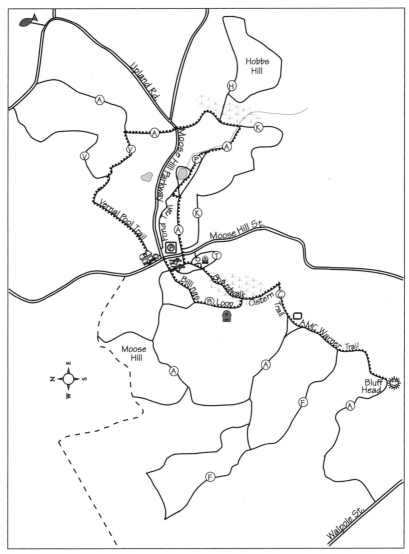

MOOSE HILL WILDLIFE SANCTUARY

Here, as on other MAS properties, blue trail markers indicate that the trail is heading away from the visitor center, while yellow markers signal trails leading back to the visitor center.

The ground cover along B Trail is **wild sarsaparilla**. In spring, clusters of greenish white flowers sprout beneath its large, umbrella-like leaves.

Early settlers boiled its roots to make a root-beer–like drink.

About 50 yards ahead on the left sits a **sassafras** tree whose roots can be boiled to make sassafras tea. The sassafras tree sports unusual leaves with three distinct shapes: one has no lobes, another has two and resembles a mitten, and the third has three lobes. In autumn, its green leaves turn a brilliant orange and red.

Sassafras

As you walk farther into the sanctuary, the sarsaparilla is replaced by several species of fern. The **bracken fern's** triangular shape, with three individual leaves growing from a single stem, differentiates it from the long, pointed delicate **hay-scented fern**. The **royal fern** derives its name from the feathery, cinnamon-colored fertile leaflets rising from its top like a crown. Its leaflets resemble leaves found on locust trees rather than the lacy leaflets growing on bracken and hay-scented ferns. The **sensitive fern** has thick, closely spaced leaves growing from a wide center membrane. Its name refers to the fern's sensitivity to the cold, which causes it to wither at the first frost.

If you spot an evergreen with shaggy red bark that has a vine climbing up its trunk and winding around its branches, it probably is an **eastern red cedar** tree hosting **poison ivy**. Most people associate poison ivy with ground-hugging clusters of three shiny green leaves, but if the plant finds a host, it will climb. Skin contact with either variety in all seasons (even in winter in its leafless resting state) causes a very itchy rash. Yet poison ivy does serve an important function: its berries feed birds during winter.

Eastern red cedar

After walking for about 0.3 mile on the B (Billings/Boardwalk) Loop and just before you reach Billings Barn on the right, look for a tree that appears to be shedding its bark. This shaggy gray trunk distinguishes the **shagbark hickory** from surrounding trees. On the ground you may find a few hickory nuts whose thick husks enclose sweet edible meats.

If you look closely at the large **sugar maple** trees across from the barn, you'll detect numerous small holes in their bark. Between the last week in February and the first week in March, pails are attached under the holes to catch the sap. Thirty gallons of this slightly sweet sap must be tapped in order to yield a single gallon of maple syrup. This tour soon will pass the maple-sugaring shack, where sap is boiled into syrup.

2. At the junction with the C (Cistern) Trail, turn right into a wetland area surrounded by **red maple** trees that thrive in this moist soil. Red maple trees are easy to identify because in every season at least one part of the tree displays the color red. In early spring, red buds emerge from reddish twigs that soon are decorated by clusters of red and orange flowers. Before the leaves unfurl, they have a reddish tint which remains on the veins and leafstalks all summer. In the fall, the tree displays its red winglike fruit. For the red maple's final performance, its foliage turns a dazzling crimson.

Farther ahead, in the drier woodlands, grows another color-coded species of tree. A thin, curly silvery yellow bark covers the trunk of the **yellow birch** tree, whose leaves and stems emit a pleasing wintergreen aroma.

Chestnut seedlings grow nearby. Look for long slender leaves with jagged edges. In the 19th century, this species dominated all trees in the forest. However, in 1904, Chinese chestnut trees infected with a blight were planted in the Bronx Zoo in New York. This disease soon invaded neighboring chestnut trees in the zoo and then traveled to other trees along the East Coast. The chestnut trees that grow here have sprouted from the surviving roots of former trees, but soon the lingering blight will weaken the trees and they too will die back.

Before the junction with the A (AMC Warner) Trail, you'll pass an unused cistern on the left. The ramp was placed there to help extricate unsuspecting wildlife that may fall in. On the right, a grove of **beech** trees stand near the path. Their elliptical saw-toothed leaves, with long veins running up their centers, resemble those on the chestnut tree; however, the beech tree leaves are smaller and their edges are not as jagged. The beech is distinguished most easily by its smooth gray bark.

Continue straight toward Bluff Head as the F (Forest) Trail joins on the right.

On the right side, opposite the path that heads into the wetland, sits a beautiful beech tree. Shoots from its spreading shallow roots have become the surrounding beech saplings.

If you are walking in the spring, keep your eye out for the lilylike **bellwort**, whose name does not do justice to its dainty, yellow bell-shaped flowers.

At the approach to the bluff, the trail starts to ascend, with granite boulders signaling the change in topography. Yellow **dwarf dandelions** push their way up between the rocks.

From the peak, the view to the west reveals Foxboro Stadium, former home to the New England Patriots of the National Football League. On the northern side you can see the continuation of the A Trail winding to Walpole Street.

3. From the bluff, descend and return along the same path until you reach the junction with the B Trail.

4. Bear right. Follow the trail onto the boardwalk that runs for a quarter-mile over a wetland filled with red maple trees.

   If you are hiking during summer, you may smell the sweet fragrance of **swamp honeysuckles**, whose clusters of white, vase-shaped blossoms decorate the marsh. Tasty blueberries grow from **highbush blueberries** near the boardwalk. In July hikers vie with the numerous birds that nest in this sanctuary in the battle for the berries.

   A **tupelo** tree sits just before the opening in the stone wall. Look for horizontal branches that grow at right angles to its trunk.

5. On the other side of the stone wall sits the maple-sugar shack where maple sap is boiled down to maple syrup. Continue past the shack, picnic benches, pavilion, and barn. Restrooms are to the right of the barn.

6. In order to proceed to the second loop that runs through the eastern side of the sanctuary, cross Moose Hill Street and turn left onto the A Trail.

7. At the fork, bear left toward the P (Pond) Trail.

8. At the intersection with the P Trail, you can either proceed straight and walk gingerly on the narrow bridge over the dam or turn right and avoid testing your balance by walking around the dam.

9. The P Trail rejoins the A Trail. Bear left and descend alongside a brook into a moist valley. Several varieties of moisture-loving ferns cover the ground. The large graceful fronds of the **cinnamon fern** predominate. You can locate the cinnamon fern by looking for numerous tall fronds growing from one thickly matted, hairy rootstock.

10. At the intersection of Trails A and K (Kettle), turn left and continue to follow A. (The marker is on the tree on your right.)

    A brook crosses the trail. To get to the other side you must either walk carefully over a log or scramble over stones and then climb from the valley to the drier woodland.

    If you wish to hike up Hobbs Hill, turn right onto the H (Hobbs Hill) Trail.

11. Upon reaching Moose Hill Parkway, turn right and walk alongside the road until you reach the continuation of the A Trail at the intersection with Upland Road.

12. Turn left on the A Trail, situated near the Moose Hill Street sign.

14. At the intersection with the V (Vernal Pool) Trail, turn left onto V. If you wish to visit the **Kendall Whaling Museum**, bear right on the A Trail for approximately 0.3 mile.

    The museum houses a collection of nautical art, history, and ethnology centered on whales. Its holdings include 17th-century paintings, engravings, and tiles; old British artwork; tribal art; a fully equipped Yankee whaleboat; ship models; and a fine collection of scrimshaw.

15. The V Trail splits; bear left to return to the Visitor Center.

    If you are hiking in spring, you'll spot a series of vernal pools to your right. These pools fill with water during spring and provide protection for such breeding amphibians as wood frogs, green frogs, spring peepers, and salamanders. When the pools dry up in mid-July to early August, the amphibians will be safe because they have matured and have learned to elude their predators.

    The trail leads to gardens behind the Visitor Center. Of special interest is the butterfly garden, filled with flowers that attract butterflies.

    For those with unlimited energy who wish to climb 534 feet to the top of Moose Hill, cross Moose Hill Street, walk between the stone pillars, and turn right onto the A Trail. Follow the A Trail for 0.3 mile to Moose Hill.

39

PONKAPOAG
POND

 Distance and Difficulty: 4.6 miles (including boardwalk) of easy walking.

If you are seeking a tranquil, scenic, "no-hassle" hike that is accessible, well maintained, and has level but varied topography, head for the four-mile loop around pristine Ponkapoag Pond in the Blue Hills Reservation. You can lengthen your walk by two-thirds of a mile if you tread gingerly on a board-walk that leads into a fascinating white cedar swamp. An added advantage of this hike is its close proximity to a public golf course that offers a large park-ing lot, snack bar, and restrooms.

Transportation: By automobile: From Routes 128/93, take Exit 2 west onto Route 138 toward Stoughton and Canton. Turn left just before the first set of lights into the Ponkapoag Golf Course parking lot.

By commuter rail: From Back Bay or South Station take the Attleboro Line to the Route 128 Station. From there it's a 2-mile bike ride southeast on Green Lodge Street (also called Blue Hill Drive). Turn right onto Washington Street. Immediately turn left into the entrance to Ponkapoag Golf Course.

By Ⓣ and bus: Monday through Saturday (the bus does not run on Sunday), take the Red Line–Ashmont subway to Mattapan, the last stop. Find the Hudson Bus that runs hourly from Mattapan to Canton. Tell the driver you want to get off at the Ponkapoag Golf Course.

Food and Drink: Snack bar and water fountain in the clubhouse.

Restrooms: In the clubhouse.

Recreational Options: Cross-country skiing, ice-skating, fishing.

The boardwalk to Ponkapoag Pond leads through a white cedar bog.

Background: Ponkapoag Pond, the largest body of water in the Blue Hills Reservation, which is managed by the Metropolitan District Commission (MDC), slowly is becoming a bog. Carved by a glacier, with few underground springs, this 270-acre pond is growing shallower and its shores are turning boggier. A floating boardwalk was constructed in 1949 to allow closer inspection of wetland plants and wildlife.

THE WALK

1. From the parking lot, walk to the right of the clubhouse. Follow the paved, shaded walkway that runs through the golf course and meets the trail that rings the pond.

2. At the end of the walkway, head for the dirt path on your right. A wooden post holding a framed map of the reservation marks the starting point of the hike.

    The trail runs through wetland. Here you'll find **sweet pepperbush**, whose fragrant upright white clusters perfume the summer air. You can distinguish this plant by the tiny blooms that form at the end of its branches. After flowering, these narrow pointed fruiting capsules dry, turn gray, and remain on the plant throughout the winter.

    Skunk cabbage, another plant that thrives in swampy areas, also can be identified by its odor, although it's not nearly as pleasant as the sweet pepperbush. Look for a ground-hugging plant with large, mottled, leathery green leaves with smooth edges. Its cabbagelike leaves appear so early in the spring and grow so quickly that they often melt the snow around the plant. Its distinctive odor, most apparent at its stem, lures insects that pollinate it.

    Off to your left, don't miss an inlet speckled with **waterlilies**. From June to September, fragrant white blooms float on flat wide leaves. But this species of waterlily works only half a day; its blooms close at noon.

    A number of different varieties of fern grow around the pond. One of the first types you'll encounter is the delicate lacy **hay-scented fern**, which indeed does emit a haylike odor when crushed.

    An **elderberry bush** sits opposite a path that joins on the right. In June, it produces wide umbrella-like clusters of small white flowers that turn later to umbrella-like clusters of purplish black berries. While its fruit yields tasty jelly and wine, its hollow stalk is used to make flutes and whistles.

    Another useful plant is **jewelweed**, growing next to the elderberry bush. Its succulent translucent stem produces a juice which is said to relieve the itching from **poison ivy** and athlete's foot. In the summer, golden orange flowers appear and later turn into swollen seed capsules. If you touch a ripe capsule, it

Touch-me-not

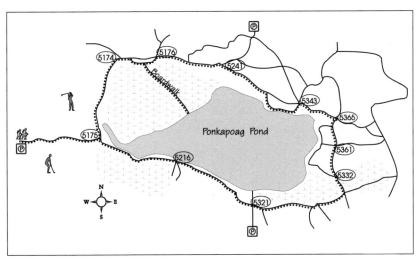

PONKAPOAG POND

explodes and disperses its seeds, which probably explains how it got its second name, **touch-me-not**.

3. Right after the cluster of jewelweed, several trails diverge. The number 5216 is attached to a tree. Bear left on the trail that hugs the pond.

A field of ferns appears. In addition to the hay-scented fern, whose single leaf grows from one stem, you'll find the **bracken fern**, distinguished by three leaves sprouting from one stem.

Growing nearby is **false Solomon's seal**, a ground-hugging flower with a graceful arching stem whose tip displays clusters of many small white feathery flowers.

About a mile into your walk, **spicebush**, another wetland-loving plant, thrives. It is quite indistinguishable unless you are hiking in March or April when pale yellow buds appear on its branches. Its smooth, dark green, oblong leaves, which appear after the flowers have bloomed, exude a pleasant spicy fragrance when crushed. Both its aromatic leaves and twigs are used to produce an herbal tea, while its fruit, when dried and powdered, can be used as a spice.

4. At the intersection with a trail coming from another parking area and entrance off Randolph Street, marked by the number 5321 posted on a tree, continue straight.

Remain on the carriage road as it turns sharply left and passes the trails to the beach and intersection numbers 5332 and 5361.

5. Descend a short hill and continue past a trail entering from the right and a tree marked 5365. Look to your left for a narrow path that veers off toward the water. Proceed on that path, marked by trees with orange blazes. This scenic side trail follows a tiny brook crossed by a narrow log bridge.

6. Turn left where the path rejoins the carriage trail. Walk past another trail (with a 5241 marker) that crosses Route 128 and connects with the northern section of the Blue Hills Reservation (see chapter 21).

Northern white cedar

7. At the junction of three paths, follow the left fork to reach the white cedar swamp. You will pass first through a cleared area within a pine grove. A plaque designates this section as a National Environmental Study Area. On your left stands the Ponkapoag Bog Boardwalk sign, directing you onto the often unstable wooden walkway that extends out into the swamp for one-third mile. Regarded as one of the state's most important natural areas, the bog is marked by the pale gray trunks of dead **northern white cedar** trees. Small and short-lived, cedars prefer swampy soils.

If you are balancing on the boardwalk during the summer, you will be greeted by bright pink clusters of flowers from the **sheep laurel shrub**. A relative of mountain laurel, a popular evergreen, sheep laurel is sometimes called lambkill because its leaves are poisonous to livestock.

Farther out on the boardwalk, look carefully for the tiny, glistening, insect-loving **sundew** plant. Binoculars or a magnifying glass best locate the diminutive insects trapped in the sticky hairs that surround a small stalk bearing a reddish flower about a half-inch wide. Insectivorous plants, such as sundew, have adapted to boggy environments by obtaining nutrients from digested insects instead of from the soil.

On both sides of the boardwalk, greenish gray sphagnum moss is accumulating and over time will transform Ponkapoag Pond, which began as a 48-foot-deep crater filled with melted glacial water, to solid land. A sphagnum bog is created when there are no underground streams to replenish the water supply and provide oxygen. The only plant that can tolerate an environment with so little oxygen is sphagnum moss. Because oxygen also speeds decay, its absence enables the sphagnum to decompose very slowly. Eventually the sphagnum moss dies, forms layers, and fills the pond. In its final stage of decomposition, sphagnum turns to peat, a fertilizer favored by gardeners because of its ability to retain water.

Ninety species of dragonflies and damselflies, considered to be among the widest variety in the United States, inhabit the area around the boardwalk.

8. Retrace your steps on the boardwalk and note the change in vegetation: from dead white cedars and sphagnum moss to live cedars and, finally, maple trees.

9. At the carriage trail, turn left and resume your excursion around the pond. During the remaining half-mile of the loop, the white cedar stumps and bog appear on your left.

10. At the paved walkway, turn right to return to the clubhouse and parking lot.

40

WORLD'S END

RESERVATION

 Distance and Difficulty: 3.7 miles of easy to moderate and sometimes hilly hiking.

The name World's End usually conjures up visions of a remote wasteland. Disregard this end-of-the-world image. From the summit of one of this reservation's four hills, which rise above Hingham Bay, the surrounding seascape gives the impression of being on top of the world rather than at the end of it.

The Trustees of Reservations does an excellent job of maintaining seven miles of trails within this 250-acre peninsula along the Weir River and Hingham Harbor. Birders flock here to view more than 75 different species, including orchard orioles, snowy egrets, bluebirds, and yellow-crowned night herons.

The tour begins at Rocky Neck, so named because of the granite outcroppings and steep cliffs that define this headland. The narrow footpaths on Rocky Neck lead to wide carriage trails that loop around the tip of World's End. The return route climbs Planter's Hill for the best view of Boston's south coast. Don't worry about getting lost; it's easy to get your bearings because the ocean remains on the right side throughout the walk.

Get there early on a sunny warm weekend, as the small parking lot fills quickly.

Transportation: By automobile: Take Route 93 (Southeast Expressway) or Routes 128/95 south to Route 3. Follow Route 3 toward Cape Cod until Exit 14, Route 228 north toward Hingham. Remain on Route 228 for 6.7 miles until you reach the intersection with Route 3A. Turn left on Route 3A for 0.9 mile to Summer Street. Turn right on Summer and proceed for 0.3 mile until it ends at the traffic light at Rockland Street. Pick up Martin's Lane almost directly across from Summer Street and follow it as it winds around for 0.7 mile to World's End.

By Ⓣ and bus: Take the Red Line toward Braintree and exit at the Quincy Center Station. Hop on the #220 bus to Hingham. Get off at the intersection of Otis (Route 3A) and North Streets. World's End is 1.2 miles from the bus stop. Go east on Otis straight through the rotary onto Summer Street. Take the third left onto Martin's Lane, which leads to the reservation.

Food and Drink: Star's and the Old Mill Grille, located near the bus stop on Route 3A, 1.2 miles from the reservation, offer burgers, sandwiches, soups, salads, and drinks.

Restrooms: The small brown wooden structure is located just beyond the northwest corner of the parking lot.

Fees: The entrance fee is $4 for adults. There is no charge for children and members of the Trustees of Reservations. A ranger is on duty and the reservation is open daily from 8:00 A.M. to 8:00 P.M. in the summer and from 9:00 A.M.to 5:00 P.M. in the winter. The phone number at the ranger station is 781-749-8956.

Recreational Options: Off-road biking, cross-country skiing, horseback riding, and fishing.

Background: Before the English influx in the 17th century, World's End consisted of two islands. When English settlers discovered the South Shore's farming potential, they built dams at two ends of the marsh (located in back of the parking lot) to prevent the ocean from flowing through and dividing Planter's Hill from the mainland. Next, they constructed a causeway, named

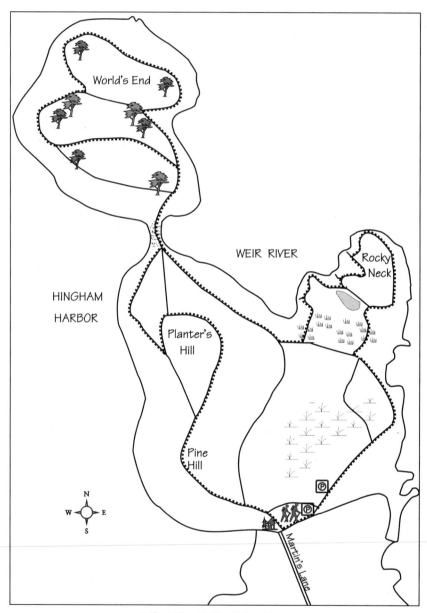

WORLD'S END RESERVATION

the Bar, to connect the outer island and began to grow hay, oats, and corn on the peninsula.

World's End remained farm and pasture land until 1886, when its owner, John Brewer, hired Frederick Law Olmsted, the designer of Boston's Emerald Necklace (chapter 1), to create a community of 163 homes on World's End to compete with a new development being constructed in nearby Hull. Olmsted designed his usual graceful landscape of wide winding roads enhanced by English oaks and native hardwood trees. However, the homes were never built. Brewer's descendants maintained Olmsted's landscape until 1967, when the peninsula was threatened again by development. To preserve the land, South Shore residents rallied with contributions totaling $450,000 which they donated to the Trustees of Reservations so it could purchase the parcel.

The Trustees, one of the oldest land trusts in the world, was conceived in 1891 by Charles Eliot, a disciple of Olmsted and a partner in his landscape architecture firm. The far-sighted Eliot saw the need for preserving land for the quiet enjoyment of the growing population. A voluntary group of trustees was appointed to govern the trust, which was empowered to hold land of "uncommon beauty and more than usual refreshing power." World's End certainly fits that description!

THE HIKE

1. From the parking lot, turn left along the wide carriage road toward Rocky Neck.

2. Remain on the carriage road for a half-mile until the right turn onto another carriage road that leads to Rocky Neck.

   Within the next half-mile, the trails pass through a variety of environments, from marsh to moist woodlands, filled with such moisture-loving plants as **sweet pepperbush**, whose fragrant spikes of tiny white blossoms perfume the summer air, and **cinnamon fern**, with its graceful tall fronds.

The path cuts through an opening in a stone wall into a field covered with various varieties of grasses and wildflowers. The blaze of color may be red blooms from the **Indian paintbrush** plant, bright orange blossoms from **hawkweed**, or clusters of pale orange from **butterfly weed**. In summer **redtop grass** tinges the fields a light pink.

Butterfly weed

3. Continue to bear right as the trail loops around the neck and the wide carriage trail narrows into a rocky footpath.

From the east side of the Neck, look across the Weir River for a clear view of Hull and Nantasket Beach. While soaking up the sun on wide granite slabs, look to the west for a preview of coming attractions—World's End.

Here, along the granite outcroppings, grow plants that have adapted to blasts of salt air. The **bayberry bush** thrives in harsh environments. Its small hard seeds feed birds that winter near the Neck.

The Brewers created the small overgrown pond, located just before the last outcropping on the loop, to supply the farm with ice. According to one of the rangers at World's End, a townsend's solitaire, a bird usually found in southern climes, was spotted near the pond.

4. After circling the Neck, the trail crosses a field and returns to the carriage road. Turn right onto the carriage road.

5. Follow the road until it meets another carriage road. Turn right and continue to bear right, hugging the water as the road loops around World's End.

Thank Frederick Law Olmsted for designing such aesthetically pleasing paths up and around the four hills that compose World's End. These hills were formed in the same manner as the Boston Harbor islands—through glacial action. As the last ice sheet advanced, around

16,000 years ago, it mounded masses of stony debris into rounded oval shapes called drumlins.

Because English colonists had stripped all the timber from the land, Olmsted convinced John Brewer, who owned World's End, to plant tall stately trees along the carriage roads and to arrange bushes randomly, so the setting would simulate an English country estate. English oaks, American elm, apple, **black cherry**, and chestnut trees are among the varieties that shade the hillside.

Private donations paid for the benches that are placed to afford the best views of Boston and the harbor islands.

6. After circling the tip of World's End, take your second left and climb the hill for a panoramic view that includes Hull to the north and east, tiny Bumpkin Island off to the northwest, and larger Peddocks Island just beyond. Directly west sit Slate and Grape Islands. Peddocks, Bumpkin, and Grape Islands are three of the seven islands in the Boston Harbor Islands State Park. During the summer a water taxi carries visitors to the islands. Most of the accessible harbor islands offer hiking trails, campsites, and beaches (see chapter 22).

Bayberry

7. Descend, turn right, and recross the sandbar, constructed hundreds of years ago to connect the two parcels of land.

The profusion of pink blossoms that brighten the bar during the summer proves that *Rosa rugosa* thrives in this sandy and windblown environment. Because of the constant wind, this normally upright shrub hugs the ground, issuing shoots and spreading.

8. Bear right at the next intersection. Hingham Harbor is on the right.

9. Turn left to ascend Planter's Hill, the highest point, with a 360° view. Look west at the Boston skyline silhouetted against the sky. An eastern view reveals four miniature islands perched in Hingham Harbor. To the north is Langlee Island, with Sarah Island directly south of it. Ragged Island is west of Sarah Island. Farthest south sits tiny Button Island.

10. Descend Planter's Hill. Bear left at the main carriage road and ascend Pine Hill.

11. Follow the carriage road as it returns to the entrance to the reservation. Turn left at the ranger station to go back to the parking lot.

Appendix A

BIKING AND

RECREATIONAL RESOURCES

Emergency numbers: Dialing 911 will put you in touch with a dispatcher who will connect you to police or an ambulance in most communities in the Boston area.

Transportation: The public transit system in Boston is referred to as the Ⓣ, an abbreviation for MBTA (Massachusetts Bay Transportation Authority), and this symbol appears on all entrances to subway and train stations. When Bostonians mention the Ⓣ, they often mean the subway, which really isn't a true subway because each of the four lines, Red, Blue, Orange, and Green runs above ground for part of its route. All four lines intersect in downtown Boston, and you can transfer at no charge. Trains that head toward downtown Boston are "Inbound;" those heading away from downtown Boston are "outbound."

Bicycles on the subway and commuter rail: A permit is required in order to take a bike on any MBTA vehicle. To purchase a photo ID permit, go to Mail Boxes Etc., 8 Park Plaza (the Transportation Building), near the intersection of Tremont Street and Stuart Street between 8:30 A.M. and 5:30 P.M. Monday through Friday, and 10:00 A.M. to 1:00 P.M. on Saturday (except in July and August). The $5 permit lasts for three years. Cyclists 16 years and older must provide proper identification showing their age. Children ages 12 to 15 must be accompanied by an adult and have their application signed by a parent or guardian. Children under 12 may ride without a permit if accompanied by a parent or guardian with a permit.

Bicycles may be transported on MBTA vehicles during the following times:

Commuter Rail: Weekdays, anytime except during the morning rush inbound and evening rush outbound; weekends, any time. A maximum of six bicycles is allowed on each train car.

Subway: Red, Blue, and Orange Lines only—weekdays, between 10:00 A.M. and 2:00 P.M. and after 7:30 P.M.; Saturday and Sunday, all day. Use only the first and last cars of the trains. A maximum of two bicycles is allowed on each car. No bicycles permitted any time at the following stations: Park Street, Downtown Crossing, Government Center, and Aquarium.

For more information call the MBTA Customer Service Line at 617-222-3200, then press 1-5-5-5.

Reduced rates: Boston Passport visitor passes are available to residents as well as tourists and can be purchased for one, three, or seven days. The passes allow unlimited use of all subways and buses. The passes are sold at North and South Stations and at information centers on Boston Common and in Quincy Market. Call 617-222-5218 for the cost or additional information.

People over 65 can get a substantially reduced fare by obtaining an MBTA ID card.

Families of up to five people can travel round-trip on offpeak commuter rail trains for a special fare if the children are under 18.

BIKE AND SKI SHOPS

All the sports shops sell and service bikes. The shops that rent bikes and in-line skates are indicated.

BOSTON

Back Bay

City Sports, 168 Massachusetts Avenue, 617-236-2222, rental and sales of in-line skates.

Back Bay Bikes, 333 Newbury Street, 617-247-2336, rental and sales of bikes and in-line skates.

Eric Flaim's Motion Sports, 349 Newbury Street, 617-247-3284, in-line skate rental.

Beacon Hill

Beacon Hill Skate Shop, 135 Charles Street, 617-482-7400.

Boston University

City Sports, 1034 Commonwealth Avenue, 617-782-5121, rental and sales of in-line skates.

Ski Market, 860 Commonwealth Avenue, 617-731-1600.

Copley Square

City Sports, 480 Boylston Street, 617-267-3900, rental and sales of in-line skates.

Earthbikes, 35 Huntington Avenue, 617-267-4733, bike rentals.

Downtown Crossing

City Sports, 20–28 Bromfield Street, 617-423-2015.

South End

Community Bicycle Supply, 496 Tremont, 617-542-8623, bike rentals.

CAMBRIDGE

Harvard Square

City Sports, 16 Dunster Street, 617-868-9232, rental and sales of in-line skates.

Cycle Sport, 1771 Massachusetts Avenue, 617-661-6880, rental and sales of in-line skates.

Porter Square

Bicycle Exchange, 2067 Massachusetts Avenue, 617-864-1300.

SOMERVILLE

Davis Square

Ace Wheelworks, 145 Elm Street, 617-776-2100. Near extension of Minuteman Bikeway.

WESTERN SUBURBS

Bedford

At end of Minuteman Bikeway

The Bikeway Source, 111 South Road, 781-275-7799, bike, in-line skate and cross-country ski rentals.

Belmont

Belmont Wheelworks, 480 Trapelo Road, 617-489-3577.

Brighton

International Bicycle Center, 89 Brighton Avenue, 617-783-5804.

Concord

Carr's Concord Sports, 69 Main Street, 978-369-4087, sales of in-line skates.

Framingham

Ski Market, 686 Worcester Road, 508-875-5253, bike and in-line skate rentals.

Lexington

On Minuteman Bikeway

Bikeway Cycle, 3 Bow Street, 781-861-1199, bike rentals.

Lexington Center

Thunder, 1726 Massachusetts Avenue, 781-674-2546, rental and sales of in-line skates.

Lincoln

Lincoln Guide Service, 152 Lincoln Road, 781-259-1111, bike, in-line skate, and cross-country ski rentals.

Newton

International Bicycle West, 71 Needham Street, 617-527-0967.

Watertown

At end of Charles River Bike Path

Farina Bicycles, 61 Galen Street, 617-926-1717.

Wellesley

Saint Moritz Sports, 475 Washington Street, 781-235-6669.

NORTHERN SUBURBS

Chelmsford

Chelmsford Cyclery, 7 Summer Street, 978-256-1528.

Gloucester

Harborside Cycles, 50 Rogers Street, 978-281-3603.

Hamilton

Bay Road Bikes, 18 Bay Road, 978-468-1301.

Lynn

Lynn Shore Cycles, 251 Western Avenue, 781-581-2700.

Malden

Malden Cycle Center, 77 Commercial Street, 781-322-1880.

Marblehead

Marblehead Bicycle Shop, 25 Bessom Street, 781-631-1570.

Melrose

Pro Cycles, 521 Main Street, 781-662-2813.

Saugus

Northeast Bicycles, 102 Broadway (Route 1), 781-233-2664.

Topsfield

The Bicycle Shop, 17 Main Street, 978-887-6511.

SOUTHERN SUBURBS

Cohasset

Cohasset Cycle Sports, 754 Chief Justice Cushing Highway (Route 3A), 781-383-0707.

Dedham

Dedham Bikes, 403 Washington Street, 781-326-1531.

Hingham

Freewheelin' Cyclery, 38 North Street, 781-749-9760.

Milton

Dave's Bike Infirmary, 440 Granite Avenue, 617-696-6123.

Sharon

Mountain Bikes & More, 700 S. Main Street, 781-784-9684.

Appendix B

Museums and
Historic Houses

Boston

John Hancock Observatory, 200 Clarendon Street. Open Monday-Saturday 9:00 A.M. to 11:00 P.M., Sunday 9:00 A.M. to 11:00 P.M.; 617-572-6429.

Nichols House Museum, 55 Mount Vernon Street. Open Monday, Wednesday, and Saturday afternoons from noon to 5:00 P.M.; 617-227-6993.

Cambridge

Harvard University Art Museums: Fogg Art Museum and Busch-Reisinger Museum at 32 Quincy Street; Arthur M. Sackler Museum at 485 Broadway. Open Monday-Saturday from 9:00 A.M. to 5:00 P.M. and Sunday 1:00 to 5:00 P.M.; 617-495-9400.

Harvard University Museums of Natural History: Museum of Comparative Zoology, the Peabody Museum of Archaeology and Ethnology, Botanical Museum and Mineralogical and Geological Museum, 26 Oxford Street; 617-495-3045.

Longfellow National Historic Site, 105 Brattle Street. Open Wednesday-Sunday from 10:00 A.M. to 4:00 P.M.; 617-876-4491.

Western Suburbs

Concord

Minute Man National Historical Park, North Bridge Visitor Center, 174 Liberty Street. Open daily 8:30 A.M. to 5:00 P.M.; 978-369-6993.

Concord Museum, 200 Lexington Road. Open Monday-Saturday 9:00 A.M. to 5:00 P.M., Sunday 2:00 to 5:00 P.M.; 978-369-9609.

Emerson House, 28 Cambridge Turnpike, Open mid-April through October, Thursday-Saturday 10:00 A.M. to 4:30 P.M., Sunday 2:00 to 4:30 P.M.; 978-369-2236.

Old Manse, Monument Street. Open mid-April through October, Monday-Saturday 10:00 A.M. to 5:00 P.M., Sunday noon to 5:00 P.M.; 978-369-3909.

Orchard House, 399 Lexington Road. Open mid-April to mid-September, Monday-Saturday 10:00 A.M. to 4:30 P.M., Sundays and holidays and mid-September through October 1:00 to 4:30 P.M.; 978-369-4118.

The Wayside, 455 Lexington Road. Open mid-April through October, daily except Wednesday noon to 4:30 P.M.; 978-369-6975.

Lexington

Minute Man National Historical Park, Battle Road Visitor Center, Route 2A. Open mid-April through November, 8:30 A.M. to 5:00 P.M.

Hartwell Tavern and William Smith House, Virginia Road. Open June-August, Saturday and Sunday 10:00 A.M. to 5:30 P.M.; 781-862-7753.

Buckman Tavern, 1 Bedford Street, 781-861-0928; Hancock Clarke House, 36 Hancock Street, 781-862-5598; and Munroe Tavern, 1332 Massachusetts Avenue, 781-862-1703. All are open from mid-April through October, Monday-Saturday 10:00 A.M. to 5:00 P.M. and Sunday 1:00 to 5:00 P.M.

Museum of Our National Heritage, 33 Marrett Road. Open Monday-Saturday 10:00 A.M. to 5:00 P.M., Sunday noon to 5:00 P.M.; 781-861-6559.

Lincoln

DeCordova Museum and Sculpture Park, Sandy Pond Road. Open Tuesday-Sunday 11:00 A.M. to 5:00 P.M.; 781-259-8355.

Wellesley

Davis Museum and Cultural Center, Wellesley College. Open Tuesday, Friday, and Saturday 11:00 A.M. to 5:00 P.M., Wednesday and Thursday 11:00 A.M. to 8:00 P.M., and Sunday 1:00 to 5:00 P.M.; 781-283-2051.

NORTHERN SUBURBS

Andover

Addison Gallery of American Art, Main Street, Phillips Academy. Open Tuesday-Saturday 10:00 A.M. to 5:00 P.M., Sunday 1:00 to 5:00 P.M.; 978-749-4015.

Robert S. Peabody Museum of Archaeology, corner of Main and Phillips Streets, Phillips Academy. Open Tuesday through Friday, noon to 5:00 P.M. and Saturday from 10:00 A.M. to 1:00 P.M. Closed August; 978-749-4490.

Gloucester

Beauport, Sleeper-McCann House, 75 Eastern Point Boulevard. Open mid-May to mid-October, Monday-Friday 10:00 A.M. to 4:00 P.M., weekends mid-September to mid-October 1:00 to 4:00 P.M.; 978-283-0800.

Sargent House Museum, 49 Middle Street. Open June to October, weekends noon to 4:00 P.M.; 978-281-2432.

Schooner *Adventure*, Harbor Loop; 978-281-8079.

Marblehead

Jeremiah Lee Mansion, 161 Washington Street. Open mid-May to mid-October, Monday-Friday 10:00 A.M. to 4:00 P.M., weekends 1:00 to 4:00 P.M.; 781-631-1069.

King Hooper Mansion. 8 Hooper Street. Open Monday-Friday from 9:00 A.M. to 4:00 P.M. and weekends 1:00 to 4:00 P.M.; 781-631-2608.

SOUTHERN SUBURBS

Cohasset

Historic House, 2 Elm Street. Open seasonally.

Maritime Museum, 4 Elm Street. Open seasonally.

Independence Gown Museum, Elm and South Main Streets. Open seasonally.

Hingham

Old Ordinary, 21 Lincoln Street. Open seasonally; 781-749-0013.

Milton

Blue Hills Trailside Museum, 1904 Canton Avenue. Open daily from 10:00 A.M. to 5:00 P.M. except Mondays; 617-333-0690.

Sharon

Kendall Whaling Museum, 27 Everett Street. Open Tuesday-Saturday 10:00 A.M. to 5:00 P.M.; 781-784-5642.

About the
Author

Lee Sinai, a Massachusetts resident, is also the author of *Exploring Martha's Vineyard on Bike and Foot*. When Lee is not writing or creating maps, she is biking, hiking, in-line skating, skiing, or playing tennis.

Before becoming a writer, Lee's other careers included college administrator, director of tours and guides for a destination management company, tennis professional, teacher, wife, and mother. She received her undergraduate degree from the University of Michigan and a master's degree from Northwestern University.

About the AMC

A Tradition of Responsible Outdoor Recreation

Since 1876, the Appalachian Mountain Club has helped people experience the majesty and solitude of the Northeast outdoors. Our mission is to promote the protection, enjoyment, and wise use of the mountains, rivers, and trails of the Northeast. To that end, we offer workshops and guided trips, maintain outdoor facilities and hiking trails, and organize volunteer and conservation efforts. A nonprofit, a percentage of all our revenue goes toward our mission.

Over 80,000 members belong to one of 11 local AMC chapters in New Hampshire, Massachusetts, Connecticut, Maine, Rhode Island, New York, New Jersey and Washington, DC. All AMC programs and facilities are open to the public.

AMC Programs

Outdoor Adventures

Each year the AMC offers over 100 workshops on hiking, canoeing, cross-country skiing, biking, rock climbing and other outdoor activities. In addition to workshops, the AMC offers guided trips for hikers, canoers, and skiers.

Volunteering

AMC volunteers maintain over 1,400 miles of hiking trails in the Northeast, perform search and rescue operations in the White Mountains, clean up rivers, monitor water quality, and negotiate access to wilderness areas with private landowners.

FACILITIES

Mountain Huts

The AMC maintains eight huts in the White Mountains of New Hampshire. Staffed by AMC crews, these huts offer hikers a place to eat and sleep during their overnight hikes. Full service huts offer hikers hot meals, warm beds, and mountain hospitality, while self-service huts provide hikers with bunk beds.

Lodging and Visitor Services

In addition to its mountain huts, the AMC offers unique lodging and visitor services throughout the Northeast. Pinkham Notch Visitors Center offers lodging at the base of Mount Washington and offers hikers updated information on trail and weather conditions. Bascom Lodge sits atop Mt. Greylock in Massachusetts, Echo Lake Camp is on Mount Desert Island in ME, while the Mohican Outdoor Center is located in the Delaware Water Gap of western New Jersey.

CONSERVATION LEADERSHIP

Outdoor recreation depends upon a commitment to protecting the land and keeping trails, rivers, and mountains accessible. The AMC has been at the forefront of the conservation movement since 1876. In 1911 the AMC fought to create the White Mountain National Forest. More recently, we have been active in protecting the Appalachian Trail corridor, securing access to trails and rivers, and protecting the Northeast Forest.

AMC BOOKS AND MAPS — SINCE 1907

The Appalachian Mountain Club published its first trail guide in 1907. Today we offer an extensive line of trail guides, maps, and books on outdoor skills and conservation. We also publish *Appalachia*, the country's oldest mountaineering and conservation journal AMC books are written by experts who have spent years living among the rivers, hills, and mountains of the Northeast. Our books are backed by the expertise of the Appalachian Mountain Club and are intended to further our mission of promoting responsible outdoor recreation. Profits from AMC books support the AMC mission.

INDEX

NOTES